REVISED EDITION

MARKET-DRIVEN MANAGEMENT

Creating Profitable Top-Line Growth

B. CHARLES AMES

JAMES D. HLAVACEK

IRWIN
Professional Publishing®

Chicago • London • Singapore

Library of Congress Cataloging-in-Publication Data

Ames, B. Charles.
    Market-driven management : creating profitable top-line growth / B. Charles Ames, James D. Hlavacek.
      p. cm.
    Includes index.
    ISBN 0-7863-0540-1
    1. Marketing—Management.   2. Sales management.   I. Hlavacek, James D. II. Title.
    HF5415.13.A455 1997
    658.8—dc20   96–9326

Printed in the United States of America
 2 3 4 5 6 7 8 9 0 DOC 3 2 1 0 9 8 7

This book is dedicated to all those who have participated in our executive development workshops. We hope you have gained as many ideas from us as we have from you.

BRIEF CONTENTS

CONTENTS   vii
PREFACE   xiii
ACKNOWLEDGMENTS   xvii

1   Attacking Turbulent Markets   1

2   Outside-In Management   19

3   Proactive Marketing   31

4   The Marketing Controller   49

5   Thinking Small to Win Big   79

6   Better Mousetraps   99

7   The Consultative Salesforce   121

8   Putting It All Together   151

9   Winning Plans   177

10   Working Smarter   197

INDEX   233
ABOUT THE AUTHORS   246

CONTENTS

PREFACE   xiii
ACKNOWLEDGMENTS   xvii

Chapter 1

Attacking Turbulent Markets 1

Roadblocks to Transformation 3
    Reluctance to Face Facts 3
    Being a Lower-Cost Supplier 4
    Bureaucratic Management Approaches 5
    Satisfaction with Existing Products 7
    Lack of Focus and Speed in Research and Development 8
    Lack of Urgency in the Sales Arm 9
Management Responses 10
    Segmenting Markets 10
    Understanding the Profit Economics 11
    Defining Issues and Priorities 12
    Realigning the Organization 14
    Reassessing Strategies 16
Summary 17

Chapter 2

Outside-In Management 19

Outside-In Process   19
Market-Driven Management Defined 21
Inside-Out Approach   22
The 6 Cs of a Market-Driven Company 23
Assessing Market-Driven Capabilities 26
Market-Driven Diagnostic   27
Summary 30

Chapter 3

Proactive Marketing 31

Why Industrial Marketing Is Difficult 32
Where Industrial Marketing Fails 34
    Understanding the Industrial Marketing Concept 35
    Walking the Talk 38
    Cross-Functional Cooperation 39
    An Obsession with the Short Term 40
    Facing Up to Deficiencies 42
Implementing the Concept 43
    Competent People 43
    Reliable Market and Economic Information 46
    Correct Business Focus 46
Summary 47

Chapter 4

The Marketing Controller 49

Six Management Principles 51
The Lower-Cost Supplier 52
Downward Trending Costs 55
Cost and Profit Pictures 56
    What Accounting Schools Never Cover 57
    Common Ranges 57
    The Cycle of Decay 60
    Reordering Cost Information 62
    Better Cost-Profit Pictures 64
    Product-Line Profitability 66
    Customer Profitability 66
    Managing Cash and Liquidity 67
Key Performance Measures 68
    Productivity Measurements 69
    Capital Use 70
    Producers to Supporters 71
Sharing Cost-Profit Information 72
Electronic Networks 74
High- and Lower-Cost Countries 75
Summary 76

Chapter 5

Thinking Small to Win Big 79

Failure to Segment 81
Foundation for Business Strategy 83
Common Errors and Mistakes 84
    Sales Segmentation 84
    Misusing Consumer Retailing Approaches 84
    Lack of Market Facts 85
    Confusing Markets with Products 85
    Thinking Too Broad 86
    Thinking Too Narrow 86
    Too Few or Too Many Segments 87
Segment and Resegment 88
    Setting Segment Priorities 89
    Responsibility for Segmentation 91
    Responding to Market Needs 92
    Shifting Attitudes 94
Aligning for Target Segments 95
Summary 96

Chapter 6

Better Mousetraps 99

Better New Products 100
Common Complaints 101
Problems in the Development and Life Cycles 102
    Product Development Problems 102
    Product Life-Cycle Problems 105
Improving the Odds 106
    Identify Customer Problems 107
    Define the Right Market/Product Focus 108
    Face Up to Deficiencies 109
    Aligning to Target Markets 110
    Match Future Products and Current Profits 112
    Cross-Functional Business Teams 113
    Go Outside for Help 115

Rationalize, Shelve, and Cannibalize 117
Protect Proprietary Information 119
Summary 120

Chapter 7

The Consultative Salesforce 121

Complex Products and Customers 122
Common Concerns 123
Success Depends on the Salesforce 124
Principle 1: Focus on Customer Problems 126
Principle 2: Determine Cost-Effective Solutions 126
Principle 3: Understand Customer and Competitive Information 128
Principle 4: Salesforce Options 130
    Geography 130
    Product Range 130
    Market Segment 131
    Special Situations 132
Principle 5: Organize Ongoing Training 133
    Industry and Application Knowledge 134
    Sales Competency Quizzes 136
Principle 6: Going Electronic 136
    Example—Compaq Computer 138
    Example—Pioneer Hi-Bred 139
Principle 7: Link Sales Compensation to Company Goals 140
    Setting Goals 140
    Sharing Cost-Profit Information 141
    Sales Salaries 142
    Commissions 142
    Seniority-Based Compensation 142
    Team Incentives 143
    Tailor the Objectives 143
Principle 8: Provide a Sales Career Ladder 144
    Conflicting Demands 146
    Inadequate Preparation 146
    Excessive Paperwork 147
Principle 9: Business Planning Role 148
Summary 150

Chapter 8

Putting It All Together 151

Why Business Planning Is Important 151
Planning Pitfalls 152
    Failure to Tailor the Process 153
    Confusion over Types of Planning 155
    Overemphasis on the System 160
    Lack of Alternatives 160
Proven Practices 162
    Planning Based on Hard Facts 162
    Direction from Upper Management 167
    Regional and Global Business Teams 175
Summary 176

Chapter 9

Winning Plans 177

Structure and Focus 178
    Strategy Statement 178
    Initiatives 180
Credibility Issues 181
    Fact Base 181
    Sales, Cost, and Profit Projections 182
    Risk/Reward Ratio 186
    Allowances for Contingencies 187
    Cross-Functional Plans 188
Management Approach and Attitude 189
    Integrated across Functions 189
    Business Team Commitment 190
Emerson Electric Company—A Shining Example 191
Summary 195

Chapter 10

Working Smarter 197

    Factor 1: Market Facts 198
    Factor 2: Market Segment Priorities 198
    Factor 3: Side-by-Side Competitive Comparisons 199
    Factor 4: Accounting Systems 200

Factor 5: Lower-Cost Claims 200

Factor 6: Quality 201

Factor 7: Manufacturing Efficiency and Capacity 202

Factor 8: Response and Cycle Times 202

Factor 9: Existing Products and Technology 203

Factor 10: New Products 204

Factor 11: Salesforce 204

Factor 12: Organization 205

Factor 13: Planning 206

Factor 14: Incentive Systems 207

Overcoming Deficiencies 207

Role of Training and Management Development 208

Cultural Changes 209

Short-Term America 209

The Business School Fix 210

The Headhunter Fix 212

The Consultant Fix 213

Wasted Training Approaches 215

Trends in Management Training 218

Role of Top Management 219

Great Companies 220

Top Management Commitment 221

False Starts 223

High-Impact Training 225

Partnerships with Your Employees 229

Summary 230

INDEX   233

ABOUT THE AUTHORS   246

CREATING PROFITABLE TOP-LINE GROWTH WITH MARKET-DRIVEN MANAGEMENT

With all the focus and press coverage about re-engineering, restructuring, and downsizing, it's logical to ask what's next. In other words, what does industry do after it has streamlined its organization, operation, and processes? Our answer is simple: "Grow the business!" You may have saved your way to improved profitability, but you have not (and cannot) achieve profitable growth with cost reductions alone. Obvious as this answer may seem, we are constantly amazed at how many companies we see where management, for some reason, doesn't seem to "get it." Our book prescribes the actions required to accelerate profitable top-line growth, and maps out a self-evaluation program to help management determine the initiatives necessary to achieve this fundamental goal.

MORE ABOUT THE PROBLEM

Over the past several years, most of the heads-up companies in American industry have gone through some kind of a re-engineering, restructuring, or downsizing effort. Whatever the effort was called, the objectives were the same: cut costs, eliminate redundant jobs, improve productivity, accelerate cycle times, and by doing so, add to shareholder value.

In most cases, these efforts have greatly increased the competitive capability of companies and put them in a much stronger position to withstand tougher competition and to be a real force in global markets. In fact, American industry has now regained its position as the strongest competitor in many industrial sectors. The companies that have lagged in taking these steps continue to suffer from bloated costs and inefficiencies that will ultimately (if they haven't already) impair their growth and profitability. We see this clearly in some slow-moving companies in the United States and particularly in western Europe where many once-dominant companies are rapidly losing the ability to compete.

Recently, a lot of "armchair" observers, including academics and politicians, have been very critical of these streamlining actions because of the resulting elimination of so many jobs. Many of us in industry can point to individual cases of "dumbsizing," i.e., clumsy and crude cost-cutting that has been done with a meat ax in a seemingly indiscriminate and unfair way—this is what the academics and politicians write and talk about. But, as we see it, these examples are the exceptions and do not in any sense tell the whole story. Most companies have been judicious in the way they have streamlined their operations, and have invested millions in separation and outplacement programs in order to treat as fairly as possible those who have been displaced.

Clearly, this whole downsizing effort has been a painful process, especially for those who were terminated because they became redundant under a new plan for the business. At the same time, there can be no question that moving aggressively to cut costs was essential for most companies in American industry. The alternative, which was to do nothing and be noncompetitive, was simply unacceptable. The resulting damage to the workforce and the economy would have been incalculable. Moreover, the improvement in corporate profits from well thought-out restructuring initiatives has been positively reflected in the stock market, where so many have invested retirement funds.

We believe, however, that many companies can be criticized for their actions or lack thereof *after* they have re-engineered, restructured, or downsized. As we see it, too many companies have taken the necessary steps to become cost competitive, only to then fail miserably in their efforts to profitably build sales. It almost looks as though management personnel in many of these companies concluded their job was done after they laid off a lot of people and cut their costs—nothing could be more wrong. Cutting costs alone doesn't build a business and generally doesn't create lasting shareholder value. You simply cannot be successful over the long term unless you have a solid upward trend in profitable top-line sales. A business has to steadily grow profits to create real value. Likewise, job creation (that should mitigate job losses from restructuring and downsizing) depends largely on organic sales growth. Thus, we would be far more critical of companies for failing to grow their business than we would of their cost-reduction efforts, which are essential to stay competitive.

MORE ABOUT THIS BOOK

This book is a "how to" guide for anyone interested in building his or her business through profitable top-line sales growth. It is organized around a set of principles that are immutable. They are just as valid today as they were yesterday and will be as valid tomorrow as they are today. The book also emphasizes the need to continuously benchmark against world class companies and to maintain unrelenting pressure on costs, since there will always be lower-cost producers entering the market with lower-priced products. But this emphasis on lowering costs is a means to an end—not the end itself—which is creating profitable sales growth. The bulk of the book focuses on all the things management must do to generate profitable top-line sales and strengthen market share after they have gotten their cost structure where it needs to be.

This book was written from firsthand experience in working with leading industrial companies that have been able to accelerate profitable top-line growth year after year by being market-driven. Jim Hlavacek points to client training companies, including Hewlett-Packard, National Starch and Chemical, Sealed Air, and Nucor, as prime examples of successful growth companies. Chuck Ames points out that his firm, Clayton, Dubilier & Rice, Inc. recognizes that lasting value is created by building companies, not by downsizing or tearing them apart. Anyone can cut costs; real leaders build and improve the business for the long term. The growth orientation reflected in these comments and examples is what ultimately separates the winners from the losers *in any industry, in any business, in any part of the world.*

Leading growth companies learn what products and services the market wants or needs. They don't live in a static world trying to sell only what they can make. Instead, they design and build what the customer wants or needs, often moving beyond existing product and process technology to do so. These same companies grow in very well-defined markets and in selective ways, while they continually make their manufacturing, sales, and logistic processes more efficient. They don't seek sales growth just for growth's sake or simply to become bigger. They seek both sales growth and productivity improvements to become and remain the most profitable in their industry. They don't just react or try to predict the future; they are proactive. In short, they plan and create the future. Let's now see how the leading industrial companies "create profitable top-line growth by being market-driven."

ACKNOWLEDGMENTS

The research, editing, numerous revisions, and word processing of this book were an enormous undertaking. We are grateful to the staff at Market Driven Management, Inc., in Charlotte, North Carolina, which contributed to this project while attending to the daily operating tasks of servicing our customers around the world.

Donis Andrews
Nancy Barrett
Nancy Burton
Karen Doran
Gery Dorazio

Finally, we would like to thank our partners at Irwin Professional Publishing who provided many useful guidelines, suggestions, and deadlines.

CHAPTER 1

Attacking Turbulent Markets

In a recent management training workshop for a steadily growing electronics company, a group of middle and senior managers voiced real concern to us over several serious threats to their business:

Increased strength of foreign competitors.

Fast response time of smaller competitors.

Obsolescence of hardware by software.

Shorter product development and product life cycles.

Customer demands for more performance and lower prices.

Growing influence of low-cost offshore competitors.

Individually, any of these threats presented a serious problem. Combined, the list was overwhelming and even frightening to this management team. Most companies—and entire industries—are faced with similar serious threats. How should management react? How can management cope with such a broad array of complex problems? They must find viable solutions soon. The emergence of forces and events such as those just mentioned is an inevitable characteristic of our more turbulent world that can threaten the very survival of many companies—and even entire industries—unless they respond faster and more effectively than they have thus far.

The world is unquestionably a much tougher place for business today than it has been in the past. Increasingly volatile changes in the business environment for any firm have greatly increased uncertainty and unpredictability for all industrial and high-tech companies. Of course, business environments have always been subject to change. What is different today is the frequency and velocity with which change is occurring and the dramatic impact these changes can have on business results. Some managers, especially those with many years of experience, will disagree, claiming that business conditions are no different or no more difficult today than those faced in other times. Managers who feel this way have either chosen to ignore, or do not truly understand, the harsh realities that currently surround almost every industrial and high-tech company. Some of these differences are listed here:

1. Global competition is no longer a scattered occurrence. Today, it is present or represents an immediate threat in every market of consequence in every region of the world.

2. Customers have become smarter and more demanding in terms of response time, performance, and services; and they resist price increases even if they are flourishing.

3. Exploding technology has shortened product and process life cycles and greatly increased the risk of payback on the development investment that must be made simply to keep pace.

4. Excess manufacturing capacity, much of it in rapidly developing areas of the world, plagues every significant market, and the scramble to utilize this capacity has created more pressure on managing than ever before.

5. Profit margins are declining at the same time requirements for new product and process improvements are increasing, and the unit costs of serving markets and key customers are trending upward.

Faced with these conditions, superior performance will only be achieved by companies whose leaders recognize the dramatic differences in today's business environment and have the fortitude to make the wrenching changes necessary to ensure that their organizations adjust to the rules of a completely new ballgame. Caterpillar is a good example of a company that has successfully made the adjustment. Caterpillar was too much of a top-down, inside-out organization. They were internally focused, functionally organized, product driven, and slow to react to opportunities and threats. After suffering losses because of aggressive efforts from global competitors (including Komatsu, Deere, JCB, Hitachi, Liebherr and others), the company finally reacted. Cat's management decided it had to move away from a centralized structure dominated by staff groups and created a number of smaller and more focused business units. They formed business units for mining, construction, paving, and agriculture, among others. The business units were empowered to make decisions, to share information, and to listen to customers and dealers; and they became more proactive to threats and opportunities. It was by no means an easy transformation.

ROADBLOCKS TO TRANSFORMATION

To achieve a transformation such as Caterpillar's, the baggage from the past—old habits, practices, commitments, and ways of thinking—must be shed. Unless such baggage is shed, the required changes cannot or will not be made. Let's examine the roadblocks that will inevitably make it difficult for many companies to make the kind of transformation we are talking about.

1. Reluctance on the part of many managers to face the real facts about their markets and competitive positions.
2. Failure to recognize the crucial importance of being a lower-cost supplier.
3. Lack of focus on target markets, key accounts, their unique requirements, and their unarticulated needs.
4. Arrogant self-satisfaction with existing product offerings that makes the business vulnerable to being "blindsided" by shifting customer needs, new competitors, and new technologies.
5. Apparent lack of urgency and confidence in research and development (R&D) and the sales groups that have become conditioned to earning a living by working on technically interesting projects and simply taking orders.

Reluctance to Face Facts

Many companies that have lost profits or market share have managers who are still waiting patiently for their business to "get back to normal." Others are looking for government assistance (e.g., import restrictions) for their declining market and profit positions. Neither of these approaches is a viable solution. What is needed is less wishful dreaming and rhetoric and a greater willingness to squarely face the true facts about markets and competitive positions. The changes that have occurred in many markets are structural, not cyclical, and it is unrealistic to expect any kind of a dramatic recovery or turnaround that will restore business practices to the "good old days."

It is extremely difficult for managers who have built their entire careers around specific products and technology to accept the fact that their former business base has now leveled out below prior peaks or, worse yet, become obsolete or irretrievably lost to new competitors or technology. Obviously, many old-line steel managers could not imagine today's world of aluminum cans, plastic auto parts and bodies, and small regional minimill producers such as Nucor that constantly "beat their pants off." Nor could managers in the high-flying and glamorous semiconductor business foresee the situation in which their markets have not only ceased to gallop ahead but have declined dramatically and in which foreign sources, including Brazil, Korea, and Taiwan, have captured the bulk of the remaining business. Unfortunately, these are the facts, and an equally discouraging set of forces applies in many other markets.

It is understandable that managers who have grown up and lived through the growth years in any of these industries find today's conditions difficult to accept. But they must change their myopic or unrealistic views of their business so that they can tackle the hard work required to maintain or regain a profitable competitive footing. Otherwise, their situations will not improve and will most likely deteriorate further.

Being a Lower-Cost Supplier

Increased competition, accompanied with the drive for greater efficiency and productivity, inevitably leads to excess industry capacity. Excess capacity, in turn, makes price an increasingly important factor in the buying decision, and lower prices rapidly cut into profit margins unless total unit costs continuously trend downward. Few managers will disagree with this point. In fact, many will claim that it is a rather obvious rehash of elementary economics. Comments such as the following are not at all uncommon: "Of course it is important to be a low-cost supplier and we are one. We have always been very competitive on costs." However, many of the managers who express this attitude have no factual basis to support their statement. Others make cost comparisons, but overlook foreign competitors that are the real long-term threats. A proprietary study on manufacturing competitiveness made by McKinsey and Company shows that many U.S. manufacturers have operated at a 30-percent-plus cost disadvantage to foreign competitors and, more importantly, have lost ground on productivity by a factor of 2 to 1. The situation is even worse for some European companies. It is not surprising that so many manufacturers are faced with such a disadvantage; they are weighed down with:

- Plant, equipment, and manufacturing methods that have not been upgraded to meet market demands for lower cost, higher quality, and shortened production cycles.
- Labor, engineering, and administrative costs and productivity improvements that are noncompetitive by any measurable global standard.
- A balance sheet that is inflated with underutilized or obsolete plant and equipment and excessive working capital.
- An unrealistically high breakeven point with a resulting profit level that does not generate sufficient funds to sustain the business and satisfy shareholders.

Even with all of the re-engineering, restructuring, and downsizing that has occurred, a surprisingly high percentage of established companies are still intolerably saddled with all of the preceding items. Also, with more and more companies scouting the world for much lower costs, the situation is unlikely to improve. A business can have the most innovative, brilliant, hard-working management team in the world; and it can pursue the most ingenious sales and marketing strategies; however, if it is encumbered with a lot of the baggage just described, there is no way it can be fully cost competitive, and no amount of hard work or management brilliance can make up for this deficiency.

Bureaucratic Management Approaches

This roadblock stems from management's reluctance to push the profit- and decision-making responsibilities deep within the organization, relying instead on large, centralized organizations with too many management levels and highly paid staff people. The real contributions of most corporate, sector, or group-level marketing, advertising, human resources, manufacturing, planning, or R&D staff activities cannot be demonstrated to our satisfaction. Most of their activities are redundant to line management responsibilities and too costly to justify. We have not been able to find proven profit contributions that offset the costs involved. These upper-level groups create unnecessary reports, memos, procedures, and nonstop meetings. Our point of view is supported by an in-depth study of 41 companies by A. T. Kearney, Inc., a management consulting firm.

As Exhibit 1–1 shows, the "lean" companies—that is, those that have the fewest management levels between the highest and lowest ranked employees—demonstrated a clear advantage in sales growth and an overwhelming advantage in earnings growth.

E X H I B I T   1–1

Is Less Management Better?

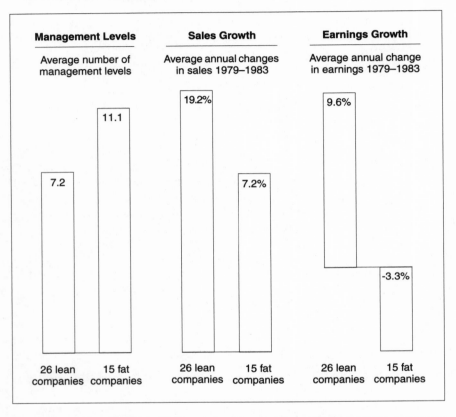

Management Levels	Sales Growth	Earnings Growth
Average number of management levels	Average annual changes in sales 1979–1983	Average annual change in earnings 1979–1983

Management Levels: 26 lean companies 7.2, 15 fat companies 11.1
Sales Growth: 26 lean companies 19.2%, 15 fat companies 7.2%
Earnings Growth: 26 lean companies 9.6%, 15 fat companies -3.3%

Results based on an in-depth study of 41 companies by a Chicago-based consulting concern. The lean companies had the fewest management levels between the highest and lowest ranked employees; the fat companies had the greatest number of management levels.

Source: A. T. Kearney, Inc.

In addition to the unavoidable cost penalties, overstructuring and excessive layering has more serious consequences for the long term. We doubt that senior managers can really know what is going on when they are several levels removed from where the action takes place—with the customer, in the plants, and in the laboratories. All they know is what they are told, and this information, whether verbal or written, has all the deficiencies of any message that has been filtered through multiple layers. As a result, the decision-making process is almost certain to be slow, unresponsive, and usually not based on the real or current facts of the situation. Ken Iverson, chairman and chief architect of Nucor Corporation, claims that two advantages his company has over larger competitors are much lower overhead costs and the ability to make and implement decentralized decisions more quickly. He attributes them to Nucor's spartan organization, with only 22 people at headquarters and only four management levels, in contrast to the multiple staff groups and seven or more levels at some of his traditional competitors. Furthermore, Nucor has no senior vice presidents, executive vice presidents, or group presidents because they believe these positions only slow decision making and add unnecessary overhead costs. In short, Nucor manages very close to the customer.

In summary, too many companies are still trying to manage their business around big chunks of business, generally defined by historical product groupings with a centralized top-down approach that stifles people, slows decision making, and adds huge costs. The expression "small is beautiful" really makes sense in today's more turbulent business climate. Any business is better off if it is broken down and managed decentrally around a number of discrete profit centers. There are several distinct advantages: the planning and decision-making process is streamlined and fast; the bureaucratic "drag" that is inevitably found in big organizations is avoided; a much better basis for planning and control is provided because people with clear-cut profit and decision-making responsibility and accountability are on top of everyday problems; and finally, more strategic options are uncovered because people closer to customers are thinking strategically about what they can do to accelerate profit growth in their particular business.

Satisfaction with Existing Products

It is easy to find numerous companies that have suffered or failed as a result of being satisfied with yesterday's products. Most manufacturers of cutting tools lost a big slice of their traditional market because they concentrated only on cosmetic changes to their products and did not respond to clear warning signals that pointed to dramatic changes in their markets. The increasing use of laser systems to drill and machine parts and of adhesives to avoid the need for holes for riveting, as well as the emergence of new coating technology that greatly extends the wear life of cutting tools, were factors that were overlooked until a large chunk of their traditional market had disappeared. Similarly, some manufacturers of hydraulic aircraft landing gear failed to develop or acquire the electronic and software capabilities necessary to participate in the shift to electronically controlled systems that are now standard design for all new retractable landing gear. These producers may continue to reap handsome profits from repairing systems in the large hydraulic after-market for some time; however, they will ultimately be squeezed out of this business as the hydraulically equipped planes are retrofitted with electronics or removed from service.

Such self-satisfaction occurs for several reasons. First, the market and technological changes are often not recognized or accepted as serious threats. Even when they are recognized, nothing may be done because the costs and risks of adopting new technologies and cannibalizing existing products are great and frequently not compatible with short-term profit goals. The root cause in most cases, however, is the simple fact that technologists steeped in one discipline are reluctant to accept the advantages or superiority of another competing technology. Why? Technical arrogance? (How can anyone have a better idea or technology than I?) Certainly this attitude is not uncommon. But a more fundamental reason is the unwillingness of many to admit that they are likely to become less needed or perhaps obsolete if the business moves toward a new technology that requires very different capabilities, which they don't understand.

Lack of Focus and Speed in Research and Development

Many industrial companies have a lot of good technological and manufacturing know-how or expertise. But these same companies often have difficulty in rapidly taking a good concept from the laboratory into the marketplace. New-product development is the seed corn of the future. Even if you acquire a business, you need new products to profitably grow the top line. Without competitive product development, a company will eventually die from severe price competition and declining sales.

A centralized R&D function is hard to justify; it tends to be unresponsive, esoteric, and too costly. Unless the business units are based on a common technology, all R&D activities should be directed by and charged to the business units. If there is a need for R&D that is not business unit driven, it should be contracted out to universities or government laboratories and appropriately charged to some business unit so it doesn't become a sink hole. Individual R&D programs should not be initiated unless they focus on specific market needs. Whether a company's R&D strategy is to be a first-to-market or a fast follower, both approaches require being very fast to market.

Many R&D people are disturbed when they are pressured to move rapidly to develop new products. However, the days of R&D as a place to "rest and dream" are over. New products must be developed as if they were perishable fruit. With shorter life cycles and the higher cost of developing new products, the productivity measures applied to other areas of the firm need to be applied to R&D expenditures. The speed or urgency of product development should be measured in terms of the number of months it takes from concept to market introduction. The estimated payback period to justify any R&D commitment should be expressed as a percentage of the expected life cycle of the new product.

Lack of Urgency in the Sales Arm

"We develop good sales plans but our sales results are dismal." "We can't seem to get the strong execution we need at the point-of-sales contact." These are common complaints of many senior executives in industrial and high-tech companies. The complaints appear to be more and frequent now because the battle for increased sales is so tough. However, the problem has existed for many years; it was obscured by high inflation rates and price increases that allowed many sales personnel to look better than they really were in terms of achieving record sales levels. Not much skill or effort was required to dine with customers, take orders, and ride the demand curve upward during this period when a lot of dollar volume was generated through price increases rather than unit gains.

Now, however, the situation is quite different. Most sales personnel are faced with the very difficult task of protecting and growing their positions in mature and declining markets against more intense competition. Products are becoming more complex and life cycles shorter. At the same time, customers have become far more demanding, sophisticated, and global in their sourcing practices. Consequently, the sales task is undeniably more difficult today than it was just a few short years ago, and sales performance must be much stronger just to keep pace.

The problem is compounded because many salespeople are not properly focused, trained, or motivated to perform the more demanding sales job that is required. Most of these deficiencies result from management's failure to recognize how their markets and the selling job have changed and to make the necessary adjustments in their sales programs. A large number of salesforces have not been sufficiently upgraded and are still overpopulated with "Willie Loman" types, who cannot make a satisfactory transition to the new demands on consultative solution selling. Also, most salespeople are not directed toward priority target markets nor armed with sufficient product knowledge, application benefits, and side-by-side competitive comparisons to enable them to sell real value to specific customer groups. Finally, most sales compensation plans are structured so there are inadequate rewards or penalties for high or low performers. Mediocrity has become an accepted way of life in many sales organizations.

MANAGEMENT RESPONSES

Overcoming these roadblocks and gearing the business for sales and especially profit growth in a turbulent marketplace requires management skills of the highest order. But it does not require a whole new array of sophisticated techniques. Rather, it demands a more rigorous application of time-proven industrial marketing fundamentals that are nothing more than common sense. However, as Thomas Paine often stated, "The problem with common sense is that it is not commonly practiced." To thoroughly understand and implement these proven industrial marketing practices means (*a*) segmenting markets to a far greater degree than was typically done in the past, (*b*) understanding the true profit economics of each product/market segment, (*c*) defining the key issues and priorities in each market segment, (*d*) realigning the organization to a more demanding marketplace, and (*e*) reassessing and adjusting business strategies to meet changing market needs. Let's look at each of these points more carefully.

Segmenting Markets

Industrial market segmentation is a "close to the customer" process of splitting industries and specific customers into groups with similar needs. The traditional way of segmenting industrial and high-tech markets by using standard industrial classification (SIC) codes is usually too broad. Moreover, such broad cuts of a market may show that intelligent marketing decisions cannot be made.

Very few general managers realize that the definition and selection of market segments is the most important strategic decision facing every industrial manufacturer. Everything else follows the selection of target markets. The selection of target markets drives competitive analysis, and it determines the type of technology race you are in and what type of manufacturing, service, and sales capabilities are needed. The definition and selection of target market segments is the first step in focusing any business unit, and the selection of key accounts should follow the target market emphasis.

There are two additional reasons for refining market segmentation to a greater degree. First, it is not unusual to find that, if an overall market that appears to be unattractive is sliced into small enough segments, one or more segments that are very attractive can generally be found. If attention is then focused on the most attractive segments, there is a much better opportunity for increasing sales and, especially, profit growth. Second, it is wise to assume that some competitors, particularly smaller ones, will segment the market, find the attractive segments, and capture market share from the companies that have not geared up to serve them. As a rule of thumb, any time a market is defined in pieces much larger than $30 million, it should probably be segmented again because many smart competitors will look for smaller pieces from which they can achieve a unique, competitive advantage. Bigger companies often make the mistake of glossing over these smaller segments, saying they have bigger fish to fry. What they overlook is that this allows smaller competitors to get a toehold that can eventually lead into their core markets. Bigger companies also forget that all large markets start out as smaller niche markets. This point is supported by the following quotation:

> IBM did not enter a market unless they could identify it as a $100 million opportunity. That is why they missed both minicomputers and desktop publishing opportunities.[1]

Understanding the Profit Economics

Understanding the profit economics is also an easy point to agree with, and many will respond to it by saying, "We know all that." In most cases those responding with these words really don't know all that, and, in fact, most don't know what understanding the profit economics really means.

Let's examine what is meant by the profit economics of a business and then look at the kind of information needed to ensure the thorough understanding essential for solid business planning. The following information is required, at a minimum, to understand the profit economics of a business:

1. How many dollars of assets are committed in each stage of each market/product business (e.g., R&D, materials, plant and equipment, finished stock, postsale support)?
2. What is the fixed-to-variable cost relationship for each product/market business; that is, for each dollar of sales, how many cents are attributable to bedrock fixed costs, how many to structured or discretionary cost, and how many to out-of-pocket costs?

---

1. Ray Alvarez Torres, "Niche Market Computer Strategies," *San Jose Mercury News*, February 10, 1990, p. 27.

3. How do costs and profit change with swings in volume?
4. What is the breakeven point at current volume? What actions could be taken to bring that breakeven point down should volume potential decline?
5. What is the rate of incremental profit on each added increment of volume? What are the volume points where new increments of structured cost must be added?
6. What are your least profitable product lines? Is additional capacity only added based on the least profitable product lines?
7. What does it cost to serve each account? Which customers are the most profitable, the more marginal, and the biggest losers?

A net profit-and-loss statement (after all allocations) for each product line and key customer is essential for generating answers to these questions. Despite their claim to know everything, very few managers actually have this information readily available. Actually, most accounting systems are not designed to provide these kinds of statements, and the accountants will argue that you can't get them because many products run over the same machines, a lot of indirect costs can't be allocated, and so on. To which we say, "Baloney!" Shared, fixed, and indirect charges often represent the most serious cost problems in business situations where a cost disadvantage exists, and they are impossible to attack in the aggregate. They must be broken down and assigned to a discrete business unit, even if done arbitrarily. Then a manager with hands-on profit responsibility can argue about fairness and whether there is value received for the costs involved.

Although this is obviously not a precise exercise, it is effective and essential. Without full-cost profit-and-loss statements for product lines and customers, managers cannot really understand the profit economics of their business. Further, they can't make the types of intelligent business decisions and plans important in today's environment.

Defining Issues and Priorities

The third step in implementing marketing practices is to ensure that the key issues facing each attractive market segment have been realistically defined in light of the current and rapidly changing business environment. There is nothing new about this requirement, but the fact is that very few management teams actually take the time to apply the discipline necessary to objectively define and prioritize the *key issues* that can make or break their business in each market segment or for each major product line. For example, the issues of higher cost products, lower productivity, a lack of new products, and slow delivery have plagued most manufacturers.

Many large companies around the world, in industries including computers, steel, automotive, machine tool, textile, chemicals, and construction equipment, have suffered badly as a result. However, only a few of these companies have addressed these issues in an effective way. Most have been unable to clearly identify the key issues, set priorities, and develop the necessary business plans to overcome the underlying problems.

While the specific issues will certainly vary for different companies and industries, the management mind-set should not vary. To deal effectively with an increasingly turbulent marketplace, priorities must be set so that the business can survive unexpected blows, adapt to sudden surprises, and capitalize on small windows of opportunity that will develop and close much more quickly than they have in the past.

Some progressive managers kick off their planning process with a session aimed specifically at reaching agreement on key issues and priorities for each market segment or major product lines. As one general manager stated:

> Our past planning has typically evolved into a number-crunching and form-filling exercise all too quickly, and we never took the time to really think about the need for fundamental changes. Now we spend the first day talking about issues facing the business in each segment and product line and the need for shifts in priorities and direction. This is strictly a thinking, discussion, and "what-if" session where we identify external opportunities and threats and examine the internal situation that may hinder us. Anybody that tries to take up much time with cost or sales projections at this stage gets shot down.

Properly identifying and defining a list of key issues provides a compelling set of planning guidelines for any business team. For example,

1. Innovation must never cease. Demonstrable product and process improvements must be achieved year after year.
2. Productivity gains per dollar of capital and per employee must be achieved annually. These gains must exceed inflation and achieve demonstrably lower costs.
3. Liquidity becomes a more important objective, often more than reported earnings. It provides the flexibility to deal more effectively with unexpected events than is possible when everything is tied up in fixed and slow-moving assets.
4. All cycle and response times must be continuously reduced (e.g., manufacturing, delivery, product development, request for quote, payback).
5. A "frightened" and relentless sense of urgency must be the way of life in all parts of the business.

These points may seem fundamental and rather obvious. However, very few managers actually pay sufficient attention to them. Ask yourself these questions:

1. How many managers demand, measure, and achieve real productivity gains year after year in each business unit?
2. How many managers are really pushing to improve liquidity and cash flow over reported earnings?
3. How many have actually driven total assets below 50 cents on each dollar of sales (a reasonable but demanding target for most manufacturing companies), and how many have concrete plans to turn total capital employed faster each year?
4. How many managers have ever considered the idea of doubling or tripling their annual inventory turns?
5. How many managers can show that product development cycles are much shorter for themselves and are improving over competitors?
6. How many can demonstrate that manufacturing and delivery cycles have been cut in half and that most requests for quotes on specials can be given within one day?
7. How many have a sufficient and relentless sense of urgency to personally adjust and encourage others around them to adjust to this much faster paced environment?

We have found that a broad cross section of managers from various industries unequivocally recognize the increasing turbulence in their market environment. On a scale of 1 to 10, with 10 being the highest level of turbulence, they consistently rate their market environment as more turbulent today than ever before, much closer to the 9 or 10 level than to 5. They also recognize the importance of shifting their attitudes along the lines described in the previous paragraph. At the same time, however, they realize there has not been a companywide adjustment of priorities or strategies to deal with this increased turbulence. Even more alarming, they uniformly express concern that their general managers and management teams do not have the knowledge or capabilities to make the necessary changes or to respond more quickly.

Realigning the Organization

Organization or reorganization schemes have been proposed ad nauseam as solutions to many business problems. As a general rule, organizational changes, especially those that simply reshuffle the same names into different boxes on the organization chart, don't improve anything. Therefore, we are not suggesting some new organization approach that is better suited for these turbulent times. However, many organizations are still too top heavy, overstructured, and overstaffed to be responsive to market needs and too costly to be competitive. The structure and staffing of any organization must be rigorously challenged to ensure it is really geared to accomplish the fundamental objectives of the business in as cost-effective a manner as possible. An honest evaluation of the answers to the following critical questions will provide a good foundation for action:

1. Is the organization structured to serve markets or simply to manage functions and sell products to large customers? Have priority markets been identified? Does someone have primary responsibility for ensuring that the product/service package is tailored to each target market? Do mechanisms exist to ensure cross-functional coordination for target markets? Is there any kind of a market focus in the selling organization?

2. Are there enough discrete profit centers? Do enough managers and cross-functional teams feel the burden and accountability of full profit responsibility? Is the business unit larger than its most successful smaller competitors? Are there any big cost centers that are not allocated or matched to someone who has a profit and loss responsibility?

3. Are there corporate, group, or division staff redundancies? Do the same titles exist at different levels (e.g., corporate controller, group controller, division controller, plant controller)? If so, does it make sense? Can staff positions or groups show how they actively contribute to profit results? If so, do line managers agree that these functions are worth the cost?

4. Are there too many layers? Are there more than three layers between the business unit manager and first-level workers? Are there managers with assignments limited to managing one, two, three, or four people? Why? Can any of these activities be combined under one manager? Why not?

5. Is the ratio of supporters to actual results producers satisfactory? How many people actually make a direct contribution to results (e.g., first-line sales personnel, direct hourly workers, sales engineering and order-entry workers, handlers of incoming materials, and storing and shipping personnel)? How many managers, staff, and support personnel are just cheering them on? If there is more than one support person for every four or five producers, what do they do? How do they contribute to profits?

These questions are not new, but the answers are more important now than ever. Traditional or experience-based answers are probably wrong because conditions have changed so dramatically. Moreover, it is doubtful whether existing management can or will ever come up with the right answers; they have vested interests, and the changes needed are simply too tough for them to swallow. These organizational structure questions are not as serious for many young and smaller sized companies since they are not as likely to be troubled with highly structured, functionally focused organizations lacking a dedicated market orientation. However, even managers in these companies must constantly fight the natural tendency to become more structured, bureaucratic, and lethargic.

Reassessing Strategies

As a general rule, a company pursuing the same strategy today that it did 24 months ago is probably on the wrong track. Too many changes have occurred in markets, competitors, products, and technologies to allow a strategy to go unadjusted for this length of time. Therefore, management should set aside a block of time to periodically address three fundamental questions.

1. What markets and business(es) are we in?
2. What markets and business(es) should we be in?
3. What markets and business(es) should we avoid?

These are not easy questions to answer any time; they are particularly difficult when so many things change so quickly. But failure to raise and respond to these questions can be fatal.

Strategies must be designed from the outside-in to overcome the product and technology constraints that tend to restrict the thinking and actions of so many companies. This is a crucial point since thinking from the outside-in opens up a wide variety of options. For example, consider a manufacturer of industrial drills. Should he simply sell a wide range of standard drills as his traditional manufacturing skills might dictate, or should he move beyond his capabilities into special-purpose drills for specific market applications or new materials? Or, going even further, should he conclude that he will help customers make holes in the most efficient way possible and, consequently, move into laser and/or fluid drilling systems that are being used to drill an increasing number of holes? Perhaps he should move in an entirely different direction and manufacture surface coatings that are used to extend the wear life of tools and many critical parts. While none of these options may actually prove to be desirable, they won't even be seen if the historical product and technology constraints are not removed. Obviously, there are a number of points to be considered in evaluating any business strategy, but the following four questions can help avoid wasted time spent arguing about "can't-win" strategies:

1. Is the strategy designed to serve specified markets as opposed to simply selling products to everyone?
2. Do the target markets offer attractive sales and especially profit growth opportunities?
3. Is the cost/profit structure attractive (e.g., breakeven point at 35 to 40 percent of capacity, gross margin of 35-plus percent, working capital of 30 percent to 35 percent of sales, return on assets of 20 percent plus, and so on)?
4. Is the plan based on demonstrable advantages over the competition? Does the strategy revolve around distinctive and needed product benefits that provide a competitive edge?

Unless these questions can be answered positively, the strategy has little chance of success as a building-block business. Time shouldn't be wasted talking about what is considered to be a can't-win plan. Can't-win situations are just too tough to overcome, no matter how effectively they are managed or how hard management works.

SUMMARY

"The Forgetting Curve," is an article that agrees with our point of view. Sir Levan Maddock states that it is easier to learn new ideas and approaches than to forget old ones. While there are plenty of schools for learning, there are none for helping you to forget. Maddock writes:

> To cherish traditions, old buildings, ancient cultures, and graceful lifestyles is a worthy thing—but in the world of technology to cling to outmoded methods of manufacture, old product lines, old markets, or old attitudes among management and workers is a prescription for suicide. A long-established business will have old plant, probably the wrong mix of skills in the workforce, surplus machinery and buildings, and will carry stock no longer relevant to the business. These constraints will be compounded by old-style attitudes toward management methods, a trade union structure inherited from earlier and different times, and an ethos ill-suited to the changing world.[2]

---

2. Sir Levan Maddock, "The Forgetting Curve," *New Scientist*, February 11, 1982, p. 12.

Two points are important to remember. First, it is essential to forget the way things were. In outside-in, market-driven management terms, the so-called good old days may now be the bad old days. Neither time nor economic recovery can restore the business as we knew it yesterday. We are now playing a new ballgame with a much tougher set of rules and much faster competitors. Second, every member of a company's management team must understand what the rules of this new game are and the changes necessary to first survive and then become a winner. Otherwise, they may not even get a turn at bat. To ensure another time at bat, most companies need a new game plan. We believe the best game plan is to become more market driven in every aspect of the business. We will next examine what it means to be a truly market-driven business unit and how to identify the specific areas in any operation that need improvement.

CHAPTER 2

Outside-In Management

There is always a risk that a term such as *market driven* will simply turn out to be a faddish play on words. This risk is very real since so much of the business literature today is overloaded with buzzwords, catchy titles, and simple solutions. And the term *market-driven management* could easily fall into any of these categories. However, it does not. We will show that it is a proven and practical approach to profitable growth. Moreover, it is based on a time-tested set of principles that have worked and will work for any business today and tomorrow.

OUTSIDE-IN PROCESS

Market-driven management is an outside-in management process that revolves around what we call the "six Cs of market-driven management." As we see it, four of these Cs should be the essential components of strategy development for any business. The first two, understanding *customer needs* and *competitive offerings,* should be the force that drives and molds the third and fourth, *capabilities* and *costs,* to meet the requirements of selected market targets. The fifth C, *continuous improvement* in costs and productivity, is a relentless process designed to improve productivity and generate customer value. The sixth C, *cross-functional teams,* is the catalyst that ensures that all key managers are actively involved in developing business plans and are committed to their successful implementation.

While this concept is easy to verbalize and theoretically makes sense, it is rarely followed in technical businesses. Instead, functional managers usually jealously regard their existing capabilities and costs as "givens" that they must live with as they go to market. For example, Xerox, the pioneer in photocopying technology, continued to push its large, rapid-copy equipment into the market when many potential customers needed only a few copies of any document. Their failure to adjust capabilities, costs, and new products to meet this need opened the door for Canon, Minolta, Sharp, and other Japanese competitors to capture this large beachhead with their desktop copiers. Xerox ultimately made adjustments to their product design, costs, and distribution capabilities, but the company failed to recover the ground they lost. Many companies fall into the same kind of trap. They view the business from the inside-out and seek to push traditional products, services, and costs without learning what customers need or what competitors offer.

As Exhibit 2–1 shows, such a view is a 180-degree difference from a market-driven approach. A market-driven approach starts outside with the customer and moves into the business to structure internal capabilities and costs in a way that leads to a distinct product/service package that meets the needs of a particular customer group.

The distinction between inside-out and outside-in was not as critical when most markets were growing and when technology was more stable because competition was less intense and because managers could ride upward with the demand curves, price increases, and long product life cycles. However, it now is crucial because many markets are not growing rapidly, customers are more demanding, technology is exploding, and

E X H I B I T   2–1

Comparison of Management Approaches

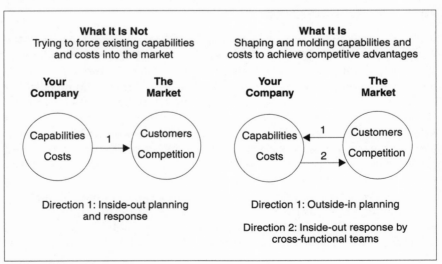

global competition is intensifying from both anticipated and unexpected sources. Outside-in industrial companies make what they can sell rather than sell what they can make.

Many people use the term *market-driven management* mistakenly, relating it only to activities in the marketing department. Bill Ward, president of Amerace Corporation in Hackettstown, New Jersey, clarified the term to his management team at one of our training sessions for his associates when he said:

> We are not talking about becoming marketing oriented. We want to become more market driven. There is a big difference. Being market driven is a much broader management concept that must start with general managers and then cuts across and up and down the entire company.

Bill Ward is right on target. However, it is useful to expand on his statement to ensure understanding and reinforce its importance.

MARKET-DRIVEN MANAGEMENT DEFINED

Market-driven management is a cross-functional effort involving all departments and levels of the organization. Properly followed, it ensures that all activities are coordinated to meet the specific needs of target market segments. R&D projects must be focused on developing solutions to common and verified customer problems; manufacturing must be committed to meeting cost targets, quality standards, and delivery cycles; and sales must be focused on identifying and interpreting customer problems and then counseling users and buyers on the correct solutions. If one were to ask individual managers within any of these functional areas how they operate, they would most likely answer, "Just as you described." It is unlikely that their counterparts in other functional areas would agree and, even more unlikely, that there would be a consensus among all managers at all levels. Achieving this market-driven focus with fully agreed-on objectives and priorities in each functional area requires the complete support of everyone in the organization. Market-driven management is much easier said than done because it flies in the face of the attitudes and actions of most managers. This point becomes clear when the common management and operating practices of most technical companies are examined:

- Most suppliers tend to view their markets too broadly, classifying them by product type (e.g., large versus small motors, truck versus passenger tires, industry categories such as agriculture, construction, retail, and manufacturer) rather than by common user requirements and unsatisfied needs.

- Suppliers are not close enough to customers to understand how they operate and, therefore, cannot tailor a product/service package that offers an attractive value proposition.

- Many suppliers' thinking and actions tend to be dominated by existing product and process features that they blindly or arrogantly assume provide unquestionable customer value.

- Most suppliers too often make sweeping generalizations about competitors but don't have the facts to make accurate side-by-side comparisons of competitor features, benefits, costs, or market positions.

- The key functional areas of the business tend to operate independently as territorial fiefdoms without any cohesive cooperation to ensure that all functions are geared to meet the requirements of target markets.

- The sales and marketing programs revolve around aggressive efforts to get large purchase orders rather than identifying and solving customer problems and providing cost-effective solutions to these problems.

These practices eventually cause profit margins and market positions to erode and threaten a company's independence or survival.

INSIDE-OUT APPROACH

A situation at Texas Instruments, the global electronics giant that pioneered the mass production of semiconductors, illustrates what can happen when management follows an insular inside-out approach and fails to recognize the dynamic nature of the marketplace:

> Long the worldwide sales leader in semiconductors, Texas Instruments had slipped to third place—behind Japan's Fujitsu Ltd. and Nippon Electric. With semiconductor sales of $2 billion, Texas Instruments had a long way to go just to get back to where it was four years ago, when its chip business earned $516 million before taxes on sales of $2.7 billion.
>
> For decades, Texas Instruments dominated the world semiconductor industry because of its overwhelming strength in technology and manufacturing. Their success caused the company's leaders to believe that TI could do no wrong, according to long-time employees.
>
> But that attitude of technical arrogance created an insularity that left Texas Instruments out of touch with its rapidly changing markets. That inside-out isolation, in turn, caused marketing blunders and big losses in such consumer products as digital watches and home computers. "We got too damn arrogant," said the president of the semiconductor division.

Under the leadership of its new CEO, the culture of Texas Instruments has been undergoing a badly needed transformation. Team spirit has been instilled at all levels of the company and a great effort has been made to get rid of the old hubris, employees, and customers that were so harmful. Moreover, top management has withdrawn to segments that they think they can still defend.

THE SIX Cs OF A MARKET-DRIVEN COMPANY

There is nothing magical about how a truly market-driven company operates, but the contrasts between a market-driven company and many other industrial companies are dramatic:

1. All thinking and actions of a market-driven company begin with a complete understanding of the applications, current requirements, and emerging needs of specific *customer groups* or *market segments.*

2. They study and document side-by-side *competitive* product and service performance to determine relative strengths and weaknesses in each market segment versus each key competitor.

3. They objectively compare their existing *capabilities* with changing market requirements and are willing to make the changes necessary to serve attractive market segments while forgoing or withdrawing from others.

4. They strive to improve their *costs* and efficiency so that they can provide their target customers with greater value and/or improve their company's productivity and profits.

5. They *continually improve* customer value, response and cycle time, productivity, and profit by constantly learning and working smarter.

6. They utilize *cross-functional* business teams with profit responsibility to ensure that all key activities, priorities, and decisions are synchronized to serve target market needs and are never stymied by functional priorities or personal biases.

As shown in Exhibit 2–2, these six principles build upon each other to form a powerful framework for any business to defend or attack any market.

In high-performance companies such as Pall, National Starch, Loctite, and Henkel's Parker Amchem, prominent positions have been built by following these concepts in all areas of their organizations. Many highly focused smaller companies have also achieved enviable results

E X H I B I T   2–2

The Six Cs of Market-Driven Management

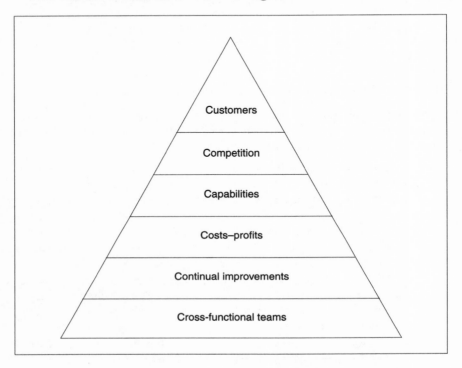

because of the way they got their start—by concentrating on a market segment and providing a demonstrably superior product/service package. Finally, a few companies such as Nucor, a steel producer, and Bandag, a tire retreader, have achieved distinguished records in troubled industries where most participants are losing ground by not being market driven.

Most technically based companies, both large and small, are *not* market driven. Many of the largest ones are so bureaucratic and poorly focused that it is not surprising that they are unable to profitably grow. Even those few companies that appear at first glance to be more market driven are not following a well-defined set of practices that are an integral part of the company's culture. Moreover, many larger companies that have been market driven have lost their competitive edge because they have lost sight of the factors that made them market driven in the first place. Exhibit 2–3 shows the natural evolution of a company as it grows, enjoys success, becomes bureaucratic, and then loses ground.

EXHIBIT   2-3

How Market-Driven Management Begins and Ends
Most Companies Evolve from Left to Right: Market-Driven
Management Moves Companies to the Left

Entrepreneurial or Market-Driven	Rapid Growth or More Structure	Mature or Bureaucratic
Everyone focuses on the most attractive market segments and key accounts that are prioritized as defend, attack, de-emphasize, or withdraw.	New products and customers added; new markets and countries entered; larger families of products result.	Volume objectives take a priority to cover fixed costs and to utilize plant capacity.
Everyone is sensitive to competitive advantages and disadvantages by market segment and key accounts.	More investment in plant, equipment, people, and overhead; more meetings occur and reports written.	Smaller but attractive market opportunities are overlooked, disregarded, or pursued too late.
Decentralized decision making and informal, cross-functional team spirit dominates; nothing is sacred—new ideas and criticisms flow freely in the company.	More people and structure added; staff and management levels added; more procedures, forms, and approvals.	Size and complacency cause a decline in margins and product line net profits; market positions begin to drop.
No company trappings, spartan surroundings; everyone acts cost effectively to improve productivity; people are empowered to make many decisions.	Increases in fixed costs, shared costs, total unit costs, and higher breakeven points; productivity improvements plateau.	Department isolation, more form filling, and bureaucracy sets in; most response, lead, and cycle times are slower than best competitors' times.
Everyone thinks and acts with a relentless sense of urgency to profitably serve customer needs, reduce threats, and capture opportunities.	Effective customer solutions and prompt service take a back seat to meeting sales quotas, getting products shipped, and keeping plants filled.	Aggressive self-starters become disenchanted, leave, or develop other interests; demoralization and mediocrity permeate the business unit, and productivity declines.

During its entrepreneurial or startup period, it has all the vital characteristics of a market-driven business. The organization is highly focused and responsive. It operates informally around teams in an open-minded environment of change.

As the business grows, more products, structure, and management levels are added. Larger families of products and bigger business units result. More investments are made in plant and equipment, and volume becomes increasingly important to absorb higher fixed costs.

When a business moves into the maturity stage, it often faces serious problems that can easily go undetected. Profits may be high even though margins and market positions have slipped. Bureaucracy sets in. Overemphasis on traditions, folklore, and past success inhibit an objective self-examination that could lead to appropriate corrective actions. As a result, good people tend to become disenchanted and plateau or leave the organization; mediocrity prevails; and productivity declines.

Constant management attention is required to fight this natural evolutionary tendency to becoming more bureaucratic and less proactive. Unless bureaucracy and all of its clues are constantly fought, it will grow and take over like crab grass, leading to all the negative consequences the term suggests. Top management must constantly be on the prowl for signs of bureaucracy and then swiftly end it. Unnecessary meetings, committees, reports, measurements, procedures, and approvals are common early warning signals that stifle people.

ASSESSING MARKET-DRIVEN CAPABILITIES

It is important to determine how market driven a business unit is and, more importantly, where it falls short. Corrective actions or improvement programs are needed where deficiencies exist. Determining the areas for improvement, however, is not a simple task. As we said at the outset, market-driven management is too often a buzzword statement that everyone espouses without really knowing what they are talking about. Because it has not been defined in operational terms, there are many conflicting views on what the term means, and there is little evidence that it has a substantive meaning, even in companies where it is commonly used.

To overcome this problem, we have developed a rating scale for the operational factors that determine whether or not a business unit is market driven in key areas of the business (see Exhibit 2–4). The scale has two sets of extremes. The left-side factors describe the worst-case situations that would represent liabilities to any company or business unit. The right side describes the ideal situations that would be advantageous for

Market-Driven Diagnostic

Liabilities	-5	0	+5	Advantages	Consensus
1. Market facts are nonexistent, unverified, or underutilized in planning and decision making.		│ │ │ │ │ │ │ │ │ │		1. The value of market facts is widely recognized as the foundation for all planning and decision making.	_____
2. Market segment definitions are too broad or based on an industry, products, technology, manufacturing, or customer sizes in each country and region.		│ │ │ │ │ │ │ │ │ │		2. Market segments and key accounts are defined by common needs and grouped as attack, defend, de-emphasize, and withdraw in each country and region of the world.	_____
3. Side-by-side competitive comparisons are nonexistent, unverified, too broad, and underutilized in decision making.		│ │ │ │ │ │ │ │ │ │		3. Side-by-side competitor analysis is done by segment, country, and region of the world and is used to develop market/product strategies.	_____
4. Accounting systems driven by generally accepted accounting principles and upward reporting rather than for management decision making.		│ │ │ │ │ │ │ │ │ │		4. Net profitability is reported, shared, and reviewed regularly for each product line, customer, market segment, and distributor.	_____
5. Lower cost claims are limited to manufacturing, are unsupported, and competitor actions and results imply otherwise.		│ │ │ │ │ │ │ │ │ │		5. Documented side-by-side comparisons show total unit costs are in line with or better than the regional and global segment competitors.	_____
6. Quality goals, product performance, and customer satisfaction measurements are nonexistent or talked about without programs for continual improvement.		│ │ │ │ │ │ │ │ │ │		6. Superior quality is relentlessly demonstrated through global side-by-side comparisons of yield rates, product performance, services, and customer satisfaction.	_____
7. Machine efficiency and capacity utilization considerations dominate product line and customer mix decisions.		│ │ │ │ │ │ │ │ │ │		7. Manufacturing is committed to continuous productivity gains that lower costs and seek a richer product and customer mix.	_____

(continued)

E X H I B I T 2–4 *(concluded)*

Liabilities	-5	0	+5	Advantages	Consensus
8. Response and cycle times in many departments are lagging, and measurement and improvement programs are not in place to reduce response times.		I I I I I I I I I I I		8. Response and cycle times in most departments are equal or superior to the best competitors, and the organization relentlessly searches for more improvements and increased speed.	___
9. Existing products and technology suppress thinking about new market needs and new opportunities.		I I I I I I I I I I I		9. People are willing to think beyond existing products and technologies to serve present and new market segments and customer needs.	___
10. New products are too late, too costly, or not demonstrably better for target customer groups and are not a major source of sales and profits.		I I I I I I I I I I I		10. New products are guided by cross-functional teams and are a major source of sales and profits.	___
11. Sales training is uneven, mostly product- and feature-driven and at odds with target market priorities, company goals, and customer needs.		I I I I I I I I I I I		11. All sales training activities are highly focused to communicate tangible and intangible customer benefits to target markets and key accounts.	___
12. The organization is too structured around functions, wide families of products, large accounts, and too many management levels and meetings.		I I I I I I I I I I I		12. The organization is relatively flat, informal, and focused on small families of products or markets, and net profit responsibility is assigned for each major product, market, and key account.	___
13. Planning is done sequentially by individuals and functions, and without necessary market focus, cross-functional integration, or team commitments.		I I I I I I I I I I I		13. Cross-functional teams develop and implement business plans for each product, market, and key account with horizontal commitments to achieve the planned sales and profit goals.	___
14. Recognition and reward programs are not aligned to market priorities, to short- and long-term goals, and to individuals, business teams, and business unit results.		I I I I I I I I I I I		14. Recognition and reward programs reward both shorter- and longer-term results and are aligned with market priorities that recognize individuals, business teams, and the business unit results.	___

28

any company or business unit. Our experience suggests that it is rare that the ideal +5 is ever plotted for any of these factors. We have never encountered a case where the majority of these factors were rated higher than 2 or 3 on the positive side. Rather, most ratings tend to be on the negative side, which demonstrates the difficulties of becoming a market-driven entity.

The advantages of using this scale to assess market-driven performance should be clear. The mystique is taken out of the concept of market-driven management, and a base is provided for discussing it in operational terms. Individual or composite ratings that can be used as a basis for gaining agreement on the problem areas can also be obtained. Once problem areas are defined, the foundation has been laid for meaningful corrective action. Properly used, the rating scale provides a solid base for building real substance into market-driven management. Without an operational definition and an objective evaluation of the current situation, market-driven management is not a useful description of anything. We have worked with hundreds of managers who know that market-driven management is absolutely essential. However, they are often at a loss to articulate it and make it a reality across all functions of their business.

Precision is not the key to using this scale; objectivity is. Our experience shows that individuals should first make their own ratings. Then consensus (not average) ratings should be developed through cross-functional group discussions. The involvement of all business areas in rating these factors is very important. With the possible exception of a general manager, most individuals in an organization do not have the firsthand knowledge to render an intelligent judgment on all 14 factors. Even the general manager is often too far removed from certain areas of the business to really know how different areas are operating. Also, differing opinions as well as constructive arguments tend to get the entire group more deeply and objectively involved than any individual is likely to be on his or her own. Moreover, a better basis exists for improving low ratings when the determination is made by a group of core managers rather than by an individual who could be viewed as simply having an ax to grind.

We have used the market-driven factors and rating scale with managers from numerous companies in a wide range of industries. The results have invariably been very useful. They have shown that some units within these companies are more market driven than others. They have enabled senior management to zero in on problems and suggest corrective actions or ways that one business unit has taken to effectively solve the problem that can help another. Most importantly, they established a reference point that can be tracked to determine where progress has been made and where more work is needed.

We suggest you first read this book before making an initial evaluation of your own situation because all chapters of the book further explain what market-driven management is. The last chapter in this book describes how to put the corrective actions to work by training cross-functional business teams with current hands-on situations.

SUMMARY

Market-driven managers recognize that a business is defined by the outside-in changing needs and requirements of customer groups and competitive offerings, not by existing products, technologies, or management experience. The advantages to this outside in-approach are enormous:

- Strategic planning is no longer simply a bureaucratic form-filling exercise with no real meaning to the business team. Substance is provided for cross-functional agreement on direction, priorities, and action programs.
- Market focuses that facilitate early assessment of threats and opportunities and much quicker responses are provided. Resources get allocated to the more attractive opportunities.
- The risk of incorrectly defining or limiting the scope of the business is reduced, and more options for improving sales and profit growth are uncovered.
- Fast-changing product and process technology is applied appropriately, and the payback odds are increased, despite shorter life cycles.

The balance of this book provides the approaches necessary to think and act as a market-driven manager for profitable top-line growth—a quintessential requirement in an increasingly turbulent business environment.

CHAPTER 3

Proactive Marketing

Many of the shortcomings described in the first chapter can be traced to deficiencies in understanding industrial marketing, particularly at the top and general management levels. The edge has been dulled, and the effects—the losses—are there: loss of productivity improvements, loss of world share, loss of entire markets, and, what's worse, loss of thousands of jobs. Today, Japan—not the United States—is producing the greatest numbers of automobiles, televisions, motorcycles, and so on. Business is booming in most Asian countries, while it is stagnant or shrinking in some of the more developed countries. Causes? There are lots of explanations: too much emphasis on short-term profits, balance sheet management, supplier reductions and dictatorial customers, too few new products, too many "me-too" products, insufficient internal growth, bureaucratic organizations, high cost structures, and work ethics, just to name a few. There is also the cultural explanation: Americans—and their work ethic—differ from both the Europeans and the Asians.

There are a lot of reasons companies are uncompetitive. We can subscribe to all of them as elements of the picture. But that's all they are—pieces of the picture, piecemeal causes; they don't frame the issue. By themselves, they don't account for the decline of our competitiveness in so many industries.

We suggest that a case can be made that there's another cause, perhaps even more comprehensive, on which there has been little public debate. We believe one could argue that our most significant miss has been in marketing—something we in America pioneered as a management concept nearly 30 years ago for consumer goods companies but haven't practiced well in industrial or high-tech businesses. Good managers know how to reduce costs, reengineer, or restructure. But great leaders know they can't shrink their way to greatness. Great leaders also know how to profitably grow the top line with the marketing concept. If any industrial company is to thrive, not just survive, it must align every business unit and every employee around the industrial marketing concept, which is much more difficult to achieve in an industrial business than it is in a consumer goods company.

WHY INDUSTRIAL MARKETING IS DIFFICULT

Where is marketing now that we really need it? The answer is less clear because, in this day and age, one rarely quarrels with the importance of marketing. In fact, it would be difficult to find someone willing to argue against the idea that gearing all the activities of a business to be responsive to user needs (a simple but meaningful description of what industrial marketing is all about) is not only sensible but is the only way to run the business. Executives and managers that we've met all around the world agree that increased marketing effectiveness is the key to being more competitive and to accelerating sales and profit growth. Despite agreement on this point, many of these industrial executives are disappointed with their companies' marketing capabilities. To quote one company president in Germany:

> I can't really say that our marketing group is doing the job it should, and I don't know what to do about it. Our sales and administrative costs are up because of staff additions and higher salaries in the marketing department, but we are not getting the market leadership we need. We are about to invest $25 million for new plant and equipment for a new product line, and I am uneasy about the whole investment. Frankly, I don't feel comfortable about our ability to retain our competitive position against foreign competition with our high engineering and labor costs. This big manufacturing investment will lock us into our current products for at least the next 5 to 10 years.

Another company president said:

> Our marketing effort or focus is simply too narrow. We concentrate way too much on selling more of today's product, and we think far too little about what our customers and competitors are doing or where new technology could lead us. Our engineering and manufacturing operations do not look to marketing for leadership, and I know a lot of the things they do would be done differently if we were a stronger marketing company. There is no doubt in my mind that marketing is important, but how do we make it work the way it should?

These executives are clearly concerned and perplexed about what they should do to achieve improvements. They illustrate an all-too-common problem. Too many industrial executives regard marketing solely as an isolated function and reason that, if they pay enough money or hire enough people, the company's marketing should improve. This approach might work in a retail goods company, but it won't work in an industrial manufacturing company. Most industrial companies have too narrow a view of marketing; even fewer executives see marketing as something that begins before you design a product and ends long after a customer buys the product. Obviously, marketing is a function, but simply pouring more money or people into this function in no way ensures a stronger marketing company. To be a significant force in a company, marketing, like quality, must start at the top. Top and general management must provide the leadership and direction to ensure that marketing considerations are woven into the very fabric of every function or discipline involved in the business.

Pat Parker, chairman of Parker Hannifin Corporation, a $4+ billion manufacturer of motion control components and systems, makes this point very clear at the beginning of every market-driven management training workshop for his managers. After noting that attendees at one session included managers from manufacturing, engineering, quality assurance, purchasing, legal, finance, and sales, he said:

> You might wonder why you are participating in a program about marketing. If any of you think you are not a part of marketing, you are mistaken. Everyone in every function in our company is a critical part of marketing. If you don't do your job right, our marketing suffers. In other words, marketing at Parker Hannifin isn't one department; the whole company is the marketing department.

This attitude is the only sound basis for the intelligent allocation of the company's resources—management's most important responsibility. Failure to think this way will lead to results that parallel those in the previous two examples. General management is increasingly concerned about their company's ability to compete; the marketing function is often expanded and costs are increased, but the company's true marketing capabilities do not improve.

In only a very few industrial or high-tech companies can executives honestly say they are happy with what marketing has done for them. More important, in even fewer can they support this belief with concrete evidence of improved results. The majority of executives in these companies talk about the concept, but it's hard to find examples where strong marketing has actually produced positive results. Most of these industrial companies haven't learned how to "walk the talk" of being market driven. In many companies, executives are downright discouraged with the results of their efforts. Very few of these executives have written the concept off; it is fundamentally too sound. But many of them are perplexed about what they need to do to get the results they want.

This chapter is designed to identify the obstacles that have prevented industrial companies from getting the payoff they should from marketing. It also presents some proven approaches on how to clear these obstacles out of the way.

WHERE INDUSTRIAL MARKETING FAILS

Marketing has not measured up to expectations in many industrial and high-tech companies because management has concentrated on the trappings and quick fixes rather than the substance. When most executives talk about what their companies have done to become more marketing oriented, they usually point to actions such as the following:

- Declarations of support from top management in the form of speeches, annual report hype, and public relations talks to the investment community.
- Creation of a marketing organization, including appointment of a marketing head and product or market managers.
- Establishment of a market research function and reassignment of some salespeople to large customers.
- Increased expenditures for customer surveys, advertising, and trade shows.
- Hirings of MBAs with "marketing" backgrounds from the better known business schools.
- Hirings of managers from other industries and companies known for their marketing skills.

These actions by themselves are no guarantee of marketing success. In fact, many of them are a waste. As Pat Parker of Parker Hannifin pointed out to his managers, effective marketing requires a fundamental shift in attitude and behavior throughout the company so that everyone in every functional area places paramount importance on being responsive to market needs. The steps taken in most companies are not very helpful because they fail to accomplish the crucial shifts in attitude and behavior throughout the organization. The most highly developed marketing departments cannot, by themselves, produce the needed changes.

Why have so few companies gone beyond the trappings to achieve the change in attitude and behavior that ensures substantive marketing? Our combined 75 years of business experience and management training suggests that one or more of these situations frequently exist:

- Top and general management have no idea how the marketing concept should be applied in an industrial or high-tech company.
- Management understands the industrial marketing concept but has not committed itself to the actions and decisions needed to reinforce it throughout the organization.
- Management has failed to install a cross-functional business planning process necessary for effective implementation of the industrial marketing concept, especially across the nonsales and marketing functions.
- The company does not know how to segment industrial markets, and it lacks market facts and cost-profit information to select target markets, technologies, and customers for emphasis.

We will discuss each of these situations in turn, illustrating the kinds of problems they can cause and pointing out the major steps required to make marketing the driving force it should be in any industrial company.

Understanding the Industrial Marketing Concept

When we say that in many cases management does not understand how the marketing concept applies to their industrial situation, you may wonder how highly paid, presumably intelligent industrial executives can fail to understand a concept that is discussed so extensively. But time and time again we find evidence that, although most industrial executives are quick to say they understand and believe in the marketing concept, most of their actions and decisions show otherwise.

To prove our point, we first define what industrial marketing is not. It is not simply a departmental operation set up to handle advertising, promotion, merchandising, and selling, as might be the case in a consumer goods company, nor does it necessarily mean striving for the greatest short-term profit contribution, going all-out for volume and large accounts, or seeking to serve everyone in the market with the best possible service. Rather, industrial marketing is a companywide business philosophy that first identifies the perceived and often unarticulated needs of each customer group. It then designs and makes a product/service package that enables the company to serve target customer groups or market segments more effectively than its competition and at an attractive supplier profit. To put it simply, marketing starts before you design or make a product and it can be defined as serving customers profitably.

Marketing in industrial and high-tech companies is much more of a general management responsibility than it is in the consumer products field. In a consumer goods company, major changes in marketing strategy can be made and carried out within the marketing department through changes in advertising emphasis, types of promotion, package design, and the like. But there are no brand managers in industrial companies! In an industrial or high-tech company, changes in marketing strategy are more likely to involve commitments for new equipment, shifts in product development priorities, or departures from traditional engineering and manufacturing approaches, any one of which would have companywide implications. Marketing may identify the need for such departures, but general management must make the decision concerning the course the company will take to respond to the market. More important, general management must see that the focus is pursued in every functional area.

This definition reveals four key dimensions of industrial marketing: (1) identifying customer requirements and unarticulated needs; (2) selecting customer groups or market segments for which the company can develop a competitive edge; (3) designing and producing the right product/service packages; and (4) aiming for improved cost, profit, and productivity. Let's discuss each point.

1. *Identifying customers' requirements and unarticulated needs.* There are many manufacturers who know all there is to know about their own technology and virtually nothing about how their customers actually operate, make money, and lose money. Most industrial suppliers are not close enough to their customers to learn about their current, emerging, and unarticulated needs. Many of these suppliers spend millions of dollars developing labor-saving parts for the least costly aspects of their customers' production processes, or they design costly features into the product without considering the benefit of each feature to groups of customers with similar needs. They then wonder why their sales personnel are not able to sell the "differentiated" new products. These backward companies try to sell what they can make rather than make what they can sell.

2. *Selecting customer groups for emphasis.* We all know companies that strive to be all things to all customers. Such companies inevitably end up with a warehouse of marginal products and a long list of unproductive customers who generate a small fraction of profits. It is not surprising that the more selective and focused companies earn better profits; they concentrate their limited resources on filling specialized needs for market segments and customers that will pay for value. These same disciplined suppliers also know when to walk away from some market segments and de-emphasize some customers.

3. *Designing the right product/service package.* We have all heard horror stories about companies that failed in the marketplace because they tried to sell a Mercedes when the customer group wanted a Ford or a Jeep Cherokee. Actually, a company does not have to be this far off the mark with its product or service package to be a marketing flop. Most industrial buying decisions hinge on minor differences, and a company is in trouble whenever the competition has a product/service package that meets the customer's needs just a little better. Smart companies know that marketing starts before you begin a product design.

4. *Aiming for improved cost, profit, and productivity.* Too many companies talk a lot about a marketing and profit orientation, but a close look at how they make decisions reveals that sales volume is still the main consideration. Many of these companies would actually have a better profit picture if they gave a lower priority to volume, even if it meant scaling back the business and de-emphasizing or firing some customers. Most companies have insufficient cost-profit information about their product lines and customers to soundly make such decisions. Furthermore, a supplier's total costs must constantly decline, or your marketing will fail. To put it simply, you must improve productivity by continually doing more with less.

Now that we have defined marketing as a total business philosophy that encompasses every aspect of the business, it should be easier to distinguish those executives who understand the concept from those who do not. The president or general manager who consciously targets market segments with profit goals and frames a total business strategy in response to each market's needs shows that he or she understands the marketing concept. The president or general manager who creates or merely enlarges the marketing department, who continually pushes salespeople to find new customers of any sort, or who indiscriminately adds more products or customers to the line does not understand the concept and has no chance of leading a market-driven business unit.

The Nucor Corporation, possibly the most innovative and best-run steel company in the world, is one of the few industrial companies that realizes that marketing is first and foremost a general manager's responsibility. With sales of nearly $4 billion and more than 6,000 employees, Nucor has no corporate marketing titles, and no one in its numerous divisions has the word "marketing" in a job title. Ken Iverson, Nucor's visionary chairman, correctly sees each division general manager as the chief marketing officer. Very few top or general managers realize that industrial marketing should be the primary responsibility of a general manager or business unit manager.

Walking the Talk

Understanding the marketing concept is one thing; following through with the commitment to make tough implementation decisions is quite another. Most companies stumble badly here. Companies with a superior marketing effort, on the other hand, repeatedly demonstrate their commitment to follow the marketing concept by their willingness to require cooperation from all functions; to invest in long-term goals; and to face up to deficiencies in product, price, or service in any department in the division.

Parker Hannifin is an example of a company that is truly committed to industrial marketing. For each of the past 20 years, top management in this hydraulic, pneumatic, and electronic controls company has invested the time and funds to make marketing a dominant force in the company. To begin with, Parker annually trains many people in how to gather and use market facts, and develop strategies and business plans. This is not an easy task since many of the company's products are sold through distribution, and a special effort was required to develop information on their end-use customers who are serviced by distributors. Parker Hannifin also requires monthly feedback from its distributors on its end users: who they are, what they've spent, and the application for which they used the part or system. Parker also regularly analyzes the strengths and weaknesses of their product/service package versus the largest and fastest growing competitors in what CEO Duane Collins calls "competitive war rooms."

To avoid the bureaucracy that often interferes with proactive marketing, Parker Hannifin made the decision to keep all divisions small, lean, and focused on market segments. Today, the company has nearly a hundred such decentralized business units with average sales of $40 million each. Each functions as a "PT boat" rather than an "aircraft carrier." More importantly, the company continues to make investments in management training programs every year to help all management functions, as well as distributors, understand what marketing is all about. Even in slow economic periods, the company invests in marketing training so that it is ready for the next up-turn to defend positions and attack the more attractive new opportunities all over the globe.

National Starch and Chemical (NSC), a $2.5+ billion manufacturer of adhesives, resins, and industrial starches and one of the most profitable specialty chemical companies in the world (subsidiary of Unilever), has earned decades of annual profit increases by creatively converting cornstarch to customer value and introducing demonstrably better new products at premium prices with a professional value-added selling program. NSC's guerrilla warfare practices include having no marketing departments and no one with the title "marketing director." NSC believes that *everybody* in the company is in marketing. Everything at NSC is done with a dizzying sense of urgency and without bureaucratic interference. The company is flat, fluid, fast moving, and able to serve customers profitability. Again, it is a strategy based on spartan PT boats that can be rapidly deployed to attack or defend rather than based on trying to maneuver lumbering aircraft carriers that are bureaucracies with communication and response problems.

Cross-Functional Cooperation

The first commitment that top and general management must make is a willingness to require and, if necessary, force all functions to make the changes necessary to be responsive to market needs. In many cases this is more difficult than one might expect because management in most industrial companies must overcome a long-standing preoccupation with business objectives that cripple the marketing effort. For example, objectives such as "get more feet on the street," "keep the plant loaded," "raise all the prices," or "move more tonnage" are common watchwords in too many companies—and often the death knell for profit-making marketing. These attitudes are extremely difficult to overcome, especially when the product is the origin and chief reason for the past success of the enterprise. People are naturally reluctant to abandon a concept that has proven itself in the past. They then become complacent, arrogant, reactive, and, at best, late followers.

Remember too that marketing recommendations lack the precision of technical data. Typically, top management is confronted with hard numbers from manufacturing and engineering—material costs, product costs, installation costs, and so on. Marketing must make its case on the basis of weak early warning signals, subjective forecasts, intuition, and judgments from working with customers. Of course these forecasts are quantified, but they can never be stated with as much precision as the performance data submitted by manufacturing and engineering. Finally, many general managers have a technical background themselves and frequently tend to assess their products from a technical rather than a user point of view. Even fewer assess their products against side-by-side competitive comparisons with customers' interests and needs as the judge and jury.

The difficulties with committing to a cross-functional approach to make marketing a companywide focus led by general management are illustrated by the case of a large industrial pump manufacturer that had historically focused on selling the largest, highest powered, most maintenance-free units possible, with the thought that this approach favored its manufacturing economics. User needs, however, had shifted toward smaller, less costly units without the rugged engineering characteristics required for maintenance-free operation. Since this trend was clear with the progressive users, the supplier was losing its market position, and marketing had recommended a major redesign of the product line. The company's manufacturing and engineering executives, who were acknowledged industry experts, argued convincingly that the current product design was still superior to any competitors and that the company just needed to "sell harder" and "put more pressure on those damned distributors."

Faced with these conflicting points of view, top management decided to stick with the original product and put pressure on the marketing group for a more aggressive selling effort. It was not until the company lost substantial market share and its entire structure was threatened that the president could bring himself to change the product-driven opinions of his engineering and manufacturing executives and force the requested redesign.

As this company discovered, the task of shifting any company that has historically been dominated by product, engineering, and manufacturing considerations to one that is truly market oriented and driven by customers and competitive offerings is always enormous. It takes a tremendous effort on the part of top and general management to ensure that the proposals are carefully thought out, are solidly documented with verified customer needs and economic facts, and demonstrate an understanding of their impact on the other operating functions in their company. It also requires top management's understanding, as well as active support with both words and actions, to make the transition successfully. This usually takes two to three years to achieve, and then it must be implanted in new employees and continually reinforced with existing employees through ongoing management training programs. This brings us to the next aspect of a market-oriented commitment: adopting a long-term view.

An Obsession with the Short Term

The idea of investing to build and strengthen the company's market position is accepted and practiced every day in consumer goods companies. In fact, "investment spending" is a term often used in describing commitments required to achieve longer term objectives. This long-term idea does not seem to be acceptable or even considered in a large number of industrial and high-tech companies, perhaps due to Wall Street's pressure for improved quarterly performance. Actually, you could argue that a longer time frame is more critical in technical companies than in consumer package goods companies because of the longer cycle times needed for the design, manufacture, and selling of any new product. Designing performance or cost improvements for an already established product is a long, hard job; developing the field test or performance data to prove these advantages takes even more time, and many industrial users rigorously evaluate the cost effectiveness of each design.

Finally, it is understandably difficult to get an industrial customer to try a new or different piece of equipment that may cost thousands or even hundreds of thousands of dollars and, more important, that may affect an entire production process. It usually takes years to gain full customer acceptance and build a solid market base for a product in the industrial world. And that, in turn, bespeaks the necessity of a long-term view. At General Electric, former CEOs Ralph Cordiner, Fred Borch, and Reginald Jones nurtured the aircraft engine, gas turbine, and plastics businesses when they were small or money-losing operations. What chance of survival would such embryonic businesses have under GE's current CEO Jack Welch's mandate that an operation must be #1 or #2 in their field, with minimum returns, or it must be quickly fixed or sold? Such short-term pressures have caused GE to exit many manufacturing businesses in favor of quicker cash crops from financial, broadcast, and entertainment services. There are no Band-Aid solutions or quick fixes to build, improve, or turn around a declining industrial market position.

Despite these realities of industrial marketing, many executives are loathe to consider spending more money to build a stronger market position if the outlays cut into short-term profits. Ironically, the same people are often perfectly willing to think in these terms when it comes to a capital proposal for a new product or plant or equipment that requires 100 times more money. Good marketing decisions might have recommended that the capital not be spent, or they could have guided the investment to make better products with needed features and focus on the faster growing customer groups.

Consider the case of a chemical manufacturer that had committed several million dollars to the development of new products to make its line more competitive. It had also invested heavily in manufacturing equipment to get the new products ready for the market. When plans for market introduction were being made, the marketing director requested a budget increase to set up a small special sales group that would focus exclusively on the new products. He pointed out that although the added costs of a special sales group would not be recovered during the first two years, by the end of the second year the added volume at that time would more than cover the cost of the new group.

The division general manager initially balked at the budget increase, claiming it would slash short-term profits. It took a lot of effort, but the marketing director finally convinced him this was shortsighted by saying, "If we don't get these products established this year, we will lose the slim lead time we have in the market—and the $7 million we sank into development and equipment will be down the drain."

Unfortunately, marketing people rarely score such wins. Usually, the overriding emphasis on the short term prevents new products from either being developed or effectively launched, even when they are clearly needed. Division managers are generally reluctant to weed out marginal products or customers so that the mix can be upgraded because they have never been trained to distinguish winners from losers when they look at products, customers, or market segments. Until more upper-level managers start thinking in those terms and adopt a long-term perspective in industrial firms, marketing's effectiveness will be limited.

Facing Up to Deficiencies

Even when top management does make a commitment to long-term thinking, it must also be willing to face up to the company's critical deficiencies in product performance, costs, price, or service. While almost all industrial managers will acknowledge that quality and service are lethal weapons in today's competitive environment, many display the natural tendency to view their own products through rose-colored glasses. They conclude that any advantages claimed for competitors' products are exaggerated or insignificant, that the competition is "giving the business away," or that it has a "cheaply engineered" or "shoddily manufactured" line that explained its ability to sell at a lower price.

One maker of electronic test equipment that we did some management training for was losing considerable business because one division's executives would not face the fact that its product was inferior to its competitors' in terms of both price and user performance. The division's major product line was losing market share, and margins had eroded several points, despite the fact that two different product managers had made the point that competitor changes in product and price had made it impossible to compete with the company's line as currently designed and priced. Both product managers recommended a redesign program to take cost out of the line and to incorporate desperately needed product features. At the same time, they proposed a lower price schedule to make the line more competitive.

Top executives, including the vice president of sales, reacted negatively. They simply could not accept the fact that their product line, which had traditionally been the top-quality product, was that far out of synch with the marketplace. Instead, they blamed the product managers for not having a good grasp of the business and for not being imaginative in their recommendations to rebuild market share with more sales volume. But they had a problem that they couldn't "just sell their way out of."

It wasn't until a new division general manager took over that the company reversed its position. This man took a fresh, unprejudiced look at his company's product as compared with the competition, concluding that the two product managers had been right and that no amount of aggressive selling, creative merchandising, or any other so-called marketing activity could overcome the basic competitive disadvantages of this product.

Admittedly, facing up to critical deficiencies is difficult. However, management cannot allow emotional ties to what has been done in the past to overrule current market considerations of what customers need and competitors are doing. Otherwise, as a CEO in one chemical company told us, "Management does a lot of talking about following the marketing concept, but in reality it's often a joke. We're too often driven by existing products, folklore, and inflated perceptions about the value of our products and our company name."

IMPLEMENTING THE CONCEPT

Implementation is a major impediment to gaining positive results from marketing, particularly in three key areas: (1) you must have competent people, (2) you must have accurate market and cost information, and (3) you must adapt your business planning and possibly your organization for the right business focus. Many executives who are vitally interested in making marketing the core thrust of the business are often thwarted because of deficiencies in these areas. Let's examine each one individually to see where the difficulties lie and how improvements can occur.

Competent People

It takes superior knowledge of customers' needs, competition, and the cost-profit economics of the business, along with a working knowledge of the technology and a healthy dose of good business judgment, to be an effective general, product, market, or business unit manager in an industrial business. A general manager cannot be a general manager for any industrial business; a competent general manager must learn the details of the particular industrial business, which usually occurs from the bottom up, not by parachuting in from a very different business. And it takes years, not a few months, to learn any industrial business. Without critical knowledge about the technology, the costs, the customers, and competitive solutions, the general, product, market, or business unit manager can never command the respect of the other executives and get them to follow marketing's lead. Effective cross-functional leadership is always based on knowledge, expertise, and professional respect from colleagues in that same business. It is usually far more effective to teach proven industrial marketing practices to people who intimately know an industrial business than it is to have someone come from outside your business and who must first learn the business (which takes years) before they can even think about developing sound marketing approaches for your business.

Yet many companies have staffed key marketing positions (marketing director, product manager, market manager) with people who clearly have none of these qualities nor the experience in the specific business. Where does management go wrong? In some cases, the problem stems from a tendency to equate marketing with aggressive selling or promotion, thus looking no further than the sales department for people to move into these positions. In fact we often see senior executives use the words "sales" and "marketing" interchangeably; many even have titles "sales and marketing manager" rather than "marketing and sales magager"—a sure sign that they do not understand industrial marketing at all. The problem is that many salespeople simply do not understand the costs and operating dynamics of the business, and their sales and volume orientation too often dominates their recommendations and decisions. As you would expect, they quickly lose the respect of other functional and top management executives and have no chance to influence major decisions.

In other cases, management turns outside the company, searching for candidates to turn the company into a market-driven operation overnight. But except in rare cases these people perform well below expectations because they typically have skills that are not applicable. Only people who intimately know the business and have a passion for the business can develop sound approaches. There is no general group of skills for industrial marketing that is readily transferable from one industrial business to another as there is in consumer goods marketing, where basic advertising and promotion skills are applicable to a wide range of product and market situations. Philip B. Hofmann, the former chairman and CEO of Johnson & Johnson, once said to us:

> I could move marketing people and general managers from baby powder to Tylenol and Band-Aids, but I could never do that in our more technical businesses that included sutures, medical diagnostics, and surgical instruments. One time we moved a bright lady from our shampoo business to our Ethicon sutures division because her husband was transferred to another city. She was first surprised how much technology was involved with the coagulation of blood and tissue wound closure. Then she was amazed at how slow surgeons were to try or change to a new product we all knew was demonstrably better. She was also amazed at how bureaucratic and complex the buying process was at large hospitals, HMOs, and government agencies. Two years later, she was grateful when we were able to transfer her back to our shampoo business.

One company equipment supplier to the telecommunications field learned this lesson after the fact. Top management decided the company needed a stronger marketing effort and recruited a successful sales manager from a chemical company whose background included three years as a product-line marketing manager and an MBA from an Ivy League school. On the surface, he appeared to be very well qualified for the job.

His performance, however, was abysmal. He did not understand the underlying technology and was unable to shepherd the company's new product program against very stiff competition, particularly from abroad. He also failed to understand the intricacies of designing and selling complex communications systems and was frequently caught off base with proposals that did not meet customer requirements. Moreover, he suffered from an insufficient understanding of how customers used and bought the product. After one year, both top management and the individual agreed that the fit wasn't good. He quietly resigned and joined a large management consulting firm, where he didn't have to live with any of his recommendations.

A number of well-run industrial companies, including Betz Laboratories and Alfa-Laval, cautiously hire some of their managers from target markets and their customers' operations. A number of companies also take their technical people and train them in customer applications and overall business economics before they become profit center managers. None of the great industrial companies we know take newly minted MBAs or people with no experience in their industry and expect them to take a lead role in developing the marketing concept. Furthermore, since nearly all marketing taught at business schools is focused on consumer goods and retailing approaches, smart companies know that people from these institutions usually have no understanding of sound marketing for an industrial firm.

Therefore, in order to have competent people implementing marketing throughout the organization, training in practical, proven, and cutting-edge industrial marketing concepts is usually needed for the entire cross-functional business team and the general or business unit manager.

Reliable Market and Economic Information

Companies generally lack three types of information. The first concerns which of their existing products and customers make or lose money. The second concerns markets and customer information—that is, which markets are growing, which are underserved, and who the most progressive customers are in each segment. They need to also learn about the largest and fastest growing competitors in each segment, including strengths and weaknesses. Finally, they must develop business plans by bringing cost-profit, market, and competitive information together.

We have conducted management training workshops for industrial business teams around the world for many years and continue to be amazed at how many companies, especially some of the largest ones, have little confidence in their cost-profit and market information. After gathering and sharing this vital information, a motion control business unit learned the following: 35 percent of all their customer relationships were unprofitable, 40 percent of their accounts were marginally profitable, and the remaining 25 percent of their customers generated the bulk of profits. Having good cost-profit and market segment information about customers and competition is the first step; it must then be widely shared throughout the organization. The wide sharing of this information—especially deep into the organization with those closest to the customers, plants, and laboratories—helps energize people and generate many what-if solutions. The wide sharing of all information must take place, or empowerment and managing close to the customer will only be buzz words. Unfortunately too many companies around the world still lack an open-book culture, and the "close to the vest" styles of many managers are obstacles. In these situations the "need-to-know" mentality should be changed to one of "Who doesn't need to know?"

Correct Business Focus

Armed with the necessary information, the cross-functional business team, led by a product, market, business or general manager, is ready to develop a focused business plan. To do this, marketing has to be set up as the lead activity and see to it that everyone understands the lead role.

This means that the marketing people have the responsibility for identifying the changing needs of the market and the opportunities these represent for the company. The marketing people, with the assistance of a cross-functional team, are also expected to translate market requirements into the actions that must be taken by the other principal functions of the company (R&D, engineering, manufacturing, finance) to capitalize on opportunities. Ed Krainer, the head of Borden Chemical, at workshops for his people, refers to marketing as "the headlights for every business unit." When we refer to marketing as the lead function of the company, we do not mean that marketing is organizationally superior to the other functions. Its role is to point the way toward better opportunities in the marketplace. The role of the other functions is to follow this and ensure that they perform in a way that is consistent with market requirements. In effect, the cross-functional business team must act as if they were a small startup business and determine where they want to attack and build market positions.

SUMMARY

There is nothing particularly complex about what it takes to build substance into industrial marketing as opposed to simply having the trappings of a marketing program. In an industrial company, however, it requires strong leadership from the top to make marketing work because marketing must be a total business philosophy from the boilerroom to the boardroom. At the same time, saying there is nothing particularly sophisticated about the concept of industrial marketing doesn't minimize the huge cultural change required to make a product-, manufacturing-, or sales-oriented company into a market-driven one. It is a very difficult job that takes time and a significant investment in the development of people. The effort will be under constant fire from those with a short-term mentality and those threatened by change. But those companies that deflect the spears and persist will reap enormous rewards in the form of a newfound responsiveness to market opportunities and competitive advantages that will accelerate sales and profits.

CHAPTER 4

The Marketing Controller

When Dennis Hayes, the man whose name is synonymous with computer modems, sought Chapter 11 bankruptcy protection, it exposed not only the deep problems of Hayes Microcomputer Products but also how any business can rapidly fall if it doesn't manage its costs, even when it has the largest market share in a rapid-growth business. Hayes was the pioneer in modems, the devices that allow computers to talk to one another over telephone lines, and it dominated the worldwide marketplace with a 65 percent market share. Just as IBM first set the industry standard for computers and later tripped, the Hayes design was followed by every other modem manufacturer in the world. And much like IBM, Hayes watched nimbler competitors with lower cost structures run away with the market Hayes developed. Hayes was too slow to respond to the lower-cost suppliers who rapidly carved out hefty shares in a high-growth market.

Hayes Microcomputer first misjudged the lightning speed and cost-pricing ramifications of technological advances in product and manufacturing technology. Like microprocessors, modems generated very short product life cycles. A modem that could handle 1,200 bits per second (bps) of data used to be standard but is now obsolete. In just a few years, 14,400 bps, with both data and fax capabilities, became common; then 28,800 bps, with data, fax, and voice, were followed by 33,600-bps modems; and then 64,000-bps modems were developed. But just as importantly, each new generation was manufactured at a lower cost and sold at a lower price. The combination of more product performance, additional capabilities, and lower prices resulted in a market explosion.

The industry is selling more modems than ever, but at lower prices, so sales revenue is growing much more slowly than modem unit sales growth, as shown in Exhibit 4–1. This is not a one-of-a-kind situation. The same pattern can be seen in personal computers, laser and jet printers, and many other industrial and high-tech products.

E X H I B I T   4–1

The Growth in Modem Sales

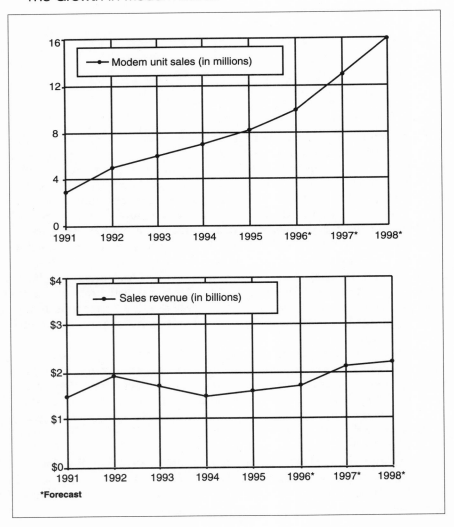

*Forecast

The Hayes bankruptcy came at a time of fierce Darwinian competition in a $2+ billion industry where market share leaders Hayes and Motorola's business units were losing money. A band of fast-moving and lower-cost suppliers, including U.S. Robotics and Zoom Telephonics, appeared on the modem scene with products that offered high performance at far lower prices. Advertisements frequently offer "Hayes compatible" knock-offs at prices significantly below the higher priced Hayes models. Smarter customers were no longer willing to pay a premium for an old name, something Hayes was counting on heavily. U.S. Robotics invested heavily in manufacturing technology that slashed costs and enabled them to undercut Hayes and other uncompetitive suppliers. They designed and made their own circuit boards (that Hayes outsourced to Mexico), created most of their own software, and got new products to market much faster than Hayes. U.S. Robotics' modem business generated gross profits of 35 percent and higher (compared with 26 percent for Hayes), and a U.S. Robotics spokesperson said, "Unlike Hayes, we don't have a lot of $100,000-a-year executives and fancy facilities that inflate SG&A costs. Our lower cost structure allows us to be aggressive in pricing and profitably grow market share."

On the day before filing for bankruptcy protection, the founder and CEO of Hayes Microcomputer, Dennis Hayes, said:

> Our past success, the growth market, and high prices attracted a lot of competitors that kept driving down prices 15 percent to 20 percent every year. The market prices came down faster than our costs. The problems of over-buying components, production snafus in Mexico from our subcontractors, and the steady descent of prices left us cash poor, even though we had annual sales of over $250 million and over $25 million in firm orders to fill. It feels a little funny having to talk so much now about cost numbers. In the earlier years, we ran the company more on intuition. If I had been paying more attention to some of the financial details, the company wouldn't have gotten into trouble.

SIX MANAGEMENT PRINCIPLES

If Hayes Microcomputer had better understood and managed six basic principles, bankruptcy would have been avoided. Few truisms apply universally in the business world, but the following six related maxims are valid in every business situation:

1. Over the long term, it is absolutely essential to be a lower-cost supplier.

2. To stay competitive, inflation-adjusted costs of producing and supplying any product or service must continuously trend downward.

3. The true cost and profit picture for each product and for all key customers and target market segments must always be known, and traditional accounting practices must not obscure them.

4. A business must concentrate on cash flow and balance sheet strengths as much as on profits.

5. Productivity must improve relentlessly from year to year, driven by a side-by-side comparison with the best competitors.

6. Cost-profit and productivity must be shared with enough people so that more "what-if" options can be generated and better decisions can be made.

These six truths are more important than ever because there is increasingly less room for error in our increasingly more competitive global environment.

THE LOWER-COST SUPPLIER

As products inevitably mature and become more similar, price competition increases and the necessity to be a lower-cost supplier increases. In today's global village, price competition comes faster, and the pressure for lower costs comes sooner. Compaq is a lower-cost supplier of PCs. Net profit margins are typically in the 7 percent to 9 percent range with gross margins between 23 percent and 26 percent, while many other billion dollar PC makers would just like to be in the black. Even well-run Hewlett-Packard doesn't make much money in its PC business. How does Compaq out-earn rivals in a marketplace where razor-thin profit margins and "profitless prosperity" are common?

To begin, Compaq keeps R&D costs low, typically only 2 percent of sales, while giants including IBM, HP, Digital, and Apple spend between 7 percent and 10 percent on R&D. In design, Compaq, unlike IBM and Digital, is careful to not overengineer any part in their machines. Whenever possible, Compaq buys off-the-shelf components, and they have standardized many parts across all their models. Compaq also saves on promotion costs by piggy-back riding on Intel and Microsoft, who mention Compaq in the marketing of chips and software. About half of Compaq's sales are outside the United States, where there is less price competition.

Another big cost advantage is from productivity gains. From 1992 to 1995, sales per employee nearly tripled from $305,000 to $890,000. Most

PC makers have long production assembly lines, while Compaq builds each machine with groups of four workers in small manufacturing cells. If a production line has 50 people, the line will run only as fast as the slowest person. In Compaq's small manufacturing cells, there are fewer bottlenecks, fewer line stoppages, and a faster work pace. In contrast to Compaq's lower cost structure, Apple Computer has had many years of declining gross margins and diminishing profits. Apple's gross profit margins plunged from 53 percent to 15 percent over a five-year period as shown in Exhibit 4–2. The difference between net profit margins of 4 percent and 7 percent at Apple would translate into $360 million a year in bottom-line profit.

No company, whether industrial, high-tech, or service, can succeed over the long term unless it is a lower-cost supplier than most others providing equivalent products or services. Proprietary advantages never last forever. All products and markets eventually mature and decline, and prices and margins inevitably succumb to competitive pressures. As competitive product distinctions fade, price becomes increasingly important in buying decisions. The more successful suppliers relentlessly improve productivity and reduce costs. Thus, even when price pressures become intense, margins will at least be maintained. When this is not done, profits

EXHIBIT 4–2

Gross Margin Slides at Apple Computer

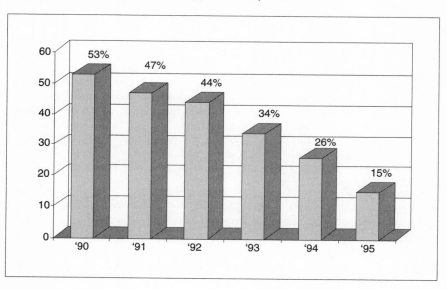

and market position almost certainly fall. Summarizing retrospectively, Paul Allaire, the CEO and president of Xerox, stated:

> We were the undisputed copier king. Finally, we realized the Japanese were selling quality products for what it cost us to make them. We learned the hard way how quickly our competition can turn market supremacy into market oblivion.

Being a lower-cost supplier doesn't necessarily mean being the lowest cost among all competitors. Nor does it mean that you can't or shouldn't have a strategy of producing at a somewhat higher cost and selling at a higher price. But it does mean that one's total costs should be at or below the average of all competitors offering equivalent products or services to the same customer segments.

Costs include more than just production costs. Overhead or other costs such as designing, selling, delivering, and technical service can throw the total cost structure out of line. These tend to overaccumulate in good times when there is no pressure to question every activity's effectiveness and efficiency.

Inflation and price increases are enemies of common sense and effectiveness. Price increases and inflation provide smokescreens for companies to avoid addressing their costs properly. In the "good old days" it was easy to raise prices when costs went up because demand was bullish and often exceeded supplier capacity. Such situations led to a lack of discipline. The health care industry is a good example. For 20 years, it was a cost-plus reimbursement industry where prices were allowed to rise with unmanaged costs. When third-party payers (government and insurance companies) and then employers finally came to their senses, a lot of health care providers who had let costs go uncontrolled got into trouble. Abbott Laboratories escaped that fate. Abbott's chairman told us:

> To simply raise prices along with the industry is not the Abbott way. Our overall corporate measure of productivity is sales per employee. Price increases don't get factored in. Paying close attention to such things as head count becomes second nature. You must develop an attitude throughout the company that you can always find a better and lower cost way to do things. Our constant effort to lower unit costs also makes more money available for new products and for price-cutting assaults. They help keep old competitors at bay and new ones away.

Logic suggests that, over time, the real inflation-adjusted costs of doing business should trend downward because, as organizations learn how to do things better, they also become more efficient. This is the underlying principle of the learning curve, and it usually works over time. The computer hardware cost of processing a million instructions per second dropped 76 percent for mainframes, 86 percent for minicomputers, and 93 percent for PCs over an eight-year period. In the manufacturing of industrial power tools, the cost fell 29 percent with each doubling of output over a 10-year period.

These continual cost reductions do not come automatically with volume, experience, or the passage of time. They require constant management attention in all matters for continual productivity gains and cost reductions. Too often products and costs drift out of competitive bounds, and no one realizes this until it is too late. Managers who quickly claim that they are a lower-cost, or even the lowest-cost, producer rarely know their true costs or how they compare with competitors. Even when clear evidence shows that competitors are selling at a lower price, many managers deny any kind of cost disadvantage. Instead, they say that "competitors are stupid," that "they're buying the business," or that "they aren't as concerned about profits as we are."

To know exactly what your costs are and to manage them well, you must carefully isolate various costs and match or assign them to specific products, accounts, or markets. Such assignments are often handled poorly. The most common mistake is to work on the basis of average costs, as if all costs were equally shared by all products and customers. Average costing ignores important differences among products and the fact that different products, different markets, and different customers require different overhead costs. The broader the product line, the more distortions result from cost averaging, which nearly always leads to average price increases or decreases. In average pricing, some products or customers are overcharged, while others are subsidized. Across-the-board price changes ignore true product-line cost differences and differences in customer price sensitivities. Average costing that results in average price changes can lead to a loss of profit, reduced volume, declining market share, and the dulling of management spirit.

DOWNWARD TRENDING COSTS

Our second management principle is that no company can be successful over time if inflation-adjusted total costs do not follow a steadily declining pattern. Management must place unrelenting pressure on the entire organization for measurable cost reductions and productivity gains, year after year. The rate of improvement may vary annually but should never fall below inflation. This means that when inflation pushes salaries and wages up x percent, productivity gains must be made to more than offset this added cost. Vigilance is critical because it is so difficult to regain cost competitiveness once it has been lost. Costs should not be allowed to get out of line in the first place. With all the company downsizing occurring, one should ask, "Who let the cost structure become uncompetitive?"

As companies grow, any increments of capacity should be added grudgingly, especially in a slow-growth business. In today's fast-moving world, life cycles are shorter and payback cycles must be shorter. Before investing in new capacity, management should make sure existing capacity cannot be stretched by going to three shifts, working six or seven days, or operating above current capacity. Furthermore, companies should evaluate capacity additions and capital appropriations against profits from the least profitable line in the plant since they can always drop the less profitable line, not undertake the contemplated addition, or both.

If your costs have become noncompetitive, then traditional incremental expense reductions alone (i.e., cutting back here and there, reducing overhead, and freezing pay) probably won't do the job. Even deep cuts along the way generally won't do. You need to think in a different way: eliminate big chunks of structured cost; design cost out of the product and system; and greatly improve efficiencies everywhere in the organization, not just in manufacturing.

COST AND PROFIT PICTURES

Our third principle is that the true cost and profit picture of each product and for all key customers and target market segments must be known and shared throughout the organization. An important reason companies get their costs out of phase with competitors' is they don't usually know their true costs. To ascertain costs, the following questions must be answered accurately for each major product line, account, and market segment.

1. What are the directly attributable and allocated costs for each major product line, from procurement to customer delivery, including postsale service and warranties?
2. What is the present breakeven point, how does it relate to capacity, and how much can volume be increased before it will have to move up?
3. What is the incremental cost and profit on each unit that is produced and sold over the current breakeven point?
4. How do costs change with changes in volume? What costs are inescapable if volume declines?
5. How do the current cost structure, capacity utilization, and historical cost trends compare with those of competitors? What cost advantages or disadvantages exist?

6. What are the total costs to serve each account? Are some of our largest customers marginal or profit losers for us? Could we make more money with fewer customers?

7. Are there certain market segments that are more attractive in terms of profits? Should we de-emphasize or withdraw from some segments?

Most managers, particularly those in multi-product-line businesses, routinely make critical decisions without knowing these facts. Managers in rapidly growing businesses are especially uninformed. Both are vulnerable to serious troubles. Many high-profit businesses have primitive or nonexistent cost-profit facts.

Consider a manufacturer of plastic injection-molding machines with a 20-year record of successful growth and profits. The company generated reasonable profits during downcycles by reducing the workforce and bringing back into its plant work that had been subcontracted out during good times. To improve margins, management heavily invested in automated equipment and greatly reduced subcontracting. Projected returns were very attractive, but in the next downturn in capital spending, losses accumulated for the first time in 20 years. The investment in automated equipment had significantly raised the fixed costs and the breakeven point. The latitude to reduce costs by eliminating direct labor hours and subcontract work no longer existed. This point had not been raised when the company evaluated the new equipment.

What Accounting Schools Never Cover

Most managers agree that it is important to understand the costs and profits of their businesses, although often they don't know what this really means. Those who do know are often frustrated because their information systems do not present the data to develop this knowledge, and they don't know how to correct it. After knowing your own costs, it is most helpful to learn about your competitor's cost structures and ranges to better analyze their positions and anticipate their future strategies and tactics.

Common Ranges

To resolve this problem, let's go back to some managerial accounting principles. In Exhibit 4–3, we add target ranges for the key cost-profit components of one kind of manufacturing operation and create a framework for developing an initial understanding of cost-profit structures and

E X H I B I T   4–3

Common Cost/Profit Ranges

Sales		100%
Cost of goods		65% and down
Gross margin		25% and up
R&D	0–15%	
Sales	5–15%	
General and	10–15%	
administration	15–45%	
Total		
Earnings (before taxes		15%
target)		60%
Assets employed		15% and up
ROA target (after taxes)		

requirements. The ranges would be quite different for a process industry because of the much higher plant and equipment investment with the attendant greater pressure for higher-capacity utilization. The opposite is true of most service businesses with lower investments and fixed costs.

The framework in Exhibit 4–3 is designed to yield a sustainable 15 percent to 20 percent pretax profit on sales, a 30 percent to 40 percent pretax return on assets (ROA) employed, and a somewhat higher return on equity, depending on the amount of debt leverage in the capital structure. These profit returns must be achieved to be a truly outstanding profit performer. Operating consistently within this framework requires the following:

1. Manufacturing operations must generate a gross margin (after all manufacturing costs, including variances) of at least 25 percent to 40 percent (and in many cases, much higher) to cover research and development and sales costs.

2. R&D activities for product and process technology obviously vary by industry but can range up to as high as 15 percent of sales, depending on the rate of technology change in the business and the stage in the product life cycles.

3. Sales expense typically runs in the 5 percent to 10 percent range—lower if sales agents or distributors are used, higher in the early stages of market development or for direct sales.

4. General and administrative costs are usually in the 10 percent to 15 percent range and should include all the overhead costs of conducting the business, including interest (at least for working capital) and allocated division, group, or corporate overhead.

5. Total assets employed for plant and equipment and working capital should not run more than about 60 cents on each dollar of sales in a manufacturing company, with variations in the split between them, depending on the type of business.

A company can be profitable if its performance does not fall precisely into this framework. In fact, the ranges show that there will probably be significant differences in the percentage for any cost element, depending on the industry and each company's business strategy. However, two numbers are crucial to meet or exceed the profit targets shown. First is the gross margin, which is the profit-generating fuel for any business. No manufacturing business can continuously generate satisfactory profits if gross margins drop much below 25 percent. Even this margin rate is questionable unless it is clear that R&D and sales, general, and administrative (SG&A) requirements are near the low end of the ranges shown. There simply aren't enough margin dollars to cover the costs of doing business and still generate a 15 percent to 20 percent pretax profit. The business may be able to generate attractive profit margins if it can operate with less R&D and/or SG&A expense. Given the pace of technology, however, most manufacturing businesses cannot sustain product and market positions while effectively managing and controlling the business with less cost in expense areas. Pursuing a "copier" or "close follower" strategy means R&D expense is probably on the low end of the range but doesn't mean it is zero or that SG&A is necessarily less.

The 60 percent of sales allowed for total assets employed is the second crucial number. While this percentage again will vary widely depending on the nature of the business, it is a reasonably good standard for most manufacturing companies. It is clear that the business must generate higher earnings than indicated in our framework to yield the desired return if the percentage of total assets to sales is higher. Conversely, the earnings could be much lower and still yield a satisfactory return if the assets were lower, as they are, for example, in many distributor or service businesses.

None of this should come as a surprise to anyone who has had profit-and-loss responsibility. But it is surprising to find so many managers who continue to struggle to improve profit results by building volume without understanding and focusing on basic problems in their cost-profit structure. The problems become readily apparent in Exhibit 4–3. While it is always nice to have increased volume, the bottom line will not be helped if the cost-profit structure is out of line, or as Jim Kennedy, CEO of successful National Starch and Chemical, says, "You can't sell your way out of a cost structure problem."

The inescapable fact is that any industrial or high-tech company must have a cost-profit structure that makes sense in order to be an attractive profit contributor over the long term. It is essential to first determine what it should be for each particular business and then to make sure the business actually operates around this structure. No amount of hard work or market/product strategies will lead to outstanding profit returns if the business's basic cost-profit structure is not sound.

The Cycle of Decay

When profits decline or disappear, companies often tighten the belt in the wrong way and in the wrong places. This can easily generate a self-feeding cycle of competitive decay. There is a natural tendency for managers to shortchange sales or market development, R&D, or training or to forgo manufacturing improvements for the short term to make the business and profits look better. Exhibit 4–4 shows how a viciously deteriorating cycle can work itself out into worsening conditions.

The most common (and almost hidden) factor that starts such a decay cycle is that of a management team operating with the wrong type of data—that of accounting rather than of cost control. Unfortunately, most data management teams use data derived from accounting systems designed primarily to meet outside financial reporting requirements and not the needs of operating managers.

In addition, these data present aggregate numbers for large chunks of the business rather than the costs or profits for a number of discrete product/markets and key accounts. Even when data present the cost and profit picture for individual product lines and some customers, they often focus only on gross or operating margins, not on the complete picture after all manufacturing, engineering, sales, and administrative overhead costs are taken into account. Finally, traditional accounting systems typically do not provide a clear picture of how costs and profits behave as unit volume moves up or down. Thus they are not particularly helpful to managers who must evaluate sales, marketing, pricing, and manufacturing alternatives that involve different levels of activity.

For these reasons, financial data must often be reorganized, reordered, and reformulated. This may require extra effort, but it is not as difficult as it sounds. First, a few commonsense cost definitions that provide the basis for categorizing all costs associated with each product line must be agreed upon. The following cost categories can provide a definitive framework for any manager:

The Self-Feeding Cycle of Decay

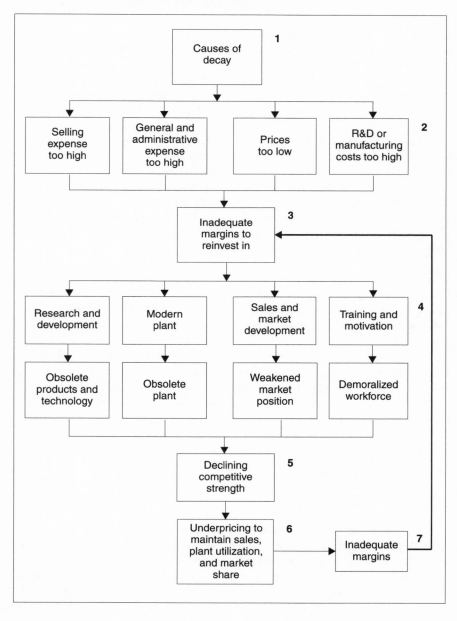

1. *Bedrock fixed.* These costs are related to physical capacity and include plant and equipment costs such as depreciation, taxes, and facility maintenance that cannot be avoided unless the facility is sold or written off the books. These are the only true fixed costs. Typically, they are not as large a factor in the cost structure of companies as you would think, although they become greater as companies automate and when newer facilities are not depreciated.

2. *Managed fixed.* These costs are largely related to people and structure—the so-called overhead of management, accounting, finance, and even activities such as advertising, sales, R&D, or market development. These costs tend to build up in good times and as a business grows. Once in place, managers often treat them as integral and bedrock fixed costs. They are not. You can and should manage them. Understanding their makeup is important to keep them under control and distinguish them from the overhead costs that organizations share.

3. *Direct variable costs.* These costs rise or fall directly in proportion to business volume. They are easily identified and can be traced back to the specific units produced or services rendered where, again, they can be better examined and managed.

4. *Shared costs.* These include all other costs incurred to support the business not immediately traceable to any one product line or activity. These normally include overhead of the corporation, division, and/or plant as well as selling and general and administrative expenses. They can also include operating costs for plant and equipment. All are manageable.

Agreeing on these cost definitions is the first step. The second step is matching the various costs to these classifications. In most businesses, few costs are either absolutely fixed or variable. Most costs lie in the vast area of "managed costs," shown in Exhibit 4–5. Make no mistake—costs in the managed category are not fixed, even though they are commonly bundled under this label. Generally, as a business expands, costs tend to be far more variable than they should be, and when it contracts, they are far more fixed than they should be.

Reordering Cost Information

Once there is agreement regarding cost categories and definitions, the next step is getting help from the accounting or controller's department to determine how to divide and match specific product/account/market businesses to the costs incurred in each of these categories. This is not easily done. Many accountants are reluctant to divide fixed costs into these categories or to allocate shared costs to specific product areas because it is

EXHIBIT 4-5

Managed versus Fixed and Variable Costs

Bedrock Fixed	Managed		Truly Variable
Depreciation	Property tax	Small tools	Materials
Patent	Rent	Lighting	Royalties
amortization	Cleaning	Materials	Overtime
	Maintenance of	services	premium
	building	Machinery	Supplies
	Insurance	maintenance	Fuel
	Executive salaries	Lubricants	Power
	Auditing expense	Sales salaries	Scrap
	Supervision	Entertainment	Commissions
	Inspection	Travel	Freight
	Payroll taxes	Uncollectible	
	Payroll services	accounts	
	Office expenses	Telephone	
	Advertising	Receiving	
	Administrative	Spoilage	
	salaries	Benefits	
	Legal expense	Wages	

difficult to do this with the precision that accounting professionals normally use to develop traditional financial statements. Accountants have a natural aversion to shifting numbers around in an imprecise manner. There is simply no way, however, to know how well or how badly a product or product line is doing without making this cost information clear, that is, without knowing which costs are bedrock fixed, managed fixed, direct variable, or shared and without matching and allocating such costs to their various business units and product lines.

At the divisional or business unit level, cross-functional teams of all department heads and the general manager should be responsible for hammering out the allocations according to the actual activity levels of each cost category. Some accountants don't like full or activity-based costing approaches because they demand a minute understanding of how a company works and a detailed understanding of all costs. It forces accountants out into the plants, warehouses, laboratories, and offices where the costs and activities are.

In most cases, general management must ensure that data are reordered along the lines necessary for intelligent product/account/market management. Shared costs are a greater problem for most companies and difficult to attack as a lump. Shared costs must be broken down and matched to discrete business units or product lines, even if it means being "arbitrary" by some standards. Managers with hands-on profit responsibility will argue about the fairness kind of allocation, but it is critical to take a stand lest discussions become endless, acrimonious, and fruitless. There is no other way. Matching costs to the actual activities and then allocating other costs is the only way to know what is really going on.

Better Cost-Profit Pictures

Exhibit 4–6 tabulates the results of changing to full-cost allocations in the instrumentation division of a large corporation. When complete, product groups traditionally regarded as the best profit producers were not as profitable as previously thought, and some of the worst were actually near the top. The instrumentation division overall had a reported gross margin of 45.6 percent and a generated 11 percent pretax profit of $30.1 million. Sales and gross margins were reported by product line, but pretax profit was reported only for the division overall. Reported gross margins for the product groups varied from a high of 54 percent to a low of 40 percent. Fully loading all production lines with their real costs resulted in adjusted gross margins that varied between 38.1 percent and 15.9 percent.

Because of their relatively lower reported gross margins, standard products D and E (at 41 percent and 40 percent, respectively) had often taken a backseat when the company assigned sales, manufacturing, and engineering priorities. When it analyzed and allocated plant, engineering, and SG&A overheads according to actual usage, however, it was clear that the standard products were being penalized by standard formulas that distributed these overheads according to sales volume. Adjusted gross margin percentages for standard products D and E improved their relative pretax profit performance dramatically; gross margins on custom-engineered products A, B, and C declined by several percentage points once appropriate overhead costs were matched or allocated against them.

Looked at in another way, products D and E contributed less than half (48.6 percent) of reported gross margin dollars but almost two-thirds (63.1 percent) of pretax profit dollars after all costs were allocated. It is obvious that the way that management assigns its sales, manufacturing, and engineering priorities can change drastically once the actual cost-profit pictures become clear.

EXHIBIT 4-6

Full-Cost Allocation (millions of dollars)

Product Group	Annual Sales	Reported Gross Margin		Reported Pretax Profit		Adjusted Gross Margin		Adjusted Pretax Profit	
A	$ 42	$ 22.7	54%	NA	NA	$ 19.8	47.0%	$ 3.7	8.8%
B	51	26.5	52	NA	NA	23.4	46.8	4.0	7.8
C	37	17.4	47	NA	NA	15.9	43.0	3.4	9.2
D	83	34.0	41	NA	NA	38.1	46.0	12.1	14.6
E	61	24.4	40	NA	NA	27.8	45.6	6.9	11.3
Divisionwide	$274	$125.0	45.6%	$30.1	11.0%	$125.0	45.6%	$30.1	11.0%

Product-Line Profitability

Net product-line profitability statements also help bring management pressure on big chunks of overhead or shared costs (e.g., SG&A, engineering, manufacturing, and overhead at all levels) that are otherwise difficult to evaluate and control. When companies allocate these costs to specific products or profit centers, they show up as a charge against earnings, and managers responsible for profits carefully scrutinize and challenge them. This can be a powerful force toward reducing overhead costs and keeping them under control that would otherwise never be scrutinized by someone with a direct profit responsibility. To do this, many companies need to create more net profit centers and have more managers with full profit-and-loss responsibilities. Rarely does a company have too many profit centers or too many people responsible for net profit.

Knowing the true cost and profit structure for product groups is also an immense help in selecting products, customers, and markets for emphasis. Remarkably few managers consider profit potentials when they assess and select product/market segments or "key" accounts. They more often focus on sales potential with the naive assumption that profits will follow. Managers can justify this in a product's early stages but can never do so later. When the fight for share in a stable, slow-growth, or declining market intensifies, managers must specialize in what is more profitable rather than in what is bigger. Most companies could make more profit if they made and sold fewer products. Lubrizol, the well-run chemical additive manufacturer, always had a sound rule of reluctantly adding capacity and only on the basis of the least profitable item made at a plant.

Customer Profitability

After selecting the most attractive market segments to defend and attack and after knowing your product-line costs and profits, the next important decision is choosing which customers in those segments to get close to, de-emphasize, or fire. Yes, those customers that mean high levels of hassle, low sales growth, and low or negative profit prospects should be fired. The notion of dropping or firing some of your customers is sacrilegious to many industrial firms conditioned to never lose an order and to keep every customer happy at any cost. These are usually the same companies that try to be all things to all people and have no understanding of the net profit of even the largest customers. These companies use the term "key account" when they talk about their largest existing customers.

The decision of which customers to concentrate on is a complex one. First, if it is an existing account, the past sales, gross profit, and net profit must be determined or estimated. Many companies have no idea what their total costs are to serve their customers. The cost of sales calls, technical service, special new products, trends, rebates, discounts, freight, consignment, outstanding receivable days, and the order transaction costs are all real costs that can be determined or estimated for every account. After completing this analysis, many companies see that between 20 percent and 30 percent of their customers are reasonably profitable, another 20 percent to 40 percent are marginally profitable, and between 20 percent and 35 percent are clear money losers. When determining which customers to emphasize, serve differently (possibly with inside people or with distributors), rationalize services to, or drop, one needs to consider both the present and potential net profit of every account.

Managing Cash and Liquidity

Our fourth management principle stresses the need to manage cash. Cash returns can be more important than reported profits. Cash returns lead to liquidity, and liquidity is a top priority whenever there are high risks and great uncertainties in a cyclical business. Cash and liquidity help withstand surprises, facilitate adaptation to sudden changes, and capitalize on the narrower windows of opportunity that are common in a turbulent environment.

Any entrepreneur or small businessperson who has survived a startup and built a market position knows the importance of cash and liquidity. Any business can go bankrupt while reporting record sales, just as Hayes Microcomputer did. But it will never go bankrupt as long as its cash and liquidity positions are strong. Most senior corporate executives and successful small businesspeople understand this but do not ensure that it is stressed or understood at the business unit level.

The results are apparent in many large corporations. Capital expenditure proposals tend to be "wish lists" justified on projected volume gains or cost savings without regard to the availability of funds or to cash-carrying costs. Working capital is allowed to build without adequate regard for its carrying costs. Overinvestment in plant, equipment, and working capital often disguises sloppy business practices and control. These are practices that inevitably lead to a bloated investment base—too big for the business and too marginal for sustaining profitability.

Many operating managers are unaware of the costs of excessive capital tie-ups. For example, most will acknowledge that it costs money to carry their inventory (these days, usually 8 percent or 9 percent, but few know that total carrying costs should include storage, taxes, obsolescence, accounts receivable, and shrinkage and that total costs, including interest, actually run closer to 30 percent. The reason so few managers know this is that the costs of working capital are not charged against their business unit's earnings, even though they are real costs of doing business.

A manager who makes pricing, capital investment, personnel, and any strategic or tactical decisions without accurate product/customer cost information—and then does not create a companywide discipline to manage costs—will face unpleasant surprises and serious questions of survival as the competitive world gets increasingly turbulent.

Cash management deserves far greater attention than it gets in most companies. Management must put greater emphasis on, and be held accountable for, managing liquidity. Planning and reporting systems should be modified to highlight actual cash flow and liquidity against objectives. Finally, the reward system should be adjusted to pay those who meet cash objectives and penalize those who don't.

None of these actions is difficult if senior management has the will to carry them out and if the accounting system is set up to do so. They can be impossible, however, if the accounting systems are designed around big divisions of business rather than around discrete product/customer/ market segments and if big chunks of structured or managed fixed costs are not matched and allocated to smaller business units.

Ideally, every manager should think like a small-business entrepreneur whose own money is at risk and who has little of it at hand. If more managers did this, we would see fewer companies with bloated balance sheets and marginal returns, and we would see a lot more with profitable top- and bottom-line growth.

KEY PERFORMANCE MEASURES

Our fifth management principle stresses the need for ongoing productivity improvements, measured by comparisons to the best competitors. Management must set goals and make action plans to facilitiate the achievement of the annual productivity improvements. After-the-fact financial measures alone do not get to the root causes of the competitiveness or uncompetitiveness of a business. Three basic types of ratios should be developed for any business and then compared with the best competitors, and improvement goals should be set with action and programs in place. If improvement goals and action programs are not developed, there is good reason to challenge any cost and profit structure. The three performance ratios deserve examination in the evaluation of any industrial business because they are clear indicators of how efficiently the business is being managed. These performance ratios vary in importance, depending on the industry and products manufactured, but it is doubtful that any business can be healthy if they are out of line with industry standards or the best-managed competitors.

Productivity Measurements

The purpose of productivity improvements is to reduce the total cost per unit. These improvements allow a supplier to increase or maintain profit margins, reduce prices, or improve operating profit. There is no single measure of productivity that applies to every business, but ratios such as sales, shipments, production units per employee, or total engineering and labor costs per unit shipped usually indicate a direction or trend. TRW has developed six productivity measures that apply to their diverse industrial businesses. These productivity measures are as follows:

1. Sales per employee (constant dollars).
2. Sales divided by total deflated employee compensation costs.
3. Value added (sales minus direct material costs) per employee.
4. Sales divided by deflated materials cost.
5. Sales per unit of energy consumed.
6. Sales divided by plant and equipment replacement costs, less depreciation.

When factory labor was a product's primary cost component, single measures such as sales per employee were helpful indicators. With increases in automation, engineering, and technical services, labor costs have often been replaced with fixed investment costs. Therefore, the productivity measures must be related to your industry and then compared side-by-side with industry averages and the best competitors in your industry. For industrial distributors and wholesale-retail businesses, the productivity measures are sales per square foot, gross profit margins, and yearly inventory turns. Productivity measures are difficult for manufacturers. The more common productivity measures for industrial manufacturers include process yields, up time, and lead times.

For example, a division of industrial parts manufacturer Federal Mogul measures its productivity in three areas and then compares itself with the best competitor in each area, as shown in Exhibit 4–7. After gathering the information, Federal Mogul creates a third column, "Annual Improvement Goal." After the improvement goals are set, action programs are developed to achieve the improvements.

Because of the "soft" nature of a service business, some people incorrectly believe that productivity measures are less useful in these type of businesses. Highly efficient United Parcel Service (UPS) religiously

E X H I B I T   4–7

Manufacturing Productivity Measurements

Measurement	Federal Mogul	Best Competitor
Quoted shipment time on standard parts	2 days	Same day
Quoted lead time on specials	20 days	5–15 days
Scrap and rework costs	4.5%	2.0%
Machine setup time	3–6 hours	2 hours
Inventory turns per year	7	10
Warranty costs (as percentage of sales)	2.4%	1.2%

measures their productivity results against package delivery rivals that include Federal Express, Airborne, Emery, and DHL. In the fiercely competitive and mature airline passenger service business, Southwest Airlines regularly measures, compares, and improves their productivity in three key areas, as shown in Exhibit 4–8. The high productivity supplier, Southwest Airlines, is also consistently the most profitable.

Capital Use

The second major performance indicator involves how efficiently the working capital is used. Enormous amounts of capital can be tied up very inefficiently if these ratios are out of line, and profit performance can suffer greatly as a result. Moreover, it is easy to develop a plan for increased

E X H I B I T   4–8

Service Productivity Measurements

	American	Delta	Northwest	Southwest	United	USAir
Cost per available seat mile	8.9 cents	9.4 cents	9.1 cents	7.0 cents	9.6 cents	10.8 cents
Passengers per employee	840	1,114	919	2,443	795	1,118
Employees per aircraft	152	134	127	81	157	111

sales that may do the company more harm than good if the costs of added working capital requirements are not adequately considered. These ratios also vary widely from business to business, but comparisons can be made with industry and competitive data. There is also a cross check against these ratios that applies in most industrial manufacturing companies. In most manufacturing industries, the investment in inventories and receivables should not exceed 35 cents for each dollar of sales. This rule of thumb may not always be applicable, but questions should be raised about the working capital investment when this amount is exceeded.

Reducing working capital yields three powerful benefits. First, every dollar freed from inventories or receivables rings up a one-time $1 contribution to cash flow. Secondly, the goal of reduced working capital forces companies to work faster because they don't have the luxury of large financed inventories to fill orders from. Finally, reducing working capital creates a disciplined approach to reviewing all areas of the business where cash is involved. For example, one DuPont business reduced working capital from $50 million to $8 million over a two-year period in which their receivables shrank from 53 days to 42 days. The receivables fell from $11.6 million to $400,000 over the two years while divisional sales surged.

Producers to Supporters

A third indicator to examine is the ratio of what might be called "results producers" or "supporters" in the organization, also sometimes called "direct" and "indirect" people. This ratio does not reflect a traditional way of looking at a business, nor does it tie in with common definitions of work assignments. It is, nevertheless, a useful indicator of any operation's cost structure and profit-making capability. Anyone contributing directly to results should be included in the category of *results producers*. This would include direct hourly workers, sales personnel with specific sales assignments, engineers involved in designing products or responding to customer requests for special features, service technicians that install and/or maintain the equipment, and anyone else who performs a function directly linked to a company's design, manufacture, sales, and service capabilities. All other personnel in the organization fall into the category of *supporters*. They provide support services to the results producers. This group includes all full-time managers, all staff personnel, all secretarial and clerical help, and anyone else in the organization who does not actually design, make, sell, or service the company's products.

As a general rule, the ratio of supporters to results producers should be something close to 1:3. Whenever the ratio gets close to or exceeds 1:1, it is very difficult for any organization involved in traditional industrial manufacturing and sales activities to generate a satisfactory profit. Too few people are producing, and support costs are increasing; for example, large capital investments may supplant many direct workers, and a large number of highly skilled manufacturing or process engineers may be required to operate and maintain the equipment. With this exception, however, the 1:3 ratio provides a good indicator of trouble when a business plan continues to show marginal profits on a growing sales base.

These ratios, of course, vary widely with different businesses, and what are correct ratios for one situation may not be correct for another. Moreover, there will always be arguments over definitions and the appropriateness of a particular ratio in a given situation. Despite these difficulties, ratios can be developed for any situation, and they can help determine whether the cost-profit structure is sound. It should not take long to determine what is a fair measure of performance for any particular situation. The value of each increment of improvement (each day's reduction in receivables, each added thousand dollars of sales per employee) can certainly be calculated to determine whether profit improvements can or should be made and whether enough emphasis has been placed on these improvements in the plan.

SHARING COST-PROFIT INFORMATION

Our sixth principle demands that the information gathered in the previous five steps be shared with enough people so that more "what-if" options can be generated and better decisions can be made. Having fact-based cost-profit and productivity information is one thing. The wide sharing of this information to encourage questions and make better decisions is another level of sophistication. Sharing cost-profit and productivity information is a lot more than just announcing year-end or quarterly results for the fickle financial community. It means communicating all relevant information monthly, weekly, or even daily to all employees within the business unit. In some companies this requires a 180-degree cultural change from a top-down, functional, need-to-know mentality. To become more market driven, organizations must put a lot more information, decision-making authority, and accountability in the hands of those closest to the customers, laboratories, and factories. These changes require a lot of learning and a change in many managers' leadership styles. In spite of all the talk about teamwork, consensus, and participative decision making, nearly every company we have worked with has a number of autocratic or dictatorial managers. These same people inevitably have a restricted need-to-know mentality toward sharing cost-profit information with associates in their organization. These managers need to have their minds reprogrammed to think and ask, "Who doesn't need to know this information?"

The old-style need-to-know management contributed to the decline of IBM. When the new CEO, Lou Gerstner, arrived, he found IBM's four information classifications to be wasteful, annoying, and dramatically opposed to an open culture. The four categories were IBM internal use, IBM confidential, IBM confidential restricted, and registered IBM confidential, the top secret category. There were different-sized and -colored envelopes used for each category. IBM spent more than $6 million on these security envelopes every year. A rulebook explained which level of bureaucracy and which job titles should have access to each category of information. IBMers ended up branding millions of mundane paper memos as "confidential." The new CEO discarded the rulebook. Now one category, IBM confidential is limited to new-product development, business plans, and customer lists. All employees now decide for themselves what qualifies as IBM confidential.

In sharp contrast to IBM's previous close-to-the-vest and limited information sharing, their successful competitor, Hewlett-Packard (HP), has always had a very open culture. Hewlett-Packard's decentralized divisions have been gathering and widely sharing cost-profit information for many years. With full or activity-based costing, HP's divisions calculate how and where overhead is being used on specific products and with large customers. At HP, cost-profit information is widely shared with the engineering labs so that everyone understands all the costs of a product before a product design is begun or frozen. Every design engineer at HP has real-time cost information at his or her fingertips. Tallies of all costs required to design, manufacture, sell, and service products are found in the desktop computers of HP design engineers.

Soon after a new product idea is hatched, HP engineers run sophisticated what-if cost, gross margin, and net profit estimates. Engineers frequently change the design on the spot to favor components that require less testing, thus reducing costs and time to market. In the bad old days, HP engineers handed the design to accountants, who required several days or longer to estimate the production and other costs. The designers were often told much later that what they wanted was too expensive. To achieve this level of knowledge in using cost-profit information, HP had to conduct a three-day workshop on "managerial finance" for nonfinancial people.

Marketing and pricing decisions at HP are guided by widely shared knowledge about a product's real and total costs. By widely sharing cost and profit information, HP often finds that two-thirds of a division's products are profitable, and the remaining one-third are marginal or losing money.

Every department in HP holds "coffee talks" on a regular basis where general and upper management meet with employees in the division to discuss product line and customer costs, margins, and profit results. HP sales, margin, profit, and productivity results are described in detail, and time is taken to answer questions from engineers, manufacturing workers, and others. The wide sharing of cost-profit information gives HP employees a feeling of being respected, trusted, and valued contributors. This culture, in turn, causes most people to come forth with money-saving ideas time after time.

Like HP, a companywide willingness to share all of the numbers of the business with all employees has existed at Nucor Corporation for decades. Nucor's CEO, John Correnti, stated to us:

> Only by sharing everything can our people do their jobs to the best of their ability. By widely sharing cost, profit, and productivity information with every employee, we have been able to unlock the creativity and power inside all of our associates. In order to lower costs or keep them in line, our people must know what their costs, profits, and productivity are. And since we have a large amount of everyone's incentive pay based upon team productivity results, they need a lot of information to manage their team. Obviously some of this information flows to the street. But I believe the value of sharing everything with our employees is much greater than any downside there might be to sharing it with folks on the outside. Our open sharing of information doesn't seem to have hurt us much over the last 27 years of profitable growth in an industry that doesn't consistently do well.

ELECTRONIC NETWORKS

As companies reduce the number of management levels in their organizations, push decision making down to more managers with full profit-and-loss responsibility, and in turn, manage closer to the customer, a more open-book culture should result. Smart top management realizes that people cannot be empowered in a vacuum. The advances in computers, software, and data networks throughout every organization are giving a whole new meaning to the words "need to know." Global electronic networks enable people to communicate across hierarchical and geographic boundaries of the formal organization with electronic networks and to interact based on ideas rather than organizational position. Electronic networks also allow people to be continually apprised of what others are thinking and doing all over the globe. With an open-book culture and wide information sharing, a more informal, faster-moving, and flatter organization inevitably evolves.

Every company's bottom line is directly affected by many factors. Department expenses, inventories, labor and sales efficiency, engineering hours, material costs, warranty costs, and so on are all key numbers. This information must be available to or be shared with many people. Employees throughout the organization must be trained in how to understand and use the relevant numbers. When this information is widely shared, every employee becomes a "knowledge worker" by helping contain and reduce cost and waste. The open-book culture of sharing cost-profit information results in continuous learning throughout the organization. As more information is shared widely in the organization, all employees must be advised against sharing certain information with people outside the organization because "loose lips sink ships." Finally, with more information, every employee becomes more of a businessperson and less of a functional bureaucrat. Upper management personnel are no longer the only ones who worry about making money because everyone is trying to keep costs contained and trying to focus on profitability as well as growing sales.

Top and general management must walk the talk of sharing more cost, profit, and productivity information by simply trusting all employees more than they have in the past. Experience from our training programs, which encourage the wide sharing of information, shows that it takes at least one to two years to make the complete transformation from limited sharing and mistrust to wide sharing and trust throughout the organization. Top management must lead this change and convert, or ultimately replace, general managers and department managers that resist the transformation to a more open-book culture that is fundamental to profitable growth.

HIGH- AND LOWER-COST COUNTRIES

Everything discussed in this chapter applies equally to countries as well as to companies. When astute businesspeople discuss cost structures and productivity, they quickly compare the costs and productivity among different regions and countries of the world. They look at the cost of labor and materials as well as the cost of highly skilled engineers and technical people. Since most industrial manufacturing businesses have a significant amount of their total costs in manufacturing employment, any meaningful decisions about sourcing, plant expansion, consolidations, and relocation must look at the manufacturing skill levels and the respective costs and productivity in various countries. It is increasingly difficult to competitively design and manufacture most industrial products from a high-cost country, not to mention the difficulty in making a substantial profit in the process.

For decades, Europe was the major source of productive and globally competitive output for industrial products. Unfortunately, much of western Europe is now uncompetitive when it comes to global cost competitiveness. Germany is a prime example of a high-cost country. Germany was once the world model of a successful industrial economy, but it has been losing thousands of jobs and future investment in markets it long dominated—advanced machine tools, telecom equipment, office equipment, optical equipment, chemicals, and automotive components. For decades, German productivity and ingenuity compensated for high corporate taxes, big government, and shorter workweeks. But in a global marketplace, German worker costs are double the average in the United States and are numbing when compared with areas in Asia. Furthermore, by law, all German workers, even recent high school graduates, get at least six weeks of paid vacation, unlimited sick leave, unemployment pay, generous layoff payments, and a mandated 37-hour workweek. German national laws prevent manufacturers from using night shifts or weekend workers to spread overhead and fixed costs over more units of production. It is not surprising that American and Asian annual output per worker and productivity is now much higher than in Germany.

Due to the high-cost situation in Germany and most of Western Europe, German chemical giants including Hoechst, BASF, and Bayer have significantly increased their investments in Asia and Central Europe where the work ethic, aptitudes, and skill levels are more competitive. The low-cost central European countries (including Hungary, the Czech Republic, and Poland) are on the doorstep of Western Europe and are experiencing a rapid flow of industrial investment. The costs in Budapest, Prague, and Warsaw are on par with the productivity levels in Malaysia, Thailand and Singapore.

SUMMARY

In Chapter 3 we defined marketing as "serving customers' profitability." This chapter spotlighted the last word *profitability*. Any marketing book, training program, product line, or customer or market segment decision that does not emphasize the cost-profit dimension is sorely lacking and is of questionable value. Without a sound knowledge of your product line and customer and market segment costs and profits, any talk of marketing or strategy is shallow and academic. Side-by-side comparisons and estimates of competitors' costs and productivity should be developed before strategies are developed or changes made. This chapter stresses that finance people in every company must be part of the up-front marketing decision-making process. And since marketing is defined primarily as a general manager's responsibility, it is critical that anyone with a profit responsibility (i.e., general manager, business unit manager, product or market manager) must lead the charge to gather, widely share, and use cost-profit information for product line and customer and market segment decisions. Profit center managers and their business teams will then become marketing controllers.

CHAPTER 5

Thinking Small to Win Big

Over the past two decades, a number of successful high-tech and industrial companies have rediscovered Demosthenes' idea: "Small opportunities are the beginning of great enterprises." Unable to compete broadly against entrenched competitors, they have adopted a successful divide-and-conquer strategy of identifying a specific market need and then focusing resources and energies on meeting that need better than anyone else. This seemingly simple, but highly effective, approach has led to a number of individual success stories in industries and markets that were losing money or going nowhere.

At a time when most major semiconductor companies suffered losses, layoffs, and plant closings, the LSI Logic Corporation broke out the champagne. When the company was only five years old, it passed $100 million in sales and was one of the few highly profitable chip makers in Silicon Valley. LSI Logic accomplished this feat by surging to the lead in a small but rapidly growing segment of the semiconductor business— the design and production of small batches of microelectronic chips customized for each user. Most semiconductor companies that churn out standard products by the millions have been battered by excess domestic and Japanese production. LSI Logic learned that many users wanted customized chips to differentiate their products from those of their competitors. The customized chips saved money and space by providing the functions of several smaller, off-the-shelf parts that had to be wired together in a circuit board. By concentrating on customization, LSI Logic developed a faster method of manufacturing customized chips at a much lower cost than the broad-line, standard chip producers. LSI Logic simply chose to concentrate its resources on a segment of the chip market that they expected to grow at 30 percent to 35 percent a year. Today, LSI Logic Corporation is a young company with sales of more than $1 billion.

In another underperforming industry, the steel business, successful $4 billion Nucor Corporation attributes its high-performing business strategy to the careful selection of product lines and niche markets. Focusing on selected products and end-use markets within efficient transportation radii, Nucor invests in state-of-the-art technology and builds minimills to the economic scale of each regional market. As a result, Nucor's costs per ton are lower for both finished manufacturing and transportation than those of their domestic and foreign import competitors. Ken Iverson, chairman of Nucor, stated:

> The major mills first ignored us. We were viewed as a flea on an elephant's back. We've never believed that bigger is better in anything we do and that you had to have a full integrated steel company all the way back to the ore mines. To be sure, the giant steel industry has been napping like Rip Van Winkle for many years. The word "market mills" is probably more accurate than the word "minimills" because we make only selective products for certain end-use markets and within a limited geographic region. This also provides Nucor with an advantage in transportation costs and response time against large centralized integrated producers and foreign competition.

Nypro is the world's largest injection molding company, with record sales and profits for each of the past 15 years. Market focus is what distinguishes Nypro: annual sales of $300 million more than the 40,000 other injection molders around the world. Most of the other companies try to be too many things to too many people. Nypro's visionary CEO, Gordon Lankton, states:

> We are successful because we are very focused. We started out by just focusing on the special requirements and injection molding needs of health care manufacturers and their products. Our global customers in that segment include Johnson & Johnson and Sandoz. Then we also focused on the computer electronics industry, and our global customers include Hewlett-Packard, Canon, and Panasonic. Our next segment, consumer packaged goods, includes Gillette, Avery, and Duracell. We have dedicated teams of marketing, sales, engineering, and manufacturing people with expertise in each segment. We are seen as insiders to these market segments because we are very active in their trade associations and industry meetings. Since we understand the needs of these segments, industry leaders have great confidence in Nypro as a true partner to serve their injection molding needs in their assembly plants around the world. We often locate our facilities in the same town or on the same street of our select customers all over the world.

Segmentation has also proven to be the key to success in many service and software businesses. The large German-based Zubin AG successfully specializes in designing and building only tunnel and bridge projects around the world. The North Carolina architectural firm of Odell Associates only focuses on the design and project management of airport construction throughout the world. Both of these firms are recognized as global experts in their respective fields. Their employees have thousands of years of in-depth experience in these defined areas of heavy construction and project management. Lexmark, a manufacturer of laser and ink-jet printers, has captured market share from both Canon and Hewlett-Packard by focusing on selected industry segments such as banking, retail, and health care. Lotus, the software developer, is especially successful in the chemical and banking industries where they have carved out a strong focus. Oracle, the network giant, has bundled together software packages and consulting support for many clearly defined market segments. Microsoft has repeatedly failed to successfully compete against Intuit's software because Intuit is so focused on small-business accounting and bill paying with its Quicken package and its other widely used products.

FAILURE TO SEGMENT

The failure to segment a marketplace and concentrate resources on one or a few customer groups is at the heart of many industrial business failures. The following examples show how market leaders and pioneers become market followers or companies with arrows in their backsides while their heads are in the sand.

Xerox, the pioneer among photocopying machines, emphasized large "national accounts," without any sound segmentation in place. Xerox also became arrogant and complacent in the copier market and then made a strategic move into financial services that diverted its management's attention and resources. Japanese competitors were the first to identify a market need and developed a desktop plain-paper copier for low-speed business needs. Xerox failed to properly segment the marketplace and allowed Canon and other aggressive Japanese competitors to do it for them. Furthermore, Xerox's high cost structure and lack of a strong distributor network helped Canon become the largest and most profitable copier company in the world.

IBM did not enter a marketplace unless it could identify at least a $150 million business opportunity, which explains why they missed the minicomputer and desktop publishing booms and other business opportunities that have grown pragmatically. IBM's "bigness mentality" was the penalty of its past success. IBM's bigness resulted in a slowness and aversion to risk taking, which had developed when the Watson family was involved. IBM chose to play it safe and became a late follower in the fast-moving electronics industry where there are only two kinds of companies—the fast and the dead. The only way a company can avoid the bigness mentality is to create more small entrepreneurial divisions or business units that focus on one or a few market segments. The "small is beautiful" phrase applies to market segments as well as to how firms organize to capture opportunities.

Herman Miller, the $800 million designer and manufacturer of office furniture, was frequently named one of the 100 best companies to work for because of its innovative product designs, worker participation, and profit sharing. The company was proud of its *Fortune* 500 list of customers. After two decades of spectacular growth, Herman Miller's engine stalled in the early 1990s. Most of its *Fortune* 500 customers had little need for office furniture as their management levels and corporate staffs shrank. Many Herman Miller customers had floors and entire buildings full of empty office furniture. The growth market segments were small businesses, home office furniture, computer workstations and medical facilities, where Herman Miller had little or no presence.

Many companies become enamored with selling to the *Fortune* 500 which guarantees success to no one. These very large customers were often the most bureaucratic, experiencing little top-line growth, and were known for pressuring dealers for the lowest prices. Herman Miller would have been far better off focusing on the emerging *Fortune* 500 customers and market segments that were rapidly growing and likely to be successful in the next decade.

To emerge as a winner in today's dynamic and highly competitive market arena, every business unit must be quick to identify new windows of opportunity and then rapidly develop a unique product/service package based on some demonstrable competitive advantage. Smaller firms are often more successful than large ones in pursuing such strategies. Frequently, it is the very reason for the smaller companies' existence; that is, someone with entrepreneurial instincts (now more popularly termed a "vision") spotted an opportunity and set up the business specifically to provide some combination of better product, price, and service. With few exceptions, larger, entrenched companies find it very difficult to develop and implement these focused strategies. Why? The vast number of these top- and general-level managers do not know two fundamental points: (*a*) Marketing in an industrial company is not one department, but the whole company, and is the responsibility of general managers. (*b*) These same managers do not realize that the definition and selection of industrial market segments is the foundation for developing and executing sound business strategies and plans.

FOUNDATION FOR BUSINESS STRATEGY

The identification and selection of market segments is the most important strategic decision facing industrial and high-tech firms. The choice of market segment(s) to pursue is the key starting block for developing overall strategies and business plans for the technically based firm. Only after the industrial firm defines market segments can they identify common customer requirements, needs, and relevant competitive suppliers. The identified market segment serves as a mirror to appraise your firm's capabilities or strengths and weaknesses in meeting the segment's present and future needs. The present and future needs of the segment determine what your "knitting" or business is or should be if you select to serve the segment.

The strategic importance of market segmentation has been ignored by most planners and academics who simply conduct macro-analysis. Strategic planning formats that do not demand specific market segments when analyzing situations and developing strategies can easily become form-filling exercises. A strengths-and-weaknesses analysis that is not conducted objectively against competitors' offerings and the requirements of an identified market segment is usually a waste of time. Similarly, if planning and strategy development is not done around the key market segments and without considering what is necessary to serve the identified market segment, the result will most likely be a broad-brush analysis and a broad-based strategy that ineffectively tries to be everything to many people.

A well-thought-out division or business unit charter should define its business mission in terms of both technologies and key market segments served. Too many divisions or business unit charters simply describe products manufactured and some broad industry groups to which they are marketed. A clearly stated mission, in terms of products and market segments served, will focus the entire business unit on customer groups with common requirements.

Simply stated, the definition and then selection of market segments drives everything! The selection of market segments spearheads competitive analysis, guides strategy development to secure competitive advantages, and determines what action programs are needed across the business unit to achieve sales and profit goals in the segment. The selection of market segments determines what type of technology, manufacturing, sales skills, and other capabilities are needed. Finally, the selection of market segments is a long-term strategic decision that cannot be easily reversed without severe penalties.

COMMON ERRORS AND MISTAKES

If market segmentation is so important, why is it so rarely practiced or performed well by industrial and high-tech firms? Market segmentation as a business practice has long been recognized and well practiced in the consumer packaged goods sector. There has been no corresponding level of interest or rigor in industrial and high-tech companies. Most industrial executives have no idea that to be market driven is an outside-in process that begins with customer groups or market segments and works back into the company. Even in industrial companies that have recently discovered marketing, many of the following common segmentation mistakes are made.

Sales Segmentation

The salespeople do the segmenting based on the size of their existing customers, which they categorize as A, B, and C accounts. Their largest existing customers are called key accounts regardless of their growth and profitability. The sales department determines how the rest of the organization selects and serves customers and distributors. These companies see segmentation as more volume, added customer service, and improving customer satisfaction to everyone. Large accounts dominate their thinking. Segmentation at best begins and quickly ends with the original equipment manufacturer (OEM) and after-market categories. Marketing is seen as a subset of sales and consists of flashy brochures, trade advertising, 800 numbers, and trade shows.

Misusing Consumer Retailing Approaches

The segmentation approaches for consumer and industrial markets are as different as potato chips are from integrated circuit chips. Household markets are segmented on the basis of personality, lifestyle, income, sex, image, social status, ethnic groups, age, and personal wants. Industrial markets are segmented on the basis of performance needs, emerging user requirements, manufacturing processes, technical services, cost-effective solutions, and the customers' customer needs. Naive academics, consultants, and advertising agencies often eloquently tout retail segmentation approaches for industrial markets that are pure nonsense for industrial applications. Any industrial manager who believes that consumer goods segmentation approaches equally apply to industrial markets is simply ignorant and wasting the company's time and money.

Lack of Market Facts

Most industrial and high-tech firms simply do not have the facts required to identify and select market segments. Most major industrial firms do not even have in-house marketing research capabilities to help develop these facts. When an in-house marketing research staff does exist, it is typically one of the most underpaid and underappreciated units in the firm. Often it is staffed with castoffs from other departments who do not have the requisite professional skills to do a competent job of market assessment.

General management rarely appreciates the value of professional market assessment and relies instead on trade or secondary information or "seat of the pants" estimates. General managers are usually unwilling to commit the time and money necessary to perform the segmentation job. As a result, the company flies half-blind, therefore missing opportunities, getting caught off-base by unexpected product or market developments, and becoming continuously vulnerable to competitors with better market information. These same companies have little information about how and when their products are used and how they compare with competitors in each market application. The cost and risk of not having this market information far outweighs the needed investment. Not until upper and general management realize that market facts are a small investment and not an unnecessary cost will the definition and selection of attractive market segments get started properly.

Confusing Markets with Products

Product- and manufacturing-driven companies have great difficulty thinking in terms of market segments. After thinking for many years first in terms of a product's composition, manufacturing method, product form, and technical features, these people have real trouble thinking about the market segment and about customer benefits and objections by market segment. These people need to first think of the requirements and emerging needs in a market segment and then match, fit, or tailor their product/service package to the segment. Not until they dispel the foolish notion of product "segments" that do not exist will they make the transition to a market-driven company. For example, a manufacturer of tantalum electronic capacitors only compared itself with other tantalum capacitor manufacturers, while the customers in the segment evaluated tantalum, ceramics, and aluminum materials. When this supplier thought first in terms of market segments, they would have quickly compared their products with the suppliers of ceramic and aluminum material. This manufacturer also gained many insights into industrial marketing segmentation by examining how their immediate customers segmented their markets.

Thinking Too Broad

An industry is a large group of manufacturers producing and selling products, whereas a market is a much more distinct group of customers or users who have similar requirements. Companies must learn to distinguish between an industry and a market segment. Product- or sales-driven industrial firms usually do not attempt to make a distinction between the two. One component manufacturer stated to us, "We serve the computer market with solid-state connectors." This kind of statement is useless since there are many distinct market segments within the computer industry, and each segment has specific customer requirements, trends, and growth rates. It might have been more useful to say, "We primarily serve workstation computer firms and some microprocessor computer builders."

As another example, an industrial firm's division charter states, "The division is a supplier of hydraulic pumps and hoses to machinery markets." Again, a general industry is being defined, not market segments. Further analysis revealed that the division was primarily supplying certain types of farm equipment manufacturers, three kinds of construction machinery producers, and heavy-duty truck makers. To avoid this kind of thinking, the president of one company told his business team that they were not segmenting properly if their total market was more than $50 million. Defining themselves this way forced them away from industry definitions, which typically report sales by the billions of dollars, not millions.

Thinking Too Narrow

At the other extreme, some sales-focused firms do not think beyond the needs of the one or few customers who dominate their business. One manufacturer of flexible machining systems developed a $150 million business with the three major auto manufacturers in Detroit. This total involvement with just three firms in one industry led to myopic thinking, which prevented the manufacturer from even considering other situations or groups of customers (e.g., farm equipment, the truck industry, and oil field equipment) with similar manufacturing requirements.

Other manufacturers think too restrictively about their markets because they are constrained by their existing products, technologies, and manufacturing methods. They think of expansion only in terms of extending their product line. They do not consider how products or services beyond their existing capabilities could help them strengthen their position or develop more attractive markets. For example, an electronic sensor producer sold chiefly to nuclear plants, where its line had been qualified and approved by the appropriate agencies. This narrow focus on a slow-growth market with a narrow customer base greatly limited sales potential. Management ultimately redefined its business to include semiconductor manufacturing and the packaging equipment segment and, by acquisition and internal development, introduced several products that filled the needs of these specific market segments.

Too Few or Too Many Segments

After conducting a segmentation analysis, some firms experience one of two extreme situations. First, they may not have identified a large enough number of market segments. If too few segments have been defined, a competitor may zero in on a segment and gain a major part of the business. Large corporations frequently segment the market into segments that are too few and, therefore, too broad. What is small to a $1 billion company might be large to a $40 million to $100 million company or division. However, if large companies do not segment small enough, competition will often do it for them. Smaller industrial firms are usually more able to think and act in terms of small, growing segments and, therefore, to position themselves within those segments to gain real competitive advantages.

At the other extreme, some companies carry the idea of segmenting beyond the point of practical value. After investing in a seven-month segmentation study that produced mountains of data, a division general manager told us the following:

> They have divided our business into 12 market segments. I think this is about double the amount we can reasonably and profitably focus on. Even if it isn't, there is no way we can develop a competitive strategy for 12 segments without spending all of our time in planning meetings. I believe we could combine some of the smaller segments where the requirements are similar. I sent the team back to work and said I wanted their top three

segments to defend and their top two segments to attack. And finally, I asked them to tell me how we should evaluate their performance in each market segment they select.

SEGMENT AND RESEGMENT

Industrial market segments are dynamic. Competitive activity, technological changes, swings in the business cycle, acquisitions, and pricing decisions can dramatically change the boundaries and attractiveness of segments. It is necessary to periodically evaluate existing segmentation and consider new or different approaches. Business history is replete with cases in which an existing competitor saw market segment boundaries as static or did not identify new, emerging segments and so lost out. Xerox failed to resegment the photocopy marketplace and, by not doing so, allowed the Japanese competitors to do it for them. The rapid use of computer printers is further redefining the photocopy marketplace.

The x-ray film market provides an example of just how dynamic a market segment can be. Although Kodak is the broadest line supplier of photographic film to most market segments, DuPont concentrated on the x-ray film segment and achieved a large market share. Now, developments in nuclear magnetic resonance technology promise to replace x rays in some applications with a process that develops the "picture" electronically and displays it on a computer screen. As the x-ray market shrinks, DuPont must redefine and resegment the market and determine what technologies and capabilities it needs if it is to hold onto this market position.

Let's look at the computer market for another example. With increased competition and new electronic capabilities, the computer market must be periodically resegmented with new approaches. One small computer manufacturer noticed that there was one type of customer that required high reliability. This market segment included banks, airlines, car rental agencies, and other businesses, where interrupted data response meant an immediate loss of customer revenue. To ensure reliability, these companies had to have backup computers or redundant systems that lay idle unless the on-line system failed. The manufacturer was able to design a fail-safe computer that would not lose any data, as the other systems did, if any part of the system went down. As a consequence, the producer enjoyed four years of excellent growth and considerable lead time before it had any real competitors in its newly defined market segment.

To pursue these new opportunities, the business firm should not concern itself with obsoleting or cannibalizing its existing technology—because if they are not proactive, a competitor may do it for them. Raychem, the $1 billion specialty chemical company and a proven segment marketer, also pursues a successful strategy of rapidly obsoleting its own products. As a result, Raychem is a moving target for its competition that is always shooting where they were, not where they are.

Segmenting industrial markets is an analytical and creative process. Management should not allow ties to previously segmented markets to strangle new ways to segment. In markets with rapid technological change, there is a need to resegment more frequently because newly emerging technologies constantly blur segment boundaries. Solid market facts help identify and prioritize segments.

Industrial marketers need to know the current size, growth rate, profit potential, and competitor market shares for any market segment of interest. This includes markets the company is currently serving as well as those it is considering for entry. Such information will enable the company to select and then gear its operations to the most attractive market segments. It also helps the company decide which products, markets, and individual customers should be de-emphasized or withdrawn from entirely. The approach for evaluating both current and potential markets is essentially the same. The difference, of course, is that more historical sales and performance data and firsthand knowledge of the marketplace are available for the markets currently served. However, many of the market facts needed to assess either markets new to the business or new to the world are typically unavailable from existing sources. Therefore, a special market analysis and study of progressive customers is essential to accurately assess the market size, growth and profit potential, customer trends, and competitive offerings.

Setting Segment Priorities

It is essential to consider and weigh all these variables (i.e., size, growth rates, profitability, and competition), along with your current share position and proprietary advantages, in order to set priorities intelligently. One useful approach to help determine the trade-offs among these variables is to calculate the present and potential profit value of a share point of each segment. This helps determine which segments are most attractive from a profit point of view instead of just sales potential. Bandag, the retread rubber and tire equipment manufacturer, religiously determines the profit value and potential of all market segments before setting priorities. Their CEO, Marty Carver, told us:

The approach that works well for us is selective profit-based market segmentation. We spend a great deal of time and effort studying market segments or niches and categorizing them by end-user type or applications, performance need, market potential, and the present and future profit potential. We then impute a present and future ROI [return on investment] for each segment before we set any product/market priorities. It brings home the point that some of the larger segments your salespeople lust after or which your engineers find technically "interesting" may not be worth a candle. Quite frankly, we have walked away from a number of larger volume or technically challenging segments that were low ROIs.

A useful way to finalize the prioritizing of market segments within each region of the world is to assign them to one of the following four categories:

1. *Defend.* This is the most important category and deserves top priority. It includes segments that are currently a major source of sales and profit and that must be defended and fortified. Sales and especially profit growth should occur in this category. These segments usually receive more services and new products. (Some of our Japanese training clients term this category "counter attack.")

2. *Attack.* This category includes segments that offer attractive long-term growth and profit potential, but current market positions and profits are low or nonexistent. These segments usually receive more services and new products.

3. *De-emphasize.* Little or no current investment is made in these segments. The near-term sales and profit growth prospects are not attractive. Prices might be significantly increased. This may be a "take-order" situation or the first "up or out" step before withdrawing from the segment in a region of the world. These situations receive fewer products and services and may be assigned to distributors.

4. *Withdraw.* This category includes markets that do not offer attractive short- or long-term profit prospects. A plan is needed to withdraw from or exit these segments or to assess them to distributors. If you are not currently selling these segments and accounts direct, a no-go decision should be made.

At the annual business planning review meeting at Unilever Chemicals in England, Dr. Ian Anderson, the chairman, was concerned that business teams around the world were not disciplined enough in selecting which segments to emphasize, de-emphasize, and exit. Dr. Anderson's following memo made the selection process clear to everyone:

Our global business planning process has identified over 80 market segments to pursue and that are supposedly all fantastic opportunities. However, I have a hunch that a good number of those will do very little for our bottom line in the short or long term. We simply must become more selective and disciplined in determining which opportunities to invest in with our limited resources. Some of our companies have been using a one-gallon watering can to feed an acre of plants. With that approach, some will die, some will be marginal, and very few will rapidly grow.

Therefore, I have asked all company presidents and their general managers to rethink and to group every segment into one of four categories—defend, attack, de-emphasize, and withdraw. I would like the people to prioritize every segment within each of the four categories and to arrive at a balance of short and longer term attractive market segments for us to invest in, de-emphasize, and withdraw from.

Responsibility for Segmentation

While an increasing number of general managers and business unit managers are aware of the need to do a better job of segmenting the market, their enthusiasm or ability to do so is often limited by short-term sales and profit pressures. Far too many profit center and general managers still regard volume gains and relationships with large accounts as the most important factors in their business. Market segmentation is regarded as some kind of theoretical exercise that is not worth much time and money, especially if it interferes with bringing in or running the business. Segmentation requires a good deal of careful thought and creativity, and it is the primary responsibility of general management to make the money and resources available to ensure that it is accomplished. Segmentation is not a theoretical exercise, and any general manager who ignores or shortchanges the need to define the discrete markets to be served is making a serious mistake. To ensure that the business is properly segmented, every profit center and general manager should be satisfied with the answers to the following questions:

1. Have we defined the segments in the best way possible?
2. Is there any evidence that competitors, especially small ones, have achieved an advantage by segmenting differently?
3. What customer benefits and competitive advantages do we have (or can we achieve) in each segment?
4. Which segments offer the greatest profit potential?
5. In which segments do we have an attractive position(s) that we should defend and grow?
6. Which segments are the most attractive to attack or build a position in?
7. Which segments should we de-emphasize or withdraw from?

If these questions are difficult to answer or cannot be answered at all, the chances are that the marketplace has not been properly segmented and then targeted.

Responding to Market Needs

Even when larger firms clearly understand segmentation and identify new opportunities, they are usually not responsive enough to capture them. Fast response time—from market need identification to product delivery—is key to this effort. The Japanese have taken an idea from American business practice that they call TAT, turnaround time. Many Japanese producers are now focusing on ways to reduce their TATs as a means of being more responsive and gaining a competitive edge. Several American companies have also been successful with this approach. Convergent Technologies, a manufacturer of desktop workstations, conceived and delivered its first computer in nine months. Similarly, Hewlett-Packard introduced its new Proprinter to the market just two years after conception, cutting the company's historical product development cycle time. Lexmark, a smaller competitor, now thinks in terms of 12 to 15 months for its product development cycle.

To pursue these small but attractive growth markets, most large corporations must break their organizations down to create smaller business units, each with profit center responsibility. This doesn't necessarily mean setting up a large number of full-fledged operating divisions, although this is certainly an alternative to consider. A matrix approach involving product or market managers can also be used to assign profit center responsibility when the business unit is small and cannot afford to carry the costs of full divisionalization. Small decentralized profit centers can stay closer to changing market requirements, are quicker to identify and pursue new market opportunities, and can help create entrepreneurial drive. Mistakes and fundamental waste are more likely to surface in smaller profit center units, and corrective actions can be taken more easily. The following paragraphs give several examples of larger companies that have achieved extraordinary success by constantly thinking small to win big by adjusting their organizations to carry out this concept as a group of PT boats and not as one large aircraft carrier.

The $17+ billion Johnson & Johnson (J&J) enterprise attributes much of its continuous growth in sales and profits to its grow-and-divide business philosophy in pursuing new market opportunities. When a J&J business unit discovers a new product/market opportunity, a totally separate, new company is often created to pursue the opportunity. Also, as existing businesses reach a certain size, they are often broken down into smaller but still very decentralized operations. This grow-and-divide philosophy has resulted in more than 200 J&J small business units, each with its own company name, president, functional vice presidents, board of directors, and policies. J&J's acquisition philosophy parallels this approach by buying small-market niche companies and then rapidly growing the business. When J&J makes a large acquisition, as it did with Kodak's medical diagnostic business, it breaks the acquisition up into many smaller and more focused decentralized business units.

Parker Hannifin is the world's largest manufacturer of motion control components and systems. Even with sales of more than $4 billion and about 1,000 hydraulic, pneumatic, and electromechanical products, Parker has never thought of itself as a big company. The key to Parker's success is that it thinks and acts like a small company in everything it does. As a division or business unit grows beyond 250 to 350 people, it often creates another decentralized division or business unit with its own business team. This grow-and-divide philosophy is like an amoebae that has spawned dozens of decentralized units. For example, in the area of industrial connectors and fittings, Parker has created divisions or business units dedicated to various markets, including military, automotive, chemical processing, semiconductor, refrigeration, and agriculture. Parker's small plant–small town strategy complements the "small is beautiful," profitable mind-set of its worldwide product/market segmentation planning.

ITW, better known as Illinois Tool Works, is a nearly $5 billion manufacturer of construction, welding, and packaging systems and products. ITW has over 300 small, focused, and truly decentralized business units. Their philosophy of small business units has been key to their process for many decades. For example, when ITW bought the $300 million Miller Group, a manufacturer of portable and automated welding equipment, they created 15 cross-functional business units, from $10 million to 25 million in size, each with a general manager and separate profit and loss statements. ITW takes a "break 'em up" philosophy when any business unit gets over $40 million in sales. ITW's small units are very responsive to customer needs, they accelerate the development of new products, and they create an obsession about maintaining a very focused market and competitive offerings.

Possibly the best larger company approach to pursuing emerging market niches is practiced by EG&G Idaho, Inc., a $1.5 billion high-tech company with 175 distinct and autonomous business units. The average EG&G business unit has less than $10 million in sales, with a total market of typically only $25 million. Each of these small businesses has its own dedicated R&D, manufacturing, and sales staffs, who focus on opportunities within each market niche. In more than 80 percent of these small high-tech growth businesses, EG&G has either the number one market share or is the technical leader in that market. In the *Forbes* five-year rankings of the top 1,000 U.S. companies, EG&G ranked second in earnings per share growth and first in profitability in the electronic category.

Company structures such as those practiced by EG&G, ITW, Parker Hannifin, and J&J, with many small business units, allow these leading companies the flexibility to rapidly leap from one attractive market opportunity to another. These smaller business units are less apt to take on the large fixed investments in production facilities and develop the lengthy product development cycles so common to most large and centralized business units. Although niche markets have traditionally been exploited most effectively by small companies, these four examples clearly demonstrate that larger companies can play the same game if they really want to. To attack and defend increasingly competitive markets, more large companies will have to pursue fast-moving market segment opportunities with smaller decentralized business units. If they don't, they will miss attractive windows of sales and profit growth.

Shifting Attitudes

One of the most difficult issues facing many high-tech and industrial companies is how to overcome the lack of strategic thinking about market segments that has historically been a serious deficiency. For years, and often for generations, the management of these companies has looked for ways to strengthen R&D, sales, and/or production activities without a clear focus on defined market needs. Now these same managers must reorient their thinking first to define specific segments and then determine what it takes to serve these segments more effectively than the competition. This attitudinal shift is much more difficult than it sounds. The many executives who have talked a good game of marketing without actually doing things differently must now provide the leadership and direction to ensure that R&D, production, and sales activities are specifically geared to the requirements of selected market segments.

To change any company's mind-set to strategic market segmentation, intensive management development programs are required for all levels and functions. When managers have typically advanced through engineering and manufacturing, or operations, a sound understanding of strategic market segmentation is even more necessary. These managers must learn that market segmentation and market selection are the starting points for all decisions and action programs. They must also realize that strategic marketing is quite different from the traditional strategic planning exercises that often involve excessive number crunching, form filling, and ritual and that quickly die out each year.

ALIGNING FOR TARGET SEGMENTS

Implementing a market segment strategy should begin with a business unit mission statement that pinpoints and defines target market segments. All the company's programs in all functional areas should then be structured and focused to effectively serve these target segments. For example, R&D programs and product development priorities should correspond to the segments being emphasized. Likewise, manufacturing, engineering, and production planning must be informed of the requirements of the target segments so that action programs to gear operations toward successfully serving each segment can be developed. Even acquisition programs should be linked to target markets. If the specific technology, manufacturing process, or expertise does not currently exist to serve the emphasized product/market segments, new capabilities must be developed and/or acquired and must be shown as action programs in the business plan. Organizationally, the technical, sales, and, often, manufacturing can be focused or closely aligned to the target markets.

In the marketing areas of the business plan, sales promotion and salesforce programs should be detailed for each target segment. Application stories for sales promotion should be developed for each chosen market segment and written in the language and economics of the respective segment. Advertising copy, trade show participation, media selection, and sales letters must all be developed specifically for the target market segments. Leads and inquiries generated by advertising and trade shows should be designed to better direct salespeople and distributors to prospects in the target segments.

Lubrizol, a successful high-tech producer of engine oil additives, regularly develops focused sales promotion literature for specific markets such as school bus fleets, long-haul tractor/trailer rigs, and mining and construction equipment. Similarly, the Swagelok Company, the world's largest manufacturer of high-pressure fittings, has used industry application stories for decades to build and protect market positions all around the world.

Direct and distributor sales representatives must be provided with the appropriate training and selling aids. The salesforce must be thoroughly trained to emphasize benefits as they apply to each respective market segment. Sales incentives or changes in compensation are often necessary to direct salespeople and distributors to the chosen market segments. Salesforces that are exclusively compensated on a sales volume basis are usually difficult to direct to new market applications that require more time to learn customers' requirements and build new relationships. New commission structures, bonuses, or incentive programs tied to accounts defended or developed in the target segments are usually necessary to ensure that segmentation priorities are pursued throughout the existing salesforce. In some situations, a specialized or dedicated salesforce may have to be created for key segments. Sometimes a different network of distributors must be recruited to penetrate the segments being emphasized.

The training of technical people, field sales, and distributors in market segment applications is often done poorly, if at all. Traditional product training, which does not concentrate on key market applications, will not help implement a segmentation strategy. Good in-depth application success stories are frequently the central focus of market application training sessions. Sealed Air, a maker of protective industrial packaging products and systems, has developed follow-on application seminars for their product training programs. Their application seminars feature company specialists in each segment with extensive use of successful case histories that they develop for each target market. The Swagelock Company developed videocassette and audiocassette job stories for salespeople to view and/or listen to before calling on accounts in various segments. Competent product and market managers and application engineers are the logical people to develop the materials and conduct the training seminars.

SUMMARY

Unable to compete broadly against entrenched competitors, new and emerging companies and those entering markets new to them have adopted a divide-and-conquer, or market segmentation, strategy. The precise definition of a target market can lead to innovative product, price, distribution, and service strategies. Selective market segmentation allows a company to marshal its R&D and engineering efforts toward specific areas rather than spread a little across a wider range of vulnerable marketplaces. At the same time, market segmentation and the selection of specific segments provide direction to the business unit, which enables it to develop the necessary capabilities to serve the identified market segment effectively.

Knowing how to segment a marketplace is, therefore, one of the most important strategic skills an industrial firm must possess. Segmentation defines what business(es) the firm is in, identifies the competition, guides strategy development, and determines the capabilities and cross-functional programs needed in the business unit. High-tech or industrial market selection is clearly a longer term strategic decision that cannot be easily reversed, so it is important that the general marketplace first be segmented into viable targets before any market selection and investment decisions are made.

Without this segmentation, all action programs and decisions tend to be unfocused and lack the impact they could have if tailored to specific segments. Once a business unit loses its focus, it is usually only a short period of time before sales and profits erode. When market positions are lost, it is extremely difficult to regain them. When most industrial companies fall behind, they never catch up. Many of management's criticisms about the failure to execute or poor implementation stem from inadequate market segmentation and departmental programs that have little or no linkages to achieving competitive advantages with specific customer groups or market segments.

CHAPTER 6

Better Mousetraps

Developing new products that perform better or cost less has always been crucial for any technically based company. New-product development is the seed corn for the future. Without new products, a business will eventually die from declining sales. In our increasingly turbulent business environment, developing the expertise and speed to keep pace with, or even ahead of, technological developments and competitors' moves is more important than ever for several reasons:

- Exploding technology is spawning new products and processes at an accelerating rate that threatens almost every product and process in place.
- Competition continues to intensify from all over the world, generating a plethora of new startups and many substitute technologies that encroach on established products and processes.
- Product innovations that result in superior performance or cost advantages are the best means of protecting or building market position without sacrificing profit margins. This is especially true today when many industrial markets are flat or where slow growth and excess capacity are commonplace. Chuck Knight, CEO of Emerson Electric Company, put it this way:

  We can compete in this country irrespective of capacity constraints because there's more than just capacity that is involved in profitably serving a customer. For example, we're in the tool business, so we make mundane things like ladders. You'd be surprised how much technology is in a ladder. We're a market leader, not because of volume but because we use new designs and new materials. Take something even more mundane such as the compressor that drives your air conditioning. Compressors have been around for a long time, but in the next five years you won't recognize them. Technology is changing mundane things that quickly. New materials, new approaches, and new technologies will make excess capacity irrelevant when that capacity is stuck on old methods. It won't do any good if there's 10 times the reciprocating compressor capacity in the world if that technology isn't going to win.

BETTER NEW PRODUCTS

No matter how superior a product might appear or how dynamic its growth, its market position is always tenuous. Modern technology is a powerful force, full of surprises, and it is a serious mistake to assume that any product has a lock on any market or that any supplier owns a market. Any product can be pushed from the growth phase of its life cycle to a mature or obsolescent position very quickly by a new product that offers the customer significant performance or cost advantages. When a successful product enjoys a strong commercial position in an attractive market, management is foolish to be complacent. In fact, the larger a company's market share, the more vulnerable it is. Not a day goes by that someone else is not working to invent a "better mousetrap" that will weaken or possibly destroy the existing product's competitive advantage. The chance of such a better product appearing in the marketplace has increased, and the impact can be devastating to the arrogant, unwary, or unresponsive.

History is replete with examples of companies that have lost their competitive advantage and perhaps even their business because a competitor entered the market with a superior product that had superior cost or performance benefits. These examples are not limited to small or weak companies; even industrial giants such as Siemens, General Electric, and AT&T have seen some of their markets eroded by competition that surprised them with a distinctly superior product. Strong competitors often emerge over the pioneers. IBM, despite its formerly dominant position in the computer market, lost position to several smaller companies that were first to develop powerful minicomputers to replace the larger mainframe computers that were the cornerstone of IBM's business. The dramatic shift in market position among the producers of computer-assisted tomography (CAT) scanning equipment in the medical equipment field also shows how product innovation can pay off. General Electric, a late entry in the field, gained significant market share over a three-year period at the expense of the pioneer companies, including Johnson & Johnson, which had developed the market but failed to keep pace with the techno-logical advancements. Now, General Electric's leadership in this market appears to be seriously threatened by competitors from Japan.

COMMON COMPLAINTS

Despite widespread agreement that new products and technology devel-opments are the lifeblood of most technically based companies, very few managers are satisfied with the results of their company's new-product activities. A typical reaction is that of Jamie Houghton, chairman of Corn-ing Glass, who explained to us:

> We're an innovative company, but if you take the whole spectrum of inno-vation, we have not had a good hit rate on successfully introducing new products. We've spent a lot of money on technology and then screwed it up either because we were late getting to the market or the market didn't want the new product. In our many joint ventures (Dow-Corning, Siecor, and Owens-Corning) we are the technical contributor, and the other partner is usually the marketer.

In our training sessions with hundreds of managers from a broad spectrum of companies and industries, we have heard many equally criti-cal expressions of discontent:

> Product development costs are too high for what we get.
>
> It takes too long to develop new products.
>
> New products are often "me-too" offerings or are too late.
>
> New-product orders are always below forecast.
>
> Products are not designed for low-cost manufacturing.
>
> Product cost targets are missed too often.
>
> Organization and reward systems (culture) have no tolerance for failure.
>
> Original product concept is often lost in the development process.
>
> Projects that lost commercial promise are not killed soon enough.

While this list is long, it is by no means complete. Every manager we worked with had a new or different way of expressing dissatisfaction. For the most part, however, these complaints represent effects or symptoms rather than root causes of the problems. As we see it, these complaints, and others like them, stem from fundamental problems in two areas of technology management. One set of problems occurs during the product development cycle; another set occurs during various stages of the prod-uct life cycle after the launch.

PROBLEMS IN THE DEVELOPMENT AND LIFE CYCLES

Exhibit 6–1 highlights the common problems in both the development and life cycles that are frequently the basis for managers' complaints. All these problems are made more acute by the increasing velocity of change that compresses the time frame. Let's look first at the problems that are most common in the product development cycle, why they occur, and how they can be improved.

Product Development Problems

The first problem rests with top management. Top management should see product development as an agent of change for the entire organization; it should create healthy tension and a sense of urgency throughout the entire organization. If top management doesn't stress the importance and urgency of new and improved products, product development will not get the necessary resources. Top management must give each new venture team great freedom to carry out a project, but, at the same time, it should set very challenging and firm milestones with the team. An executive at Hewlett-Packard stated:

> It's like putting the team members on the second floor and removing the ladder. I believe creativity and speed are generated by pushing people against a wall and then pressuring them. Pressure and necessity are the mother of many successful new-product innovations.

To ensure proper emphasis on new products, top management must set challenging goals as a percentage of sales for products introduced within a five-year period. It is also the responsibility of top management to help business units measure and shorten their time to market by asking them three questions:

1. What is the average concept-to-market time in months?
2. What is the best competitor's average concept-to-market time in months?
3. What is the time reduction goal in months?

Top management must also anticipate, encourage, and expect new-product risk taking. Top management should serve as sponsors for product champions that are willing to stick out their necks. The company cultures at Johnson & Johnson and Nucor exemplify the proper role of top management to encourage risk taking in product and process development, as described in the following discussion.

EXHIBIT 6-1

Development and Product Life-Cycle Problems

From Idea to Launch

Product Development Cycle

Top management does not
Stress the importance and urgency of new products
Encourage risk taking
Serve as sponsors

Cycle times and profits not aligned with
Shorter windows
Shorter time to market
Shorter payback periods

Projects not focused on
Good product ideas
Verified customer needs
Important benefits
Significant opportunities

Critical linkages missing
To a leader or follower strategy
To a focused business plan
To technical or commercial strengths
To cross-functional integration

Time to Market

From Launch to Effective Life

Product Life Cycle

1. Introduction   2. Growth   3. Maturity   4. Decline

1. Introduction
Field trials with lead customers in target markets are not well managed
Time to gain new product approvals and new sales are underestimated
Introductions are penalized by lack of market focus, application, and selling power

2. Growth
Existing products
Are too costly
Don't satisfy customer needs
Demonstrate insufficient customer benefits
Cost reduction not started soon enough
Next-generation products and enhancements not begun early enough
Not enough emphasis on enhancements to extend the life cycle
Failure to manage products, programs, and products from concept to postlaunch
Failure to cannibalize one's own products

(These problems affect all 4 phases.)

Compressed Life-Cycle Time

103

Years ago, when Jim Burke, a young product manager at Johnson & Johnson, was summoned to CEO Phil Hofmann's office, Burke thought he was going to be fired. His first new product had failed miserably. Instead Hofmann said:

> Are you the one that cost us all that money? Well, I just wanted to congratu-
> late you. If you're making mistakes, that means you're making decisions
> and taking risks. And we will never grow the top line if you don't take
> some new-product risks. You also saved us a lot of money by suggesting
> that we pull the plug early.

To continue this risk-taking culture, when Jim Burke became CEO of Johnson & Johnson, he frequently reminded employees of their multimillion dollar new-product failures in CAT scanning equipment, baby diapers, and adhesives—not to admonish anyone but rather to emphasize the lessons learned.

Ken Iverson, the chairman of successful Nucor Corporation, tries to meet with as many recently hired engineers as possible each year. He often makes the following risk-taking statement to young managers:

> We expect people to make decisions, try new processes, and take risks at
> Nucor. During your career, we expect you will probably make three or four
> mistakes or try processes that have to be abandoned. Each of these will
> probably cost the company $80,000 to $100,000. In a sense, if you don't do
> that, you're not doing your job. All I would ask is don't make all those mis-
> takes or try all those processes in your first year here.

Upper management must also be involved in new-product development as sponsors and reviewers. At Sealed Air, CEO Dermot Dumphy and all general and upper managers are members of at least one new-product team. At the Fluke Corporation and Hewlett-Packard, upper management receives a one-page monthly summary of every R&D project. At 3M and National Starch and Chemical, all upper management personnel attend weeklong semiannual R&D project reviews.

The second problem—cycle times and costs not aligned with realities—occurs because management and product development personnel have not adjusted their sense of urgency and pace to the accelerating rate of technological change. Today, market opportunities develop and evaporate quicker, and acceptable payback periods have decreased, in many cases, from years to months. This means that the time to market must be quicker and the time periods for all product development activities compressed. Some companies have reduced their time to market but fail to reduce the launch period and market development time. Yesterday's standards for developing new products and achieving a payback simply no longer apply. Our rule of thumb for an acceptable payback period in today's world is that it should be no longer than one-half the anticipated life cycle. This allows a payback that will support continued investment in new-product and -process technology.

The third problem—a lack of market focus—is probably the single most important reason that so many new products miss the mark and so many product development dollars are wasted. Achieving a market focus is unquestionably difficult because it requires both a deep understanding of stated and unarticulated customer needs as well as a knowledge of how the technology can solve those needs. Generally, this customer and technical knowledge does not exist in any one individual but is scattered among many. Pulling these scattered fragments of information together is a difficult but essential step to achieving a proper market focus.

Weak or missing cross-functional linkages, the fourth problem, is a frequent source of complaints and frustration. It occurs because the activities of many product development groups are not linked as closely as they should be to the priorities, needs, and commercial strengths of the operating units. Achieving this linkage is not as easy as it might sound. Product development personnel are likely to have advanced degrees and knowledge of technology that no one else can match. Moreover, their interests are frequently focused more on their professional associations and on advancing the technology than on meeting customer needs or financial goals. Getting this group to subjugate their natural interests to those of the business unit's and customers' needs, without limiting their ability to stay at the forefront of technology, is a crucially important responsibility of general management. R&D people must get very close to customers in their workplace. They must listen to and observe what progressive customers need and help them define their perceived and unarticulated needs. In a small but increasing number of companies, there is very little distinction between marketing and R&D people. In a few leading new-product companies, R&D reports to marketing to achieve the needed technical and commercial coupling.

Product Life-Cycle Problems

Now let's examine the problems that occur in the product life cycle. In the introduction or launch phase, problems inevitably result in disappointing sales and profit shortfalls. Our experience suggests that many new-product sales forecasts can be cut in half and still be too ambitious. Most managers inevitably overestimate the value of their new products to their customers and underestimate the time their customers will take to evaluate the product and finally place a significant order. Also, most companies simply do not do an adequate job of training the salesforce on the product's advantages or of directing and focusing the salespeople to the high-potential applications.

Few companies launch new industrial products as if they were perishable fruit. Even fewer do any kind of postlaunch review. Sealed Air does both. For every new product Sealed Air launches, salespeople are required to take a proficiency test on the new product's customer benefits and how they compare with competitive substitutes. The salesperson must retake the proficiency exam until a predetermined score is achieved. Our experience has found that many industrial salespeople and sales managers resist such proficiency training. Pharmaceutical companies have required new-product proficiency training and testing with their salespeople for decades.

It is in the growth and maturity phases of a product's life cycle that products are often allowed to drift into a noncompetitive position. In today's world of accelerating and competing technologies, this can happen very quickly unless management keeps abreast of changing customer needs, stays a step ahead of competitive moves, and pursues the right technologies. Cost-reduction programs, product enhancement, and even next-generation products must be defined much earlier in the cycle than ever before. As product life cycles shrink, second-generation products must be started well *before* the first generation is launched.

The decline phase is where huge amounts of money are wasted. It is not uncommon to find 80 percent of the effort going to the defense of products that are more important for what they have contributed in the past than for what they are going to contribute in the future.

The dollars lost or wasted in inventory write-offs and customer returns are also critical because management often overlooks the importance of following an orchestrated plan to phase out old products. Again, both problems are made more acute by the increasing number of new products and technologies and the rapid obsolescence of old ones.

There is no magic formula for overcoming these problems. However successful companies generally follow several practices that improve their chances of breaking through these road blocks to achieve a major payoff from their technical activities.

IMPROVING THE ODDS

Although few companies are completely satisfied with their new-product efforts, it is clear that some companies do a much better job than others, as shown in their growth rate, market share, and profit picture. Just look at multibillion dollar industry leaders such as Intel, 3M, Rubbermaid, and Hewlett-Packard. A number of newer or less well-known companies such as Pall, LSI Logic, and Sealed Air have achieved phenomenal success through new-product leadership. All have a record of new-product introduction that has contributed much to their success. Why are they able to achieve better results with new products than their competitors? How do they work around, or at least minimize, the risks and pitfalls in new-product development that plague most companies? Each of these companies has its own development priorities and needs, but they all follow nine fundamental principles:

1. They identify and verify perceived and unarticulated customer problems and areas in which they can make or save customers money.
2. They think through their market/product focus to provide the maximum commercial opportunity.
3. They face up to fundamental cost and performance deficiencies and develop demonstrably better products.
4. They ensure that product development efforts are directly linked to a business unit and to market/product strategies.
5. They strike the right balance between investing in future products and generating current profits.
6. They utilize cross-functional teams to guide new-product and market planning.
7. They are willing to go outside for new technology, expertise, or specialized skills.
8. They rationalize, obsolete, and cannibalize their own product lines.
9. They protect their proprietary positions and respond quickly to any encroachments.

We will look more closely at each of these principles to see what they involve.

Identify Customer Problems

This is the outside-in approach we described in the first chapter that, in turn, is the foundation for any market-driven company. Examples of companies that have succeeded with this approach are legion. Bob Jasse, founder of Chomerics, a successful electronics company that is part of the complex of high-tech companies near Boston, attributes much of its success to understanding the magnitude of the electronic contamination problem in both commercial and military communications. Chomerics developed this in-depth knowledge by conducting a series of educational seminars (80 in one year) for design engineers working on these problems. These seminars enabled them to see the range of problems much more clearly. Chomerics' response was to design and market lines of electronic shielding products that reduced radio interference and enhanced the quality of both voice and data communication. Their design engineers had to get very close to customers before they made recommendations and developed solutions.

A less glamorous example is Post-it Notes™, one of the most successful entries ever in the office supplies field. Art Fry, a research director in the commercial paper division of 3M, first recognized the possible need for the product when he was directing the choir in his church. He saw how difficult it was for choir members to locate hymns. He noticed a similar problem throughout 3M's offices where paperclips, cards, and rubber bands were used to separate and identify pages and paragraphs. He linked this "unarticulated market need" to 3M's adhesive capabilities and came up with the Post-it Note product as a possible solution. The adhesive technology that enabled Post-it Notes to be a success had been shelved for 10 years because no one had connected the new technology to a market need. Obviously, additional research and refinements to the product and manufacturing technology were necessary before the product was actually ready for the market. The key point, however, is that it all started with the recognition of a need or problem, which then created the opportunity. The identification of new market needs and new business opportunities is what makes marketing the entrepreneurial function in every industrial manufacturing company.

Remember, no one in the industrial world buys products or services because they want or enjoy them for themselves. Business products or services are purchased only to perform a specific function that directly or indirectly makes or saves the customer money. Therefore, it is essential to understand the economic or functional needs of the customer or user and to keep these needs foremost in mind so that functional substitutes cannot erode the supplier's market without its knowledge and thus without an opportunity for counteraction. We believe that 90 percent to 95 percent of all R&D expenditures should have a commercial focus.

Define the Right Market/Product Focus

In most technically based companies, a market/product business can be defined in different ways, and there are vast differences in the size and potential of any market, depending on how it is defined. It can be defined as a component, a finished product, or a system based on the integration of several products. It can be defined to include various stages of production and distribution. It can be defined to meet specific customer needs in specific market segments in a way that goes well beyond the existing capabilities. If a company only defines its business and focus around existing products or technologies (an inside-out approach), it is bound to be caught off guard time and time again.

A company's business strategy and the scope and flow of new-product activities are greatly influenced by how the market/product business is defined. Consider the case of an industrial company that is a market leader in industrial drilling and cutting tools. Its management and engineers have traditionally seen themselves as being in the business of simply making and selling more and better drilling and cutting tools. It is obvious, however, that no one really wants to simply buy drilling or cutting tools. What the customer or user wants to buy is the ability to make holes or fabricate parts in the most efficient way possible. In fact, from the user's point of view, drills or cutting tools are far from the final answer. They are costly, they break, they wear out, and, in that sense, they actually interfere with the manufacturing process. If the company had defined its business objective as helping its customers or users make holes or fabricate certain parts more effectively, instead of as making and selling more and better tools, it would have been on much sounder strategic footing. Instead of confining itself solely to improving or expanding its line of drilling and cutting tools, its engineers would be looking for different methods of drilling holes or cutting materials, including such new approaches as the use of lasers, electron beams, and ultrasonic waves. It would also be aware of the increasing use of materials that are easier to cut and drill with these new and unconventional methods. If the company had pursued this broader business objective, it would have been better able to respond to the equipment manufacturers that introduced laser, electron beam, and ultrasonic machines to "drill" holes or cut material far more efficiently in many situations.

Face Up to Deficiencies

Many companies fail to objectively evaluate their products against competitive offerings in rigorous side-by-side comparisons. If they do go through an evaluation process, it is often superficial or biased, leading to a continuation of business as usual rather than dramatic cost or performance improvements. Management is not always presented with the real facts because it is easier not to rock the boat. In other cases, management may see the facts but not accept or face them squarely since it is not easy to admit that a product is no longer competitive. As a result, a surprising number of companies continually try to get by with products that are not competitive, and they make only the fundamental, essential changes in design or cost. For example, a major manufacturer of tapered roller bearings failed to compare their products with spherical, needle, and ceramic bearings in each application. In many applications, their sophisticated tapered bearings were overengineered and too costly. Not until they developed or acquired these other types of bearings did they stop their market-share losses.

There are many product development lessons to be learned from smaller and often very focused manufacturers. The major electric motor manufacturers such as Westinghouse, General Electric, and Reliance saw this clearly when Baldor Electric, a much smaller company, designed a narrow range of products and a manufacturing process that gave it cost, performance, and lead-time delivery superiority. Baldor was able to capture market share because its larger competitors were slow to recognize and react to its strategy, which was based on unsatisfied customer needs. The managements of these large companies spent too much time rationalizing their loss of position by claiming Baldor was losing money, selling inferior products, and giving the business away and far too little time getting a factual picture of what was really happening.

These examples highlight three important points that successful new-product companies follow. First, it is often more useful to scout and learn from the smaller rather than just the largest competitor. Second, it is essential to ensure that products are designed for efficient manufacturing and assembly. Finally, me-too parity is never a solid basis for gaining or regaining position. Even if a company is not first to market, it can learn from the competitor's mistakes and develop a better product from the customer's perspective. Technical programs should be designed to leapfrog the competition rather than play catch up or match itself against moving competitive targets.

Aligning to Target Markets

Companies with excellent records of successful new-product introductions are likely to ensure that new-product programs flow from and are controlled by agreed-upon market priorities. While this sounds obvious, we can cite several multimillion dollar product development programs that resulted in the following products:

- An anaerobic adhesive that was three times as expensive as any competitive offering and far exceeded the requirements of any identified customer group or market segment.

- A 12-axis, high-speed machine tool that worked perfectly once set up but that could only be used by a small handful of machine operators with the requisite skills in the shrinking military aerospace market.
- An expensive robot designed to assemble computer printers that was a technology overkill because humans in even high-cost countries could assemble printers faster and cheaper.

Many other ludicrous examples could also be cited, but these are sufficient to make the point. Unless product development efforts are linked to a carefully conceived market/product strategy for defending or growing the business, technical management will often assign the wrong priorities to development efforts or be led to products and markets that have no real commercial value. Literally hundreds of millions of dollars are wasted each year because technical efforts are poured into products that are out of touch with market needs and opportunities. This is the chief reason the success ratio of new-product development efforts is so low in many companies. R&D programs should focus on market segments and progressive customers that have been selected to defend or attack. The plain truth is that, left on their own, product development engineers will spend a lot of money developing products that interest them or on what they think is right for any market. They will not just sit still waiting for direction. General management's responsibility is to provide sufficient direction by ensuring that development activities and priorities are defined by cross-functional teams and focused on market segment(s) and verified customer needs.

Many executives argue that the idea of linking every new development project to a commercial need or plan is impractical and too restrictive. We remain adamant that this is not so. The only rare exception is when senior management makes a conscious decision to spend money on basic or exploratory research. This is an expensive process, however, and a company that follows this route must have plenty of money to support "interesting" research that may lead nowhere. We believe that 90 percent to 95 percent of all R&D expenditures should have a commercial focus. Our point of view is supported by Dr. Roy Vagelos, Merck's longtime chairman and CEO, who was formerly head of Merck's R&D department:

> We have many scientists, but they have objectives to do something about some specific diseases or disorders that have been targeted. We challenge these people with the clear objective of making a drug for a specific need and not to just discover interesting facts and publish in journals. Since cost-justified procurement pressure and competitive substitutes have significantly shortened the effective life of every patent, we can't afford a lot of serendipity in R&D.

Match Future Products and Current Profits

In companies known for new-product success, management has mastered the ability to strike the right balance between investing in future products and generating current profits. This raises some obvious questions. How much should be invested? How much is too little? How much is too much? New-product leaders are now answering a number of questions to better measure, evaluate, and plan their new-product development efforts. The following questions help:

1. What percentage of companywide sales came from external acquisitions and internally developed new products over the last five years?
2. What is this percentage for each business unit?
3. What percentage of each business unit's and the corporation's profit come from products introduced in the last five years?
4. What is the effective patent life of the top 5 to 10 patented products?
5. What has the overall success rate been with new products?
6. What percentage of planned sales and profit growth can be expected from new products introduced in the next five years?

The penalties are severe if a mistake is made either way. A company can get by and may even prosper in the short term by spending too little because money not spent obviously increases short-term profits. It is not uncommon for managers, under pressure to meet certain profit goals, to take this tack in an effort to make their results look good. However, such an approach is shortsighted and foolish. If the market is attractive, enlightened competitors will introduce new and improved products that will quickly erode the company's market position and cut into its future earnings stream. On the other hand, many managers overspend for new products without sufficient regard for achieving satisfactory short-term profits. These managers are so enamored with the promise of tomorrow that they spend a disproportionate amount of money on new-product efforts that can ultimately undermine the financial health of the company.

Managers in rapidly changing high-tech industries face the added problem of deciding which technology to invest in as well as when to invest. By investing too early in a new technology, the firm faces the risk of premature entry before the market is ready. By investing too late in a new technology, a company may fall behind its competitors and lose market position that is tough to recapture once a new technology is established by a competitor. By failing to invest at all in a new technology, a company runs the very real risk of seeing its products become obsolete in a relatively short period of time.

The medical electronics field demonstrates how quickly companies must move in rapidly advancing technologies. When the CAT scanner was introduced, it was immediately recognized as the most significant breakthrough since the discovery of x rays. Technicare, the first U.S. CAT scanner company, saw sales grow from $20 million to more than $200 million in five years. The number of employees grew from 200 to more than 3,000 in the same period. The CAT scanning market then went through several technology life cycles, each of which made products obsolete in less than 18 months. The rapid obsolescence of technology, coupled with the swift growth of sales, fueled Technicare's need for cash, which nearly caused disaster for the startup company. Johnson & Johnson then acquired Technicare. Without J&J's acquisition and infusion of cash, most believe Technicare would have soon declared bankruptcy. Reflecting on the rapid developments in this industry, Richard Grimm, founder and former chairman of Technicare, made this comment to us:

> The way this technology moved was unbelievable. There were four major developments in three years that basically obsoleted all prior CAT scanning devices. We were smaller than some of the other competitors and if we were not quick on our feet in terms of product development, we could have been out of the picture overnight.

Deep pockets or the willingness of J&J to spend a lot of money on CAT scanning was not the answer. After five years and millions of dollars of additional investment in people and technology, J&J threw in the towel. They sold the remains of the business to General Electric. J&J's former CEO, Phil Hofmann, said to us:

> CAT scanning was a glamor business that attracted us. But the rest of J&J had little experience designing, making, selling, and servicing large capital electronic equipment. We basically sell consumables that have little or no after-sales service requirements. I doubt if GE, Siemens, or Toshiba, the CAT scanning competitors, would get in our pill, suture, or bandage businesses.

Cross-Functional Business Teams

Peter Drucker, the well-known management visionary, stated, "Successful innovations in all fields are now being turned out by cross-functional teams with people from marketing, manufacturing, and finance participating in research work from the very beginning." What he is saying is that leader companies recognize the fallacy of relying on any one individual or department to mastermind its new-product activities. They know how important it is to have inputs from all areas of the business as market opportunities are identified and product solutions are developed. Therefore, they put together cross-functional teams to accomplish the following:

- Identify and verify customer problems, cost-effective solutions, and market potentials by market segments, key accounts, countries, and regions of the world.

- Develop an integrated business plan (never just an R&D brief or a marketing plan) for taking the product to market and for achieving sales and profit objectives in the launching.

- Agree to firm technical, sales, and financial milestones in the business plan and use project management techniques to keep concurrent activities on time.

- Define product features, performance, customer benefits, costs, and designs globally by maintaining commonality as long as possible in the manufacturing process.

We must emphasize that we are not talking about a loosely formed committee that is not accountable for results. We are talking about a carefully selected cross-functional business team with the combined knowledge to define market needs and product solutions; the authority to set priorities, budgets, and deadlines; and, most importantly, that is accountable for business results. 3M recognizes successful cross-functional new-product teams with their Golden Step Award. The award is presented to teams of scientists, technicians, marketers, manufacturing engineers, and salespeople who have worked to develop, make, and sell a successful new product. Cross-functional teams should always include one or two key customer members for guidance and feedback. Leading new-product companies also include key suppliers on the cross-functional team before any design is frozen.

Speeding to the market with a new product requires a multidisciplinary team approach, called the "parallel method" in Japan. Masters of the team approach to speeding new ideas to the market include Canon and NEC in Japan and Compaq Computer in the United States. The cross-functional team stays with the project from start to finish in a manner that resembles a rugby match, where the ball is passed back and forth down the playing field, rather than the more traditional relay-race approach, in which responsibility is passed sequentially from department to department. Designers start to work before feasibility testing is over, and manufacturing and marketing are deeply involved long before the final design is set. One of the best examples of the parallel or cross-functional team approach is seen in action at the Compaq Computer Corporation.

Compaq is fast to the market because it is slow to lock itself into a final design. In Japanese terms, this is called working slow up-front so that you can work faster in implementation. A product definition team of managers from engineering, manufacturing, marketing, sales, and finance must reach a consensus on features, performance, and costs before development engineers get the green light. This team approach allowed Compaq to develop and introduce one successful computer in just nine months. Compaq starts its nine-month cycle with a one-page product description. As soon as top management approves the concept, Compaq organizes teams in engineering, manufacturing, and marketing. The teams work together under a project manager. When team members hit snags, they are required to return to their departments to resolve issues instead of thrashing them out in a cumbersome and slow-moving committee. The central virtue of the Compaq approach was stated by a Compaq vice president, who led a new-product team:

> Our process minimizes formal communications, overhead, and the normal types of empire building: nonstop meetings, turf battles, and people claiming ownership to some idea.

At Compaq, this cross-functional management approach is simply called "the process," and it involves informal team meetings where members discuss a problem or policy. Every department involved gives its view. Then the group attempts to separate facts from instinct, examines the trade-offs, and arrives at a decision. At a recent new-product meeting, managers from Compaq's international group argued against the date the domestic division had chosen for a new-product launch. Furthermore, the sales department staffers worried about the product's effect on dealers' inventories. As a result, the date was set back. It is rare that a single member or group will dominate at Compaq. "Most organizations have winners and losers," states Eckard Pfeiffer, CEO of Compaq, "but not here." He further states:

> Compaq tries to continually create and foster an environment of teamwork and open communications in product development and throughout the organization. Our managers have a certain type in mind when they recruit individuals to work in this team environment at Compaq. Applicants must be smart and motivated, but above all, they must be easy to get along with and have an "open attitude." It is not unusual for anyone newly hired to have been interviewed by 15 people who represent all departments of the company and a variety of senior levels. Who is not hired? Loners, or those who wear their ego on their sleeve and use the word "I" a lot. The number one issue is whether they fit into the cross-functional team approach here.

Go Outside for Help

Most technically based companies—particularly if their products are developed around different disciplines (electronic, mechanical, chemistry)—find it impossible to stay abreast of all the technological developments that can affect the business. Recognizing this, enlightened management continually monitors and searches for ways to capitalize on technological achievements outside the company as a means of sustaining or improving their market/product position. While this seems logical, many companies do not do this, usually because their management has the self-centered or arrogant attitude of believing that anything "not invented here" (often called the NIH factor) can't be very good. Such an attitude doesn't have much virtue in any situation, and in today's constantly changing world, it can easily lead a company into a position in which its products or technology is suddenly and unexpectedly obsolete.

There is no mystery to keeping up with outside developments. One way is to develop a relationship with the appropriate university engineering professors and people at government laboratories. University engineering departments and government labs throughout the world are involved in a variety of research programs. As a general rule, they welcome and actively seek arrangements with companies that will support their efforts; in turn, they provide the company with a window into their developments. More companies should follow the lead of many biomedical companies, which have built entire new businesses around their close relationships with leading scientists in medical and engineering schools and government labs working on a mutually beneficial area. However, before plunging into such outside relationships, it is necessary to avoid sticky patent situations by agreeing up front who owns the intellectual property.

Another way to stay abreast of new technology is to participate either as a sub- or prime contractor in government-funded projects that focus on or require advanced technological development. Many companies have successfully used this approach to capture technology for their own commercial use. Harris, Raytheon, and Motorola are good examples of companies that have concentrated on government-funded contracts that later provided technological advances for the commercial side of their businesses. Technical personnel in these companies are routinely transferred from government projects to commercial business units to ensure the effective transfer of technology.

Licensing is yet another way to gain new technology. Many inventors do not have financial resources or the interest to commercialize their developments and can realize an attractive return without risk by entering into a license agreement with a manufacturer with the necessary capabilities. University research laboratories offer opportunities in which researchers are more interested in advancing the state of the art than in commercial accomplishments. The key is to follow an organized and focused approach that covers all the sources in which new ideas are likely to develop and that ensures early identification of developments with promising commercial potential.

Suppliers are increasingly being looked to for technological advances. Key suppliers should be involved very early in the concept stage before a design is frozen or prototypes are made. A great deal of two-way trust, cooperation, and sharing of information with these suppliers must exist as it does with the long-term *keiretsu* relationships many Japanese firms forge with suppliers. For example, in the United States, Kimberly Clark aligned with National Starch and Chemical, who then supplied most of Kimberly Clark's adhesive for their new-product development programs around the world. Both parties signed secrecy agreements. National Starch was one of the few adhesive suppliers with sophisticated development labs in North America, Europe, and Japan that could adapt technology to Kimberly Clark's global and regional needs.

Finally, new-product technology can be gained through outright acquisition or the formation of an informal or formal alliance with another company. Sometimes acquiring a product platform or piece of new technology is the best approach. However, the company with the technology may not want to be acquired, it may be too big or too expensive, or the needed technology may be such a small part of the whole that an acquisition doesn't make sense. Whatever the reason, an alliance that provides the basis for coupling new technology to a commercial base is a very feasible alternative.

The most successful companies pursue some combination of these avenues to achieve technological superiority. They recognize that no one has a monopoly on technological ideas or developments, and they constantly search the world market for new technologies and key technical people to strengthen their ability to serve their target markets and key customers.

Rationalize, Shelve, and Cannibalize

Many companies have too many existing product lines. Before adding more new products to cluttered families of products, most companies should rationalize or prune their existing product lines. Some older product lines should be priced much higher, phased out, sold as specials, or completely eliminated. This will free up resources for new-product development.

Many companies have too many active R&D projects that move slowly if at all. These same companies wonder why they are slow to market new products and why they haven't had many true new-product successes. Most companies need fewer R&D programs and need to stop reprioritizing or reordering a long list of projects. Companies need a mix of incremental product improvements and one or two big programs, sometimes called "Manhattan" projects, with dedicated people. R&D projects should be shelved when some of the following clues emerge:

1. There is little or no enthusiasm among the cross-functional team.
2. The project repeatedly misses milestones, budgets, and planned activities.
3. The cross-functional team is oblivious to major shortcomings in the project.
4. There is no longer a product champion for the project.
5. Lead customers are no longer enthusiastic about the new product.
6. Design trade-offs significantly alter the product's original intent, definition, costs, price, and performance results.

A surprising number of top and general management people have difficulty shelving or saying no to a team that continually misses milestones in their business plans. Management simply must abort a project that has little chance of technical and commercial success. Furthermore, if a lagging project is a "pet" project of an influential executive, it should face the same project review scrutiny as every other project.

Progressive companies are increasingly cannibalizing their own products. When a manufacturer introduces a product improvement that is interchangeable and better or lower priced than their existing product, cannibalization occurs. The new product might help one business unit while it takes sales and profit from another business unit in the same company. When the new product will replace an existing product at a lesser profit, there is even more resistance to developing or launching the new product. Sometimes timing and different pricing to specific market segments and individual customers can control the rate of cannibalization. However, product cannibalization should be increasingly pursued if you are either defending or attacking a market segment.

The failure to productively practice cannibalization is seen by late followers in the automotive industry. Ford scrapped its innovative plan to develop the first minivan in the mid-1970s for fear of cannibalizing strong sales of its full-sized station wagons. GM's truck division (GMC), which had no car sales to lose, was held back from developing a minivan in 1978 by the Chevrolet division. Ford, GM, BMW, and all the Japanese manufacturers have played catch up to Chrysler for 10 years! Today minivan sales outnumber station wagons nine to one, and most are made by

Chrysler. Many auto manufacturers are ending production of their station wagons because customers are choosing minivans and 4x4s.

Denny Sullivan, executive vice president at Parker Hannifin, explains why the company makes multiple technologies available to the same customers:

> Some people wonder why we make products that overlap some applications. In some situations you can control motion with either hydraulic, pneumatic, or electromechanical technologies. We have full-fledged divisions for each of these technologies that compete for the customer's business. Our group salesforce offers the customer all three technologies. We then help the customer decide which of our technologies or solutions are best for their application.

In another approach, Lew Platt, CEO of Hewlett-Packard, explains why they intentionally obsolete, cannibalize, and kill their own products:

> We've developed a philosophy at HP of killing off our products and rendering them as obsolete with new technology. We have learned the hard way that it's better that we do it than have a competitor do it. To make sure we have killed the technology, some business units conduct formal funerals to signal to everyone the technology is obsolete or dead because it is usually hard to kill an old product or technology!

Protect Proprietary Information

Many companies make the mistake of developing first-class products that provide significant competitive advantages and then fail to protect their positions or react quickly enough to competitor moves. As a result, costly and hard-won market position gains are often lost, never to be regained. For example, VisiCalc developed the market for computerized spreadsheets. After developing the first spreadsheet product in Cambridge, Massachusetts, the founder did not take enough precautions to protect the intellectual property. Meanwhile, a young VisiCalc product manager, who had overseen the spreadsheet development, formed Lotus Development. The Lotus Development product was renamed Lotus 1-2-3, and it quickly swept into first place for spreadsheet programs after VisiCalc declared bankruptcy. VisiCalc was an idea whose time had come. The idea was sound, the technology was sound, but strong marketing and intellectual property protection were lacking.

Successful companies aggressively protect their proprietary positions, reacting quickly and with real force when competitors threaten. Companies such as 3M, National Starch, Nalco, and Abbott Laboratories are almost paranoid about information leaks that might get into the hands of competitors. They perceive every competitor as a hostile enemy seeking to injure or overthrow them. They routinely seek the strongest possible patents, get international trademark protection for brand names, limit the access (even to employees) to many restricted areas, and make noncompete agreements a condition of employment. They usually also develop and sign secrecy agreements with key suppliers and customers. Individually, none of these activities is particularly unique. Taken together, and coupled with a watch-dog attitude that is part of the culture, those companies are a formidable force.

These companies also take a number of other actions to reduce the possibility of competitors hurting their positions with some kind of a surprise blow. They continuously gather intelligence about their competitors all over the world. Since a new technology always starts in one country of the world and market application, employees scout trade shows around the world. In addition, they keep competitors off base by starting work on product enhancements and even next-generation products while the growth of existing products is still healthy or before the first product has been launched. They sometimes keep these improvements in reserve and wait for the most propitious time to introduce them. An executive from a highly successful medical equipment company told us:

> We always try to keep well ahead of our competitors with new products or enhancements. When they come at us with something that threatens our existing product, we then jump out of the grass and kill them with something they didn't know we already had on the shelf.

SUMMARY

Keeping pace with demonstratably better new products is a risky, difficult process under the best of circumstances, but it is vital to the long-term success of every enterprise, especially in a time of rapidly changing technology and intense global competition. There are some proven steps firms can take to better the chances for their products: They should identify customers' perceived and unarticulated needs. They should carefully think through their market/product focus to zero in on significant value added opportunities. They should face up to cost and performance deficiencies in their product line. They should prune marginal products from the existing line. They should ensure that all development efforts are linked to strategies to defend or attack a market segment. They should ensure that cross-functional teams play an important role in the entire development process. And, finally, companies should increasingly cannibalize their existing products before competition does it for them.

CHAPTER 7

The Consultative Salesforce

Salesforce performance has always been a very important contributor to the success of industrial and high-tech companies. Other elements of the marketing mix—that is, advertising, promotion, and merchandising—simply do not have the same impact for these companies as they do for consumer goods manufacturers. Unlike consumer products, there are very few situations in industry in which the buying decision is made impulsively by some especially creative advertising campaign. In many consumer or retail goods buying situations, a live salesperson is not involved in the process. Industrial selling is usually accomplished by a salesperson demonstrating the value of the manufacturer's product and services to many buying influences with factual information. Industrial buyers don't usually make emotional or purely impulsive decisions to buy. They make more rational buying decisions to improve performance or save or make money for their companies.

Industrial salespeople must go through many lengthy steps in the consultative selling process that ultimately lead to a purchase order. It often takes several calls to secure an initial order, and, given the high cost of the average sales call (estimates of $400 to $500 are not unusual), the minimum cost to close a new sale can be several thousand dollars. This lengthy, costly, and often very technical buyer-seller process is dramatically different from many arms-length and often impulsive retail or consumer goods transactions.

The task of selling industrial products ranges from the extreme of being an order taker and expediter to the other extreme of being a creative consulting engineer. As we see it, the order taker/expediter type of salesperson is an endangered species. Selling jobs that are at the order taker extreme can be accomplished with telemarketing, electronic ordering (EDI), and faxes and are better handled by inside sales and customer service people.

Since many industrial products have become more complex and since most customers' operations and procurement also have become more sophisticated, today's industrial salesperson must have more technical knowledge about his products and an aptitude to understand the customers' operations. Today's industrial salesperson must be a creative consultant to the client, suggesting a cost-effective solution or a value proposition that puts money in his customer's pocket. The salesperson should be perceived as a counselor who improves a customer's costs, performance, and productivity. The industrial selling process should be like a physician who questions, listens, and diagnoses a patient's symptoms and then prescribes a remedy. Our discussion in this chapter focuses on how we see today's and tomorrow's industrial salesperson—as a trusted and respected consultative problem solver to the customer, not simply as an order taker, expediter, or someone that just schmoozes with customers.

COMPLEX PRODUCTS AND CUSTOMERS

Industrial sourcing decisions are becoming more sophisticated. The quality movement, vendor ratings, supplier reductions, sharper customers, and various types of buyer-supplier alliances have permanently changed the role of industrial selling. Customers aren't interested in only the "feeds and speeds" of industrial products; they have less time to babysit salespeople, play a round of golf with them, or take long lunches. Customers are asking suppliers to help them in many areas. They are increasingly choosing only those suppliers who can help streamline their operations, reduce their costs, and put speed in their new-product development efforts.

All this requires a salesforce with a different aptitude, mind-set, and skills than the stereotype image of the high-pressure, fast-talking salesperson who can't be trusted and who is pushing hard for an order. Unfortunately, many product- or engineering-driven industrial salesforces are also only interested in pushing their products, regardless of what the customer really needs. Consultative selling takes a lot of time, it demands intimate application and product knowledge, and it requires making sophisticated presentations to many different audiences in the buying organization. The quantity or number of sales calls a person makes each day or week is far less important than the quality of the sales call.

Unfortunately, many industrial suppliers are still selling the old-fashioned way. A 23-year IBM veteran salesperson described the old ways that still persist at many industrial firms:

> I sold systems that people didn't want, didn't need, and couldn't afford. We were so articulate that we could persuade people to act against their own interests. Pushing metal or selling boxes and meeting product volume quotas set by our regional sales managers was our mission. We were a legendary army of well-paid generalists selling hundreds of different products to dozens of different types of customers while some of our more successful competitors had more specialized salesforces that helped solve customers' problems. As competitors like Hewlett-Packard helped customers develop solutions to capture, move, and share information, many IBM salespeople lost the confidence of many customers.

Some major customers were equally critical of IBM's sales approaches. The senior vice president of GTE, one of IBM's former top 10 customers, stated:

> When we needed to move from just buying mainframes to information management systems with many networks, IBM reps tried to talk us out of these approaches. IBM's well-scrubbed and white shirt salespeople made flashy presentations, used a lot of buzzwords, but had little substance. Hewlett-Packard's salespeople were different. First of all, they listened a lot, asked probing questions, and took a lot of notes. They learned about our information needs at all levels of the organization and forged strong ties with top, middle, and lower management and with the people that actually operated our computers. HP's telephone support people were often more helpful than IBM's direct salespeople, who were less effective than a fax machine. We now use HP for most of our information technology needs.

COMMON CONCERNS

In the many training sessions we conduct every year across the globe, we hear many of the same concerns about industrial salesforces. The common uneasiness about each salesforce is expressed in the following statements:

> Our salesforce is evaluated and rewarded on tonnage or sales volume, while the rest of the organization is measured and rewarded on profit results.

> Our salespeople spend too much time on paperwork and expediting and too little time in front of customers.

We have had productivity improvements in all areas of the organization except in our selling organization, where we spend a lot of money with questionable returns.

As we add more product lines to our salesforce, I'm afraid our salespeople know less and less about each product line . . . our best competitors are much more focused.

After some product training and a basic selling course, we don't do much to make our salespeople more professional and current.

We talk a lot about value-added or consultative selling, but many of our salespeople lack the aptitude and have no training, no tools, and no incentive to invest the time required to do solution selling.

We sell a lot of our products through distributors, but our salespeople don't know how a distributor makes or loses money, and we don't develop business plans with distributors to help them sell our products.

SUCCESS DEPENDS ON THE SALESFORCE

A focused, well-trained, trusted, and motivated salesforce is always a powerful competitive advantage for an industrial supplier. Looking ahead, several factors are certain to make the role of the salesforce even more important to marketing success:

1. Buying practices all over the world are becoming sharper and more sophisticated as companies have more supplier choices and recognize the tremendous profit potential of building more analysis into all buying decisions.
2. The technical complexity and sophistication of products, systems, and services continue to increase and require more in-depth industry, application, and technical knowledge.
3. Competition from substitute technologies and foreign suppliers is increasing and making the selling task both more complex and important.
4. First-hand market intelligence from customers and about competitors is increasingly important to develop distinctive product/service offerings and presentations that help a customer make or save money.

The first two considerations place a much greater premium on intelligent selling to help customers articulate their needs and then to demonstrate the tangible and intangible benefits from a product/service package in meeting those needs. The third consideration means that many companies will become far more dependent on value-added selling presentations to overcome unit cost or performance claims and demonstrate the benefits (not just features) of their products. Finally, the need for more and better intelligence about market requirements and competitive actions means sales personnel will have to be more resourceful and better trained on how to draw this information together and rapidly share it within their organizations and they develop team presentations.

Most senior executives are quick to agree with the importance of having an outstanding selling force. However, only a few are fully satisfied with the effectiveness and productivity of their selling organizations. Most see their selling arm falling short of the performance they want in many ways:

1. They (the salesforce) do not have a clear view of the important market segments in the various sales areas and do not understand the unique needs of each customer group or market segment.

2. They do not effectively identify and demonstrate the total value of their products and services to customers for existing and, especially, new products in a way that takes pressure off unit price as the key buying consideration.

3. They do not prospect for new customers to build a solid sales base; they mostly try to sell more products to their existing customer base.

4. They do not improve their productivity at a pace sufficient to keep abreast of constantly increasing selling costs.

5. They do not provide a useful flow of market intelligence about customers and competitors to aid planning strategies and new-product offerings.

6. They do not understand how distributors make money or how to evaluate and improve a distributor's sales of the company's product lines.

The salesforce in many industrial manufacturing companies functions more as a collection of independent sales agents and distributor principals than as an extension of the marketing arm. The problem can be traced back to the failure to follow one or more of nine essential sales principles of a truly market-driven company. The balance of this chapter discusses each of these nine principles in detail.

PRINCIPLE 1: FOCUS ON CUSTOMER PROBLEMS

We don't know of any customer in the industrial world who gets really excited about any supplier's product. In fact, no matter how well designed or low priced a supplier's product is, the prospective buyer would rather avoid the purchase entirely. The product usually has no personal appeal to anyone in the user's organization. Its main purpose is to reduce costs, improve production, or increase sales revenues. Thus, the buying decision is more analytical, rational, and economic, with personal considerations playing a less significant role. The following example illustrates this point:

> A few years ago, a sales team [including one of the authors who was then president of Reliance Electric] from the Toledo Scale Division of Reliance Electric met with a manufacturing team from Frito-Lay™, the world's largest supplier of chips and other snack foods. The meeting was set up to discuss a manufacturing cost problem that was very significant to Frito-Lay. The problem centered around the need to ensure that chip buyers were never "shortchanged" on the stated net weight of the package. To eliminate this possibility, the bag-filling operation was set up to overfill by as much as 10 percent. When considered against the tremendous volume, the overfill costs represented millions of dollars each year. The question was how to minimize the overfill cost and still ensure that no customer would ever be shortchanged.
>
> Shortly after the problem was described, a Toledo Scale sales representative said, "What Frito-Lay needs is our check weighing system that automatically kicks out any package that doesn't fall within a prescribed weight band." The product idea may have had merit. But the comment rubbed the Frito-Lay procurement team the wrong way. The team leader responded, "We don't want to buy your product. We want a solution to our problem and you don't know enough about it to recommend anything yet."

The Toledo Scale sales team had lost credibility, which was then very difficult for them to regain, because they were not sufficiently sensitive to the customer's problem.

PRINCIPLE 2: DETERMINE COST-EFFECTIVE SOLUTIONS

After hearing from many customers that their salesforce was "just raining new product features on them,"[1] Hewlett-Packard™ set out to upgrade their salesforce over a three-year period. First, it structured the salesforce so that it paralleled the company's marketing strategy by aligning the

---

1. "Mild-Mannered Hewlett-Packard Is Making like Superman," *Business Week*, March 7, 1988, p. 111.

salesforce by industry rather than organizing it by geography. In the previous geographical sales organization, a salesperson called on anyone in a defined territory. Industry or market concentration allowed for more in-depth customer contact, and with more knowledgeable salespeople, in Hewlett-Packard jargon, they became "trusted advisors." HP salespeople calling on just the financial services sector are required to take an average of at least two weeks of classroom training every year to understand everything from the basics of banking to what happens in each phase on the trading floor. Dick Justice, Hewlett-Packard's head of American marketing and sales, explained to us:

> Customers want to solve business problems, not just buy analytical instruments or computers. Our reps can now go in to a customer and say, "I understand your business, and my job is to apply technology to improve your competitiveness or reduce your cost." We realize that customers' careers are at risk today if they buy the wrong technology. Customers are looking for suppliers to work with them and help in their total operation. We had to become industry experts. In the old days we sold just the sizzle to customers with fancy presentations. Today we must sell documented cost and performance improvements to many horizontal and vertical buying influences.

The approach taken by AMP, the world's largest electronic connector company, is another example of what a professional industrial salesperson should do. In order to focus on customer problems and the fastest-growing customers, AMP has added more electrical engineers to its sales staff. AMP's vice president for U.S. marketing and sales stated:

> We want to have more cerebral discussions with customers who are in the planning and product development mode. All of our reps have laptops so they can tap into their business unit and do connector design and circuit simulation right at the customer's facility. For a few of our truly key customers, AMP has a resident sales engineer permanently at their site to interface directly with the customer's engineering, manufacturing, and purchasing people.

Industrial and high-tech manufacturers should provide their salesforce with the necessary tools to analyze a customer's needs and make recommendations much like a doctor does with a prescription or remedy for a patient. The Timken Company, the world's largest manufacturer of precision tapered roller bearings is an excellent example of the kind of consultative selling tools that make salespeople true professionals. The Timken Company developed a software program that enables their salespeople to help customers, including Caterpillar, Boeing and Mercedes, select the proper antifriction bearing with Timken's Select-A-Nalysis™

program. With customer information about as many as 20 conditions or constraints, including the RPM, radial load, heat generation, fatigue life, OD, bore size, torque, and lubricant type, the Timken sales engineer can sit beside the customer's design engineer and select the proper bearing for his problem. The right bearing is quickly determined and the customer immediately receives a bearing drawing. As the customer considers different "what-if" conditions, the Timken sales counselor can immediately generate the appropriate bearing selection and the Select-A-Nalysis shows the Timken part number.

PRINCIPLE 3: UNDERSTAND CUSTOMER AND COMPETITIVE INFORMATION

Achieving an understanding of a user's operations, requirements, future needs, and competitive information is the most important activity that industrial sales representatives perform. Salespeople are the primary source of competitive intelligence and a helpful source for segmenting markets, identifying customer problems, and designing new product/service packages. To achieve the degree of understanding necessary, the salesperson must become intimately involved with and really learn about the customer's business. This means learning where costs are incurred, what bottlenecks are worrisome, and where operating problems occur. Achieving this level of understanding inevitably requires more time than some salespeople care to spend asking questions and listening to the people responsible for running the business. Despite the salesperson's natural aversion to this activity, it is an absolute must for any market-driven company because it is the only way to identify customer problems and come up with the best solutions to lower costs, enhance productivity, or provide some other important advantage to customers.

The right salesforce must be recruited, trained, and given incentives to provide organized feedback on such questions as these:

- How does the product fit into the OEM's and end user's operations, fill an economic need, and compare with competitive offerings?
- What benefits from the product's performance (e.g., initial cost, life-cycle cost, failure rate, support service, total system cost) are really key in the immediate customer's and end user's minds?
- What current or potential developments in the end-user's business could change cost or design requirements, and how can these needs be met?
- What changes in the end user's operation or the competitive environment could affect the customer's business, and how could

these changes, in turn, affect the requirements or demand for the product?

Management must do more than simply tell the salesforce to provide such information; it must take three important steps to ensure this information is properly developed:

1. Sales assignments must be made in a way that gives each salesperson a fair chance of achieving an understanding of what is going on at the immediate customer and end-user levels. In effect, the professional sales assignment should be structured to encourage the salesperson to become, to some degree, a market specialist with in-depth knowledge of specific end uses. However, it is unlikely that any salesperson can develop the kind of detailed product and application knowledge required if he or she is expected to sell a broad line of products to all customers in all markets. A salesperson in such a situation will naturally gravitate to the less complex environment and devote a lot of time to negotiating price instead of identifying and communicating value. As a result of insufficent product and application knowledge, any salesperson will become more of an order taker and expediter.

2. A formal system for distilling and interpreting the account information received from the salesforce must be installed. This sounds like a very basic point—and it is. However, time after time we have heard a salesperson say, "I send the market information into headquarters or the regional office, but nobody ever listens to me or believes what I say." Before long the sales representative will not bother. Call reports that are cut and dried, or list only company visited and product sold, are of little value. Unfortunately, many of the end-of-the-week calls or activity reports are instruments of torture for sales reps and tell his manager and others in the organization next to nothing. The Warner Electric division of the Dana Corporation requires every salesperson to list on each monthly sales report the three best ideas that he or she learned from customers. The division top management reads every idea.

3. The company's value system must reflect the high priority management places on a clear understanding of user needs. If not recruited carefully, some salespeople may not have the technical background or aptitude to understand a supplier's products or the technical complexity of the customer's operations. This priority must be reflected in recruiting the right people and in an ongoing commitment to training. Unless every industrial salesperson receives at least one to two weeks of training annually, they are probably not current. This priority must be reflected in an ongoing commitment to product, application, market segment, distributor management, and personal skills training, including using laptops, listening, and making effective technical and business presentations. This priority on training and keeping current may be manifested in a recognition and compensation structure that pays a premium for developing business in certain end-user groups or for certain applications. Then, again, it may simply be reflected in the way management compliments those who do a good job, or, more importantly, chastises those who do not. Training and continuous improvement of the salesforce must be nonstop and must occur in both good and slow economic times.

PRINCIPLE 4: SALESFORCE OPTIONS

When organizing an industrial salesforce to implement marketing strategies, the firm should choose from three basic structures: purely geographical, product range, or market segment, or a combination of the three. We now describe each structure and the advantages and limitations of each.

Geography

In the most basic sales organization, each rep is assigned an exclusive territory in which he or she then represents the supplier. The sales rep is responsible for all current and potential business in the defined geographic structure regardless of the type of customer (market segments) and the size of each account. If a company manufactures one product for one market segment, this approach works well. This approach minimizes travel expenses because the geographic region covered is limited. A major function of sales management then is to design territories with similar sales potential, travel time, and workload. However, when a salesforce carries a larger number of products or more complex products for many market segments, this approach can rapidly deteriorate to order taking. It can result in having geographic coverage but little or no penetration in specific market segments because the salesperson does not have the in-depth knowledge of the customer's operations and requirements necessary to fully service the customer. In order to bring more focus to customer problem-solving for a wider range of products, separate salesforces can be structured around fewer products or around common market segments.

Product Range

Product specialization is typically necessary when the products are more technically complex and/or are very numerous in number. For example, Parker Hannifin created separate salesforces for its seal, connector, and pneumatic product lines even though they sometimes call on the same customer. As a company broadens its product lines and since different technologies are often involved, such as with Parker's seal and pneumatic businesses, more specialized product and application knowledge is needed. A company will often aquire new product lines or entire companies and then just add the product lines to those handled by its original salesforce, and then claim it has achieved efficiencies from the "pooled" salesforce. Unfortunately, as a company adds new product lines to a salesperson's responsibility, the salesperson often becomes less knowledgeable about the individual products. Furthermore, if the salesperson now contacts different people at the same geographic customer location, the risk associated with trying to intelligently represent too many products or technologies is even greater—even though, on the surface, it often looks very efficient to have one salesforce call on the "same customer" at one geographic location.

As Johnson & Johnson expanded its products, it created different salesforces to call on the same hospital location because the buying influences and technologies for surgical instruments are different from those for prescription drugs, which differ from those for surgical gowns or glucose monitoring equipment, although all are at the same hospital location. Johnson & Johnson knows that sales effectiveness must be considered ahead of the efficiencies that might come from a pooled salesforce. Similarly, Betz Laboratories has two different salesforces selling water treatment chemicals at the same papermill location because the buying contacts, chemistry, and specifications are different at the "wet" and "dry" ends of the same papermill.

Market Segment

Industrial companies are increasingly specializing their salesforces by industry or market segment. Pall Corporation, the world's largest and most successful maker of filtration products, has separate salesforces for their aerospace, industrial hydraulic, chemical, electronics, and biomedical markets. Sometimes the same Pall product is sold to different market segments by different salesforces and at different prices because the benefits and values of many of their products vary across market segments. The market-specific salesforces of Pall have been key to running trials and demonstrating lower total life-cycle cost (not unit price), and they have helped Pall rapidly introduce new products by showing customers how they will save or make money with the new product.

A market-focused salesperson should be an expert in the industry or segment on which they concentrate. Market-focused salespeople are especially well suited to run field trials, perform consultative selling, and launch new products. Quest, a unit of Unilever Chemicals that makes brewing ingredients, has a global salesforce that only calls on breweries around the world, even though that means crossing over the geographic territories of other Unilever Chemical salespeople. Unilever's product development and acquisition's candidates for brewery ingredient products are guided by suggestions from the brewery salesforce. Furthermore, nearly all of Unilever's brewery salespeople are ex-brewmasters.

The major disadvantage of the market-specific selling approach is that when customers in a market segment are widely dispersed throughout a country, more extensive travel time and costs may be incurred than if they were organized only by geography. Sales organization by market or industry segment emphasizes sales effectiveness over sales efficiency, and, if successful, the added travel costs are a good trade-off.

Special Situations

In multidivisional companies there are often some product, customer, or market situations that require special attention. A few senior sales reps might be assigned to national or global accounts that need close coordination between multiple customer facilities and the supplier's many manufacturing locations. In another situation, a market or industry specialist might be located in Detroit to work with just automotive customers and another one located in Charlotte to work exclusively with textile accounts, while the rest of the salesforce is organized on a geographic or product basis.

In another specific approach, 3M creates some market focus within their geographically organized coated abrasives salesforce. How? The 3M sales rep located in High Point, North Carolina, sells to all accounts in his geographic territory, but he also serves as a market specialist in the woodworking industry throughout the United States. Similarly, the 3M salesperson located in Pittsburgh is responsible for a geographic territory but is also employed as a national resource for steel manufacturing customers.

In still another situation, specification work and approvals might have to be performed at a central buying location or technical center before the product can be bought and used in another region. In this case, a missionary specialist might be assigned to running trials and obtaining approval at a customer's facilities but would have no responsibility for sales. The primary job of a missionary salesperson is to provide customers with product and application information and get products approved and specified. These salespeople don't usually take orders from customers, and they are typically low-key and low-pressure "salespeople." For new products that require a lot of technical education with immediate customers or with customers' customers to "pull" the demand for a product, a specialist might conduct seminars throughout the country, or a region of the world, to begin the buying process, which is then handed over to a local salesperson. In such cases, one or a few product or market specialists would be added to do the education and missionary work. Finally, where a division or business unit believes its products are not suited for the existing geographic, product, or market-focused approaches, it will strike out on its own with a dedicated salesforce for its limited set of products and defined customers.

PRINCIPLE 5: ORGANIZE ONGOING TRAINING

As we mentioned earlier, today's sales job is far more complex than simply making calls to sell the product or taking an order. In addition to achieving sales goals, management rightfully expects their salespeople to build a strong commercial or proprietary position with key customers by really understanding the business, by providing market feedback on customer needs and new application opportunities, and by selling a desired product mix.

Rarely, however, does management give the salesperson sufficient training to accomplish these objectives. Usually, the sales representative is provided with product knowledge, given a sales quota along with a pep talk, and told to get out there and sell. This is not very helpful to the typical salesperson, who is constantly faced with a choice of how to allocate his or her time among various products, customers, users, or other contacts that could influence the sale. Nor does it help him or her to think through the specific actions that should be taken when the priorities have been decided.

Many sales executives take comfort in the thought that their sales training programs are designed to tell their salespeople all they need to know to do their jobs. But most sales training programs focus almost entirely on product features and fundamental selling approaches, such as how to tell the product story, combat customer objections, refute competitor claims, peak customer interest, and close the sale. This kind of sales training is, of course, useful. Every salesperson must have knowledge of the basics before he or she can make an effective sales call. But such knowledge alone is no longer sufficient in most cases to help the salesforce do an outstanding job. To accomplish this, the salesforce must have guidelines that help resolve such issues as the following:

- Which market segments offer the greatest sales and growth potential, and which specific accounts should be targeted based on documented value in that segment?
- What points should be emphasized (e.g., cost savings, product reliability, product performance features, ease of operation) with each market segment to provide genuine value and take the emphasis off price as the dominant buying consideration?
- How should selling time be divided among servicing existing accounts, prospecting for new ones, making introductory calls, arranging and making capability presentations, and so on?
- How much emphasis should be placed on new-product introductions, which applications represent the best targets for the new product, and how can an agreement for an initial trial be secured and the trial managed?

Training the salesforce is not an easy task. Battles are won because the troops are properly trained. Today's sales troops need new and better sales tools and ongoing training oriented to specific markets, applications, and customer problems; need side-by-side competitive comparisons; and must be less focused on just their own product lines and closing a sale.

Industry and Application Knowledge

Once market segments are selected to defend and attack, in-depth knowledge about each segment and application must be gathered and disseminated in training sessions for the salespeople. Sometimes a salesforce can develop this knowledge from past experience and specialization. Often they cannot. Hiring people away from leading customers in each target market is one sound way to build the industry knowledge base among your salespeople; these people would then train the other salespeople. Those hired from the target customer market segments should have at least three to five years of experience in the operations or technical area that you compete in; they do not usually come from the customer's marketing or sales areas. People recruited from customer operations have an in-depth knowledge of the manufacturing process, bottlenecks, customer economics, and competitors' products and services. Of course, a company should never hire a person from a current customer unless that customer is first notified and is in agreement with the switch.

The following examples show how hiring people from your customer's operations (or your customer's customer) can bring the customer's heart and soul to the center of your business:

- Crosfields, a U.K.-based supplier of catalysts to segments including the petroleum industry, hired process and maintenance engineers from petroleum companies to train their salespeople and develop user-friendly literature in the operator's language.
- Johnson & Johnson's business units, including Ethicon (sutures), Endo-Surgery (small incision products), and Codman & Shurtleff (surgical tools), have had a long-time practice of hiring former operating room nurses for sales positions.
- Quest, a Holland-based unit of Unilever Chemicals, has built a strong global position selling enzymes and processing aids to the brewing industry because nearly all of their brewery salespeople are ex-brewmasters with 5 to 10 years of brewing experience.
- Betz Laboratories, the well-run, U.S.-based water treatment company, makes and markets chemicals to water, papermills and steel mills and hires salespeople with a technical background and three to five years of operations experience from the key markets they serve. Five of Betz's top 10 managers, including their CEO, Bill Cook, came to Betz from customers early in their careers.

One of the better market-driven transformations we saw first-hand happened over a three- to four-year period at the Cabot Corporation, a $2+ billion chemical manufacturer of carbon black, fumed silica, and tantalum products. Cabot was an old-line, product-driven company. Ken Gilson, an officer in the company, led the transformation from being product driven to market driven. After targeting a number of key market segments, Cabot carefully hired a number of sales and technical people from progressive customers in the segments as follows:

Target Market Segments	Employees Hired from
Automobile and truck tires	Major global and regional tire manufacturers
Coatings and adhesives	Dexter, Nippon Paint, Henkel, Valspar, Lord
Semiconductors	IBM, AT&T, Rockwell

Companies such as those just described find it much easier to take experienced people from a customer's operations and train them in their own products than it is to do the reverse. Equally important, salespeople from the respective market segments will be able to develop an in-depth rapport with the users because they intimately understand their business and operating conditions, speak the same language, and have credibility.

Sales Competency Quizzes

Attending a sales training workshop is one thing. Remembering what one learned may be another. After every training school at Sealed Air Corporation, they administer a two- to four-page multiple-choice quiz that covers the important points in the training program. Also, every Sealed Air new-product training session concludes with a short quiz that covers the new products' features, tangible and intangible customer bene- fits, and side-by-side competitive comparisons. If a score of at least 80 percent is not achieved on each Sealed Air competency exam, the partici- pant has to study and retake the quiz. Sealed Air also conducts a distribu- tor management workshop for sales reps that concludes with a five-page competency examination.

The notion of competency quizzes after any sales training has been commonplace for years in the pharmaceutical industry, where "detail" salespeople are extensively trained about the benefits, negative side effects, and competitive product offerings of the new drugs they present to physicians, who then test and prescribe those new products—much like an engineer who writes a new-product specification. Since a physi- cian is usually a technically astute buying influence, a well-trained drug salesperson is mandatory. When we suggest to industrial clients that they administer competency quizzes at the end of any sales training program as Sealed Air and others do, many sales managers strongly resent the notion.

PRINCIPLE 6: GOING ELECTRONIC

When today's consultative industrial salesperson opens his or her brief- case, the last thing he or she might bring out is product samples or order forms. The first item he or she often removes is a laptop computer, which contains background information on the account. Laptop computers, soft- ware programs, company databases, information networks, electronic data interchanges, voice and e-mail, faxes, 800 numbers, modems, pagers, and portable telephones have dramatically redefined the industrial sales- person's effectiveness and efficiency. All these electronic technologies are enabling factors that have permanently changed nearly every aspect of the salesperson's job. First and foremost, these electronic tools have allowed the sales rep to respond to customer needs faster and better. On- line networks help the salesperson instantly know how much of which items are located where. Previously, many telephone calls and call-backs were needed to provide the customer with the most basic shipping and scheduling information. When planning any sales call, salespeople had to dig through file folders and telephone many departments to gather current pieces of information that they then manually updated. Sales reps can now just "key up" and log new information into their computers.

Laptops are also especially helpful in working with a customer to solve a design problem. Sales reps and customers increasingly sit down together in front of a computer screen, and with menu-driven software options, they can view what the configuration will look like, what customer benefits will result, and what the customer's total cost will be. For example, GE plastics sales engineers use laptops with the customer's engineers to apply failure analysis and to apply design to manufacturing and assembly models to determine the optimum design and understand the system's total cost. As a result of this type of technical help, GE can frequently sell a higher-priced plastic thermoset because the sales rep can demonstrate how it lowers a customer's total system cost more than a lower-priced option. Furthermore, if the customer is not thoroughly convinced that the solution is the best for his needs, they can be shown, using GE's database, an application story or testimonial from someone in that market segment who benefited from buying the same product. While in front of the customer, the GE rep can also access information about competitive products, prices, configuration notes, and the status of deliveries.

Even the traditional product training schools are being affected by computers. The time and cost to fly people off to week-long product training schools is being reduced or replaced with CD-ROM training programs. For example, as copiers became more technical and buyers more sophisticated, Canon Copier's traditional week-long training programs were getting expensive and time consuming for the independent dealer salespeople. Canon developed interactive CD-ROM training programs that last for 16 hours and reduced or eliminated some of the training schools. The CD-ROMs walk salespeople through the steps of selling copiers, and they give people the opportunity to interact with other people acting as customers. If a salesperson is having problems handling a certain objection, he or she can type in questions and get a series of possible answers. Common troubleshooting procedures and solutions can also be handled via electronic and videotape modules.

Sales representatives who are equipped with the available electronic technology have seen their customer effectiveness and productivity increase. Two short case study situations, one at Compaq Computer and the other at Pioneer Hi-Bred, a farm seed developer, show how electronic technologies can significantly improve an industrial salesforce's efforts to be more effective and efficient.

Example—Compaq Computer

Compaq Computer is a $9.1 billion manufacturer of computers. A few of its products are sold by mass merchandisers, including Wal-Mart, but 90 percent of its sales are to business firms and dealers, where most of their salesforce productivity gains have been achieved. Compaq claims that their revenue per sales rep is far above Hewlett-Packard and light years ahead of IBM and Digital. Compaq's CEO, Eckard Pfeifer, describes its situation:

> Our reps were spending too much time commuting bumper to bumper getting to and from a sales office. Two years ago we moved every one of our salespeople into home offices. In the process we also cut our salesforce by a third, from 359 to 224 people in North America, and saved $10 million annually in salary and rent.
>
> We decided to automate instead of populating the street with more inefficient salespeople. If we had replicated IBM's high-cost infrastructure of large sales branch offices in big cities, we would have been in trouble. We first asked our customers. Many said they could not find our salespeople, or it took too long to reach a live one. Some of our reps were getting more than 40 voice-mail messages every day. The typical big-company response would be to hire more salespeople. We concluded that all of our existing salespeople were utilizing their time badly.
>
> We shut down four of eight regional offices. Every salesperson's home office was equipped with a portable notebook computer, a 486 processor, a 200-megabyte hard disk, a color monitor, a wide keyboard, a backup drive, and a laser printer. Each home office also got a fax/copier, cellular phone, two phone lines, a desk, a bookshelf, and a credenza for a total cost of $8,000; a noncomputer manufacturer would pay about $10,000. To eliminate information bottlenecks, we set up toll-free numbers to answer routine inquiries about products, pricing, and availability, freeing salespeople to focus on developing new business and servicing accounts. We paired inside customer service people with outside sales reps and call it "hunting in pairs"!
>
> Every workday our reps log into our client/server network with a billion bytes on-line. The database includes a centralized account listing where Compaq people from different departments record their contact with each present and prospective customer. All customers have market segment codes. The system also contains marketing material, technical reports, application stories, and electronic mail. Sales managers, engineering, customer service, and other staffers can scan the network for updates.
>
> Reps typically download the material they will need for their current day's meetings into a notebook computer or what they call their toolbox. They also have appointments, contacts, telephone numbers, charts, and graphic presentations on their notebook computer. They don't have to carry around overhead projectors and transparencies. If they want to leave a

brochure or schematic with a client, they just produce one on the laptop computer. If they get into a pinch on the road, they can just plug into our database from any phone jack and a modem.

When the reps return home, they type and print letters, respond to e-mail, and update the common database with the latest information about current and potential customers. If they need an engineer to follow up with more information, they input the contact's name, and when the engineer looks at his accounts in the database, he'll call the contact.

Automating our salesforce and moving them into home offices reduced Compaq's sales, general, and administrative expenses (SG&A) from 22 percent of revenues to 12 percent over two years. As a result of this lower overhead and, more importantly, higher sales productivity, even though Compaq's gross margin fell six points in one year, net income still climbed as a percentage of revenues. In fact, we hope to get SG&A down to 10 percent, making it possible for Compaq to live well amid further price cuts.

Example—Pioneer Hi-Bred

One of the most automated and best consultative salesforces in the world is found at Pioneer Hi-Bred, a $1.3 billion developer and grower of farm seed corn. Most industrial salesforces' uses of laptop computers, software, networks, and information technology pale next to Pioneer. Pioneer has used its salesforce finesse and information technology to become the most profitable and largest corn seed company in the world, with a 45 percent market share in the Americas. Tom Urban, Hi-Bred's chairman and CEO, explains how their electronic salesforce works:

> To begin with, Pioneer tracks over 800,000 current customers and prospects in its database for the United States, Canada, and South America—a group responsible for 45 percent of the world's corn production. Our in-house database, which is consistently updated by the salesforce, records who runs which farms, how many acres they grow of which crop, what type of seed corn they are currently buying, and who they are buying it from. Another Pioneer software program helps our reps track the yields (customer benefits) from 17,000 plots on which 150 different corn hybrids are grown, providing detailed comparisons of Pioneer seed yields versus the yields of our competitor's seeds. When Pioneer's reps (who are usually all former farmers) meet with customers, they are armed with laptops and printouts of customized reports generated from PCs at their homes. If a farmer doesn't currently plant a Pioneer line, the sales rep's goal is to get the farmer to plant a trial strip of Pioneer seed. The reps use other reports to show how farms with similar conditions have improved their yields with Pioneer.
>
> Every rep can call up our databases to identify any of 50+ hybrids designed for unique soil or climate conditions, resistance to particular

diseases or pests, fast maturation, and high protein or starch content for livestock feed or corn syrup end-use markets. The software packages also help farmers plot expected soil moisture and corn market prices. In addition to improving our customer effectiveness, information technology has also dramatically improved the efficiency of our sales reps. Fifteen years ago, each rep typically had 70 to 80 customers. Today they have as many as 300, and they also update all the customer information and process all the orders electronically. We have also significantly reduced the number of first-level sales managers we now have in every country. Largely due to our computer-assisted approach to sales, our market share has significantly jumped every year since 1990.

PRINCIPLE 7: LINK SALES COMPENSATION TO COMPANY GOALS

Many sales compensation arrangements work at cross purposes to management's overall businesses objectives. For example, many companies still pay their sales representatives totally or largely on the basis of their sales volume, even though achieving a richer price or product mix, opening new accounts, or developing certain end-use markets and account profitability may be an equally or more important objective in terms of ultimate success in the marketplace. But what person in his or her right mind would spend time on longer-term sales development activities when the payoff is simply for volume taken today? Also, who would spend much time negotiating value for a higher price when revenue is the pay lever? In fact, who wouldn't constantly complain to headquarters that prices are too high when lower prices could provide a basis for meeting a quota based only on revenue or volume?

Setting Goals

Setting goals for a salesforce has traditionally meant just setting sales revenue quotas. The quotas are usually expressed in sales volume and are too often dictated from the top down by a regional or national sales manager. Sales goals should be mutually developed by the salesperson and his or her supervisor. Any sales goal that is based purely on sales volume is wrong. One-dimensional sales goals based solely on volume can undermine the profit and other goals of any business. If salespeople are rewarded solely on the basis of volume, they will focus on the largest customers and then negotiate the lowest possible unit price. Of course sales volume must be in every salesperson's goals but there must also be goals in other areas, such as territory and account profitability, new business, customer trials, new-product sales, customer satisfaction ratings, and distributor management, where appropriate.

The role of sales management is to develop the appropriate multiple goals and weights for each salesperson. The switch to some of a person's pay being tied to profits is intended to stop salespeople from cutting deals that hurt the supplier. Intense discussions usually occur when deciding how much of the pay should be tied to profits and where it should be capped. When IBM first moved its 30,000 salespeople from a pure-volume goal to pay-for-profit, only 6 percent of the compensation package was tied to account and territory profitability. Very little change occurred. One of Hewlett-Packard's salesforce, which competes against IBM, pays its people a variable commission of up to 40 percent. Our belief is that at least 20 percent of the variable pay should be tied to profit to encourage sales reps to behave more like businesspeople and less like bounty elephant hunters chasing volume.

Tying incentive payments to gross margin dollars generated is another way to pay salespeople. It links both volume and a profit measure into the account, and it's easy to explain and measure.

Sharing Cost-Profit Information

Part and parcel of any sales compensation package tied to profits is the need to widely share product and customer profit information with the front-line salespeople. Salespeople need to know how much profit they are making, or giving up, at every account and on each transaction. Without product-line and customer profit information, salespeople have little reason to care about how unprofitable an account may be. When a salesperson knows the margin on various products and the past and potential profit prospects at every account, they can rationalize services, emphasize the higher margin products, and better manage account profitability. We often hear managers say, "You can't trust salespeople with profit information," or "They will tell or go to the competition with the information." Salespeople, like all other employees, must be trusted, empowered with information to make decisions, and evaluated as a businessperson. It makes good sense to drive profitability measures down into the salesforce, giving reps the same accountability as upper management. Salespeople simply must have access to financial information about the business and their customers to do this. We also strongly suggest that each salesperson's territory be managed as a profit center—account by account and in total for his or her territory.

Sales Salaries

In some cases, sales salaries are so high relative to the incentive opportunity that incentive really doesn't mean much. Many companies have drifted into this situation by steadily granting salary increases instead of holding salaries constant at some level and increasing incentive opportunities. The company is then locked into higher structured sales costs that are tough to swallow when volume turns down and, more importantly, that make the salesperson too comfortable even if sales goals are not achieved. In other situations, the incentive is so small that it doesn't motivate the high performer. Many company bonus plans for salespeople are seen as inequitable and unfair.

Commissions

The idea of earning a commission on sales appeals to many aggressive people and has a lot of merit in many situations. However, some commission arrangements that start paying off on the first dollar of sales encourage sales representatives to "skim the cream" or "cherry pick" from the territory by concentrating on quick volume from accounts—when the emphasis should be placed on developing the potential in the more profitable accounts. Several salespeople from one company that sold chemicals freely admitted that they set a daily volume quota for themselves that would yield enough commission to meet their standard of living. They were very comfortable with a lower, but adequate, income, and they frequently bypassed high-potential accounts that required more development in preference to sure-thing orders.

Seniority-Based Compensation

Other compensation systems are designed in such a way that they reward seniority rather than performance. This arrangement has a double-edged effect: Senior people relax their efforts, and young, aggressive people become frustrated and go to competitors. A company that sold in the semiconductor equipment market provides a classic example:

> Incentive payments were made out of a group bonus pot, and each person's award was based on a percentage of his or her salary. Since no adjustment was made to reflect individual performance and since senior people tended to have higher salaries, many hard-working younger people became discouraged and left. Equally important, when management looked into the situation, it found that many of the senior salespeople were relying on the younger people to build up the pot and thus were not pulling their own weight.

Team Incentives

Since many industrial buying situations require that upper management, technical people, customer service, and office staffs all work together to serve customers, incentives and recognition systems for just the outside salespeople can demotivate other members of the customer team. As companies form sales teams or cross-functional groups to serve key accounts, the sales rep becomes more of an account leader and less of an account manager. In such team-selling situations, all team members should participate in the rewards. When everyone has a share of the rewards, strong peer-group pressure comes into play. Less supervision is needed with self-managed work teams with group incentives. Self-managed sales teams take on tasks such as scheduling people and equipment that are traditionally done by supervisors. Team-based sales incentives motivate people to help each other and share ideas and information.

Every compensation plan has weaknesses, and some team compensation plans allow the lower-performing individuals to receive the same rewards as the heavy contributors. But, over time, peer-group pressures help many people improve their performance, and the team composition may eventually have to be changed. The sales team members may even have a hand in hiring and disciplining team members. Where everyone in the business unit or division has an incentive based on the profit return of their unit, individual and team-based performance is aligned. When team-based incentives do exist, it is necessary to share all sales, profit, customer satisfaction, and productivity information with all the employees in the business unit. Team-based incentives make everyone serving the customer work like a business owner and less like a hired hand.

Tailor the Objectives

In many cases, sales executives are so concerned with keeping their compensation plan simple that they fail to take into account key variables that affect sales performance. It is not at all uncommon to hear executives say something like, "We know our sales compensation plan is not right, but it is simple and we don't have any difficulty getting our salespeople to understand and believe it." In other cases, executives feel that once a system is in place, it should not be changed because the salesforce will become confused or suspicious. Of course, making changes in midstream that are unfair to the salespeople should be avoided at all costs. But the fact is that marketing objectives do change frequently, and unless the compensation system is adjusted to reflect these changes, it is certain to drift out of phase with the company's business and marketing goals.

The paramount objective is to tailor the compensation system to meet the particular requirements of the sales situation in your industry. Thus, there is no way to prescribe a compensation plan that is right for everyone. However, every compensation system should be designed around five areas:

1. Achieve monthly, quarterly, and annual sales and profit objectives from direct sales, and, where relevant, for distributor sales.

2. Ensure a balanced selling job by paying for new account openings, new applications, new-product introductions, and other sales development activities essential to strengthen the company's short- and long-term market position.

3. Provide an attractive entry level for new salespeople, who will then provide adequate raw material to build the kind of organization necessary to achieve marketing objectives.

4. Provide an especially attractive earnings opportunity for career sales representatives so that there is a cadre of highly skilled, trained, and motivated people to serve as the cutting edge of the marketing effort.

5. Draw a sharp distinction between the rewards for average and outstanding salespeople and the penalties for below-average performers.

PRINCIPLE 8: PROVIDE A SALES CAREER LADDER

A highly respected, professional, and high-performing consultative salesperson is absolutely essential for any industrial business that wants to sustain sales and profit growth. And those people who love the daily challenge and freedom of industrial sales and do it very well should not have to change careers in their company or go to a competitor for advancement and higher remuneration. Unfortunately, most industrial companies have no career path, and pay steps are based on expertise and performance within their sales organizations. Sales for many industrial companies are too often a dead-end street or a cul-de-sac. This problem is usually greater in Europe than in the United States because many European industrial companies have not recognized the need for a really professional and high-performance salesforce. A few progressive companies have developed a career ladder for professional salespeople (see Exhibit 7–1). Any advancement up the sales ladder should be based on performance and not just longevity or seniority.

E X H I B I T   7–1

Sales Career Ladder

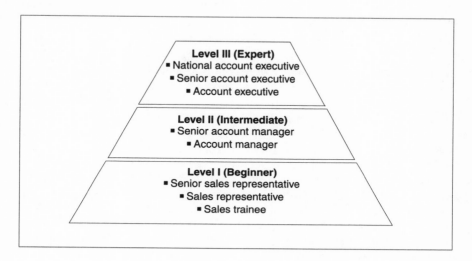

As companies equip sales representatives with more electronically automated information and empower them in decision making, it is less necessary for them to frequently report to a sales manager for permission or authorization. Furthermore, with the use of laptop computers, electronic mail and networks, faxes, and portable phones, the reps have less need to be in a traditional sales office, and the span of management control can also increase for sales managers. When the salesperson is able to obtain customer and application data from a corporate or business unit computer, develop training sessions through computers, videotapes, and other communication options, and use e-mail or voice mail direct from headquarters, the sales manager's position as primarily a communication conduit, data analyst, and information source about prices and profit has significantly diminished. The more sales reps a sales manager has reporting to him (often from their car or home office), the less face-to-face contact time he has to spend with each.

However, most sales executives agree that strong first-line sales supervision is still a key ingredient in their efforts to build an outstanding selling organization. The salesforce is typically made up of a cross section of men and women with widely diverse backgrounds, experience levels, and perceptions; and many are separated from headquarters by thousands of miles. The first-line supervisor is the only manager physically close enough to them to define and interpret company policy, direct their week-to-week efforts, and coach them in the company's sales approach for various products, markets, and customers.

Conflicting Demands

In some cases, the performance of first-line supervisors falls short because their job is structured such that they are supervisors in name only. They are really only super salespeople or bureaucratic administrators, with the bulk of their effort focused on direct selling activities and/or paperwork.

We know of one company that relied on its branch sales managers to handle the first-level supervisory role. Each manager was expected not only to watch over three or four salespeople but also to take on a full sales territory of his or her own as well. The results were not at all what management expected. The branch managers spent the greater part of their time selling and developing their own territories, and thus they provided little, if any, real supervision for their salesforces. Actually, this should not have been surprising—any time salespeople must choose between doing the sales job that is second nature to them and carrying out the difficult tasks inherent in any managerial role, they tend to take the path that is easiest and most enjoyable. Our experience shows that most people who have a combined sales/supervisory role quite naturally and honestly get so deeply involved in their own direct selling activities that they have little time for the coaching, training, and follow-up activities that are the heart of the supervisor's job.

We are not suggesting that it is totally inappropriate for a sales manager to have any direct sales or account responsibility. In fact, a good case can be made that every sales manager should have some account sales responsibility to keep current with selling problems and requirements. But this responsibility must be limited so that it does not take up a disproportionate amount of the manager's time.

Inadequate Preparation

In other cases, first-line sales managers fail to perform well because they do not know what the supervisory role is or how it should be carried out. This is frequently not their fault; surprisingly few companies provide any kind of training programs to help new supervisors learn how to perform their new responsibilities. Most sales managers need training in the sales management process that represents the heart of their job. In particular, they need to be shown the following:

1. How to make territory, market, account, or distributor analyses and determine sales potential.
2. How to administer sales compensation and incentive programs.
3. How to evaluate the performance of their sales personnel, or distributors, identify training and development needs, and determine who can and cannot improve.
4. How to make new hires and dismiss poor performers.

In some cases, former star salespeople can never make the transition to manager, no matter how much training is provided. Often those who fall in this category are allowed to stay in their supervisory positions far too long. Eventually, the management career path becomes clogged with people who are going nowhere. Understandably, this frustrates the outstanding younger salespeople looking for early promotions and inevitably leads to a high turnover of people who should not be lost. A vicious circle ensues, resulting in mediocrity at the supervisory level and ineffective training and direction for the salesforce. The sales career ladder, suggested earlier, would alleviate some of the problem.

Excessive Paperwork

In many companies, the call report mailed weekly to headquarters is sacred because it gives management a feeling that they are on top of what is going on in the field. More than likely, however, all management has is a massive paper flow that is useless to headquarters personnel. Many companies look to their call reporting system as a reliable means of control. In reality, however, some salespeople simply go through the motions of filling out their forms while spending their time as they please. Clearly, some type of planning and control system is desirable in every sales organization, but it should be designed around a weekly or monthly cycle to minimize the paperwork. And it should primarily help the salesperson plan his or her time and set priorities. It should not be designed as an elaborate system for centralized control or Big Brother intimidation.

A good call report captures the right account information. Good call reports meet three criteria: (a) They are easily generated and updated on a laptop computer that is networked to many databases. (b) Call reports should clearly identify all the contacts at the account and identify the market segment and applications, competitive purchases, and your company's historical sales at the account. (c) Finally, the critical issues or problems at the account, the status of trials, and the next step should all be clearly communicated. A sound call report is a vital part of consultative selling that summarizes the important transactions at the account. The benefits of a good call report extend beyond themselves. If a sales rep is transferred, injured, resigns, or dies, such complete and automated information can give a new rep a three-month edge at the account by not having to spend time reconstructing the vital information.

PRINCIPLE 9: BUSINESS PLANNING ROLE

The top sales management of any industrial company—that is, the national sales manager and his or her subordinates, who typically have responsibility for sales results in the largest geographic region—should play an important role in the entire business planning process. They should be an integral part of any cross-functional team set up for any important strategic assignment. In developing target market plans, front-line sales reps experienced with accounts in the market segment should participate in the business planning process. Their participation is essential to ensure that the company's product and market plans reflect the customers' changing needs.

It is also essential to gain the wholehearted commitment of sales management to successful execution of the company's overall target market plans. If the salesforce is enthusiastic about the plan and genuinely believes it can sell the volume and mix that is expected, it will do a good job. If the salespeople feel that sales expectations are unrealistic, or that unfair sales goals have been imposed on them, morale will suffer, and the plan will not be achieved. It is not unusual for sales representatives and field supervisors to charge, "Our sales goals have no rhyme nor reason and have nothing to do with the marketplace. They are just 10 percent to 15 percent higher than last year." With this attitude, how can they be expected to do all the hard work necessary to achieve demanding sales targets?

Considering the importance of sales performance to the success of target market plans, it is only logical to give sales management a real voice in the development of these plans. At the least, they should be included in the following activites:

- Closing the feedback loop from the field by distilling and interpreting information on user requirements, local market conditions, competitive standing, and expected sales at key accounts.
- Discussing sales needs and opportunities with other functional managers and recommending alternative actions to build or defend the business overall and at key accounts.

- Participating in cross-functional discussions to evaluate the commitments and programs required to carry out various options and to weigh these against expected results.
- Agreeing on realistic volume and share of market targets under various options and helping to decide which options are most attractive.
- Suggesting product-line gaps and evaluating the merit of specific product development and acquisition candidates.

The experience of Owens-Corning Fiberglas, a large company serving the building products field, proves that significant results and improvements can accrue from tying the sales managers more directly into the business planning process. The top executives of this company were very concerned about a general deterioration in the company's marketing effectiveness. Share position in traditional markets was slipping badly, and important new markets were emerging in which the company had no position at all. The company's product edge had been lost, and new-product developments were not coming along as they should. Finally, sales costs were increasing steadily while productivity (i.e., average sales per salesperson) was trending downward. In short, the current marketing situation was bad and the outlook worse.

In recognition of the gravity of the situation, the general manager called in the product managers and key sales managers for an emergency planning session. Including sales management in the planning session was more of an afterthought than anything else since planning had traditionally been an isolated headquarters function while sales had responsibility for execution. To the general manager's surprise, the most imaginative and effective ideas came from the sales managers closest to the target markets. They recommended product modifications that could be made quickly, well before new products could become available to meet important needs of emerging markets. In addition, they suggested dropping a collection of low-profit products so that manufacturing could be simplified, the salesforce cut back, territories enlarged, inside salespeople added, and overall productivity increased. These sales managers also proposed a volume discount plan that would provide the basis for recapturing business that had been lost with large customers while still preserving the integrity of the company's pricing structure. The general manager and the product managers were so impressed with the contributions made by the sales managers that they made it a regular practice to include them in planning sessions from that point on.

SUMMARY

Clearly, a host of things must be done to build an outstanding industrial salesforce. Much has been written about the importance of motivating salespeople, territory layout, key account planning, and other important considerations for personal selling. We have taken a different approach by emphasizing management principles that enable the salesforce to function as consultative problem solvers and businesspeople and be at the cutting edge of a market-driven management team. We have found that these management principles equally apply to independent distributors or dealers that market a manufacturer's products.

When management follows these principles, all the other activities necessary to make the salesforce an effective implementation arm will be carried out as well. Neglecting any one of these principles will jeopardize the success of the business, no matter how well other sales activities are performed.

In nearly every company, implementation requires overcoming long-standing traditions and mind-sets. Extensive training of sales managers and salespeople alike is mandatory, and possibly even personnel changes must be made. However, all of these efforts are clearly worthwhile, for failure to manage the salesforce according to these management principles can cost a company a fortune in lost market opportunities and excessive selling costs.

Many successful industrial companies have taken a hard look at their selling effort and have made the changes necessary to build these principles into their sales organization. In so doing, they have converted their volume and order-taking salesforce into a legitimate consultative selling organization. This, in turn, has given these companies power in the marketplace to significantly strengthen their competitive position and sustain profit growth.

CHAPTER 8

Putting It All Together

Corporate life would be a lot easier if management could simply forget or wish away the whole idea of formal business planning, but no one yet has been able to figure out how to get business plans into written form without a great deal of hard work. If anything, planning is likely to become a more important management tool in the future because it is the best way to deal with the increasing risks and uncertainties that are so directly tied to a turbulent environment.

WHY BUSINESS PLANNING IS IMPORTANT

Business planning, both strategic and operational, has been an accepted part of the business management process for many years. The discipline of planning helps avoid the mistakes that are bound to occur when managers simply try to ad-lib their way through a complex business situation. Planning has taken on added importance in recent years as the world has been caught up in a maelstrom of change that has greatly increased the risks and chances of failure for any business venture.

Many argue that it is impossible to plan in an environment characterized by such volatile change and uncertainty. Actually, these conditions have made planning a more critical function because it is essential to try to anticipate changes and think through possible responses before the changes actually occur. This is what *contingency planning* is all about: It is the only way to avoid getting caught off base with no idea of how to react. It is essential for management to devote much more time to considering (*a*) what positive and negative trends are likely to impact the business (there is always some good in a negative trend), (*b*) what can be done to minimize the risks or capitalize on the opportunities that are likely to occur as a result of these changing conditions, and (*c*) what alternatives are available if things turn out differently than expected. Developing answers to these questions is essential for survival in a period of accelerating change and increasing uncertainty.

Despite the obvious need for, and inherent logic of, formal business planning, very few companies are truly satisfied with the results achieved compared with the time and effort involved. The comment of a general manager for an electronics company exemplifies the frustration and disappointment of many executives:

> We knock ourselves out every year with a major time commitment and massive paper flow to put together a strategic plan for the business that is heavily based on marketing input. But we can't really point to any substantive benefits that are directly traceable to all the extra effort. As I see it, our marketing [department has] not done the job it should in thinking through a strategy. If it had, we'd have a lot stronger edge in the marketplace. At this point, I am not sure whether it is something important that we ought to do better or whether it is just an exercise that conventional wisdom says we should do.

Why should his reaction be the rule rather than the exception? What are the pitfalls that cause planning results to fall short of expectations? Most important, what lessons can be learned from the experiences of those companies that can honestly point to concrete results from their planning efforts?

PITFALLS

Ignorance of planning theory or mechanics is not the cause of the disappointments so many companies are experiencing. Most managers are well aware that effective planning depends on market and economic facts, that it results in detailed operating programs, not just budgets, and that it provides the best basis for measurement and control. Most managers are also very familiar with the various approaches to formal planning that have been emphasized in business literature and the academic world over the past several years.

Yet major problems continue to crop up when many companies try to put some kind of formal planning approach into practice. These problems fall into four categories:

1. Failure to tailor the process to the company's specific needs.

2. Confusion over types of planning and who does what.
3. Overemphasis of the system at the expense of content.
4. Lack of alternative strategies.

Let's examine each of these categories a bit more closely before moving on to see what steps have been taken by companies that have successfully integrated an effective approach to business planning into their management process.

Failure to Tailor the Process

To a large extent, the disappointing results encountered by many industrial and high-tech companies reflect their failure to recognize two distinguishing characteristics that dictate the need for a planning approach tailored to their specific needs. The first is the large number of product, market, and channel options that are available to most industrial and high-tech companies. A typical multiproduct industrial or high-tech manufacturer sells multiple products into a wide range of different markets, often through different channels. For example, it would not be uncommon for a manufacturer of electronic components to sell a broad array of different products in as many as 30 distinct markets (e.g., automotive, aircraft, marine, military), facing different technologies and competitors in many of these markets. It doesn't make much sense to try to cover this complex network of products, markets, and channels with a broad-brush business plan for the company as a whole. Instead, there should be a number of discrete plans, one for each market/product business that should be treated as a separate entity.

Juggling a large number of market/product businesses is not the only problem facing managers in high-tech and industrial companies. Since the success of individual market/product plans is dependent on activities in all key functional areas and on the share of total company resources each market/product business receives, it is unrealistic to expect product managers, market managers, or even general managers to develop plans for selected market/product segments by themselves. It requires a cross-functional team effort with the full participation of operating managers throughout the entire planning process. Thus, the role of the business unit manager in an industrial or high-tech company is to analyze and interpret market/product requirements for the business and then, with key functional managers, determine whether and how these requirements can be met. A product, market, or business unit manager may play the lead role in drawing plans together for the assigned market/product, but the market/product plan must be a total business plan, never just a marketing plan. General management must also be involved throughout the process to set priorities and settle disputes that are bound to occur whenever several discrete market/product businesses depend on common resources.

Obvious as these points may seem, they are frequently overlooked. Many general managers try to turn the entire job over to a marketing person or the division controller. Traditional marketing people just prepare sales forecasts and controllers just develop budgets—neither develop focused business plans. After several years of frustration with the resultant plans, they are ready to write off the whole planning effort as a monumental waste of time. The real source of their disappointment lies not in the planning concept, however, but in the way it has been applied. Here is a good example of how this can occur.

A major chemical company ran into trouble when it added a group of six market managers to its marketing organization, gave them a planning format to follow, and told them to develop a written plan for achieving a stronger and more profitable position in their assigned markets. Half of the six market managers had MBAs from some of the "best" schools but lacked an in-depth knowledge of their markets and respect within their own organization. All six managers, eager to earn their spurs, embarked on a massive fact-gathering and writing effort. Some MBAs were referred to as "Masters of Business Analysis." After several months, hundreds of pages of plans and supporting documentation had been written, but no one in top management was much impressed. The general manager of the materials manufacturer put it this way:

> I'm being generous when I say the end products are only slightly better than useless. Admittedly, we have some better market facts now, but the plans are based on a lot of ideas for product and market development that just aren't in line with our idea of the direction this business should take. On top of that, they've left out a lot of technical and capital considerations that really count. I've concluded that our market managers are simply too far out of the mainstream of the business to do an intelligent job of planning for us.

Not surprisingly, the market managers felt that they too had good cause for complaint. As one of them put it:

> The first month of effort was worthwhile. We were putting a fact base together that is essential for intelligent planning. But after that we were flying blind. We never had any idea from top management on the kind of business the company wanted or didn't want, the minimal profit return it expected, or the kind of support it would be willing to make in various markets. Worse still, we had no cooperation from the development group, the plants, or even the salesforce, where decisions are made that really influence the business. The planning we did was bound to be a bust.

Unfortunately, this has been the experience of a great many otherwise well-managed companies. Far too many planning activities get plenty of lip service but little real attention or involvement from general management and the line decision makers who have to make the plan work.

Confusion over Types of Planning

Confusion about the distinctions among strategic planning, long-range planning, operational planning, corporate strategy, and market/product strategy also leads to major difficulties in accomplishing the planning job. These are all distinctly different types of planning, and the terms cannot be used interchangeably without creating confusion. To start with, it is useful to point out the differences and relationships between strategic planning and operational planning.

Corporate Planning versus Market/Product Planning

The distinguishing feature of strategic plans is that they typically involve this commitment of resources (both human and capital) to a particular course of action. And, once these resources are committed, it is difficult to change direction without some kind of penalty. This is not to say a commitment to a strategic course of action is irrevocable, but a penalty is most certainly incurred if directions are changed once a company begins implementing a strategic decision. For instance, it is impossible to reverse a decision on a new production plant once ground has been broken or to retract funding commitments for new-product or market development once the project is under way without suffering considerable time and cost penalties.

The time frame involved is another distinguishing characteristic of strategic planning. Generally, strategic planning covers a period of several years. Three to five years is a reasonable period for strategic planning in most manufacturing companies since most strategic decisions or actions (e.g., building a new manufacturing facility, developing new products or a position in new markets) can be implemented within this period. Heavy manufacturing or resource companies that are dependent on long-term R&D programs or natural resource development may need to plan over an even longer period.

Operational planning, on the other hand, is typically done annually and should be designed to implement strategic business decisions. Operating plans also provide management with an annual budget for controlling performance year to year, quarter to quarter, or even month by month. Many of the cost and time commitments reflected in the operating plan are the result of strategic decisions to develop and introduce new products, build new plant facilities, strengthen positions in new markets, or make acquisitions. The operating plan is a vehicle to help implement the strategic plan; therefore, it is obvious that these two types of plans must be directly linked together. In effect, the first year of a strategic plan that covers a three- to five-year span should serve as the foundation for next year's operating plan.

Market/Product Strategies

Besides the distinction between strategic and operational planning, there is a distinction between two categories of strategic planning that should be carried out in any multibusiness company.

The first category of strategic planning is market/product strategy. We noted earlier that a separate plan is needed for each identified market/product business. A well-defined market/product strategy should show where the business is heading and what kind of growth and profits can be expected. Product, market, or business unit managers have the major responsibility for developing market/product strategies by answering the following 10 questions:

1. Is the basic cost and profit structure of the business competitive? If not, what does it take to get marginal operations on a competitive footing?
2. Is the business focused on the right market segments to defend and attack positions? If not, how should the focus be shifted by de-emphasizing or withdrawing from some segments?
3. What external factors or trends are likely to affect sales growth and profit potential favorably or unfavorably in each target market segment?
4. Is the company's technology even with, ahead of, or behind the fastest competitors in the targeted segments?
5. Should investments be made in engineering, sales, or manufacturing to enlarge the business?
6. Should investments be made to integrate forward to strengthen market positions or backward to improve the profit structure and/or ensure a stable source of supply?
7. Is plant capacity available to handle increased volume expectations? If not, when and where will new capacity be needed and how much?
8. How much new capital is required for which projects, and what is the expected payoff?

9. What is the sales, profit, and cash-flow outlook for the business, and what is the probability of achieving these results in different countries and regions of the world?

10. Finally, does the market/product plan meet or exceed the corporate profit goals? If not, which market/product situations would be more attractive?

Corporate Strategy

Once market/product strategies are developed for each business unit, general management has the basis for deciding what strategic moves, if any, are required at the overall division level. This leads to the second type of strategic planning typically done by top or corporate management, which is designed to answer two fundamental questions:

1. Does the aggregate outlook for all the company's business units meet overall growth and profit goals?

2. If not, how big is the gap, and what are the alternative ways to close it?

Exhibit 8–1 illustrates how a gap can be calculated by aggregating the planned performance of all business units and comparing the result with overall corporate goals. As you can see, the company's operating divisions have projected earnings well below the corporate objectives of 15 percent compounded growth each year, and an earnings gap of $1.20

EXHIBIT 8–1

Calculating the Aggregate Outlook

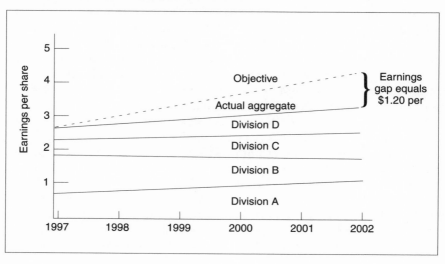

per share is expected. If we assume that there are 5 million shares outstanding, the company needs to pick up $6 million of after-tax earnings over the next five years to close the gap. In this kind of a situation, corporate management has basically three alternatives:

1. Change the corporate earnings target.
2. Restructure division plans to close the gap.
3. Redeploy capital into new technologies, market segments, or businesses with sufficient earnings power to close the gap.

Clearly, some combination of these alternatives is often the most prudent approach to follow when a strategic planning gap occurs. Whatever the decision, it is likely to change the direction or structure of certain business units and perhaps of the entire company.

Strategic planning gaps can cause companies to expand certain businesses, make acquisitions, form alliances, or take other strategic actions that reshape the character and earnings stream of the company. When you read about a company that has sold one of its business units or moved into a new business area, you are seeing real-life actions resulting from corporate strategic planning. The company's corporate management has decided that the present structure of its businesses is not satisfactory to achieve its goals and has carried out a strategic decision to change that structure.

How Sales Forecasts Tie In

The pivotal factor in any operating plan is the sales forecast. Manufacturing levels as well as expense budgets are related to the sales forecast when the operating plan is put together. The sales forecast is also the most variable or least controllable set of numbers in any business plan. Manufacturing costs are far more predictable; generally there is an experience base from which manufacturing costs at various volume levels can be predicted with a fair degree of accuracy. Also, expense levels for most SG&A activities are known from prior experience and are therefore more predictable. Sales results, on the other hand, depend on a host of uncontrollable factors such as the economy, competitor actions, industry or user developments, sales force effectiveness, and so on.

There are a variety of techniques for making sales forecasts, ranging from simple trend-line extrapolations to sophisticated statistical and computer-based projections developed around relevant market and economic indicators. The more accurate sales forecasts are a bottom-up process that starts with key accounts and market segments in each country you plan to defend and attack market positions. Regardless of how the sales forecast is made, however, it is still a guess about future events with all the risks and uncertainties of any prognostication. In most manufacturing companies, multiple forecasts are prepared by different individuals or groups within the organization, and it is general management's job to sort out these forecasts and ensure they are properly used to plan, manage, and control the business. Let's examine the different types of sales forecasts that are likely to be made in any industrial concern.

To begin with, most sales representatives are asked to make a "grass root" sales forecast for their accounts and territories. The aggregate of individual or bottom-up sales forecasts typically reflects the optimistic view of an enthusiastic salesforce and is generally an unrealistic set of numbers for making strategic, operating, or financial commitments. Recognizing this, sales management usually scales back the sales representative's forecast and recommends a lower set of numbers for planning purposes. If market, product, or business unit managers are involved in the organization, they will make sales forecasts for their assigned areas based on their best estimates of market conditions and the competitive situation. The aggregate of the account/market/product forecasts is a good cross check against the forecast made by sales management, but it also may be on the high side since it is unlikely that all the markets or competitors will act exactly as all managers expect.

Many companies have additional sales forecasts made by independent market or economic research groups to get still another picture of sales expectations. Finally, it is not unusual for manufacturing management to second guess any or all of these forecasts and make a forecast of its own to schedule its manufacturing operations. A manufacturing manager for a medical equipment company put it this way; "The sales guys always have a 'pie in the sky' forecast that they never make, and I am not going to build inventory or product to a forecast like that."

It is general management's job to make certain that everyone in the organization has a clear understanding of what forecast is going to be used for what purpose. Probably the best approach is to use one of the more optimistic forecasts as a basis for setting sales quotas, establishing incentive programs, and evaluating individual sales performance. Then sales goals fall in line with what the salespeople feel they can achieve and, hopefully, will stretch the salesforce toward better performance. A second, more conservative forecast, however, should be used to make operating and financial plans and commitments. It is always much easier to adjust these plans and commitments upward if higher sales are achieved than it is to scale them back if actual sales results fall below forecast. Following this approach will help management avoid the embarrassment of explaining that profits suffered because sales were lower than forecast and because operating and expense ratios got out of line.

Overemphasis on the System

Many companies have developed comprehensive planning systems that define formats and procedures in great detail. Although some structure is unquestionably necessary, in too many cases the system is so detailed and so highly structured that it acts as a hindrance rather than a help to the planning process. The bulk of the time and effort goes into completing the analyses, schedules, and forms defined by the system rather than into the thinking and discussion that leads to innovative plans.

Of all the roadblocks, this is the most frustrating for managers charged with the responsibility to do a good job of planning. They recognize that good planning is hard work and cannot be done without a certain amount of pencil pushing. But they bitterly resent demands for excessive writing or forms completion that serves no practical business purpose. A product manager for an electronic equipment manufacturer voiced his frustration over a planning system prescribed by a corporate planning group:

> As part of my planning responsibility, I have to follow a format prescribed by the corporate planning group that calls for a point-by-point discussion of history and a laundry list of problems and opportunities and a whole series of analyses and schedules that are irrelevant for my business. I'm "gigged" if I don't cover every point and complete every form, and there's no way to do it in less than 30 pages of schedules and text. That takes a lot of time to prepare—mostly wasted time. All the product managers are sore about it. Much of what we end up writing is a rehash of the same old things year after year. In effect, we're being discouraged from concentrating on the aspects of the business that are really critical. What they want to see, apparently, is a nice, neat set of plans that all look alike. It just doesn't make sense.

Unfortunately, situations like this are not unusual. Some overzealous staff person or corporate group designs a series of forms that are completely out of balance with the realities of the business. The resulting paperwork eats up great blocks of precious time without producing anything more than a lot of accounting schedules and a written description of what would have been done anyway. Planning is more than simply completing forms. In fact, most forms are a hindrance to planning that should be kept as simple as possible.

Lack of Alternatives

Given the dynamics of most business situations and the turbulence surrounding us, it is surprising that so many managers have tunnel vision when thinking about alternative ways to respond to change and improve the business. We believe this causes many industrial and high-tech companies to be chronically out of position and plagued with poor results. They continue to plan for and run the business by making small incremental improvements to what they have been doing in the past. Their thinking is blocked by their past experience, and they don't realize that what they have been doing is wrong in light of their changed environment. They need to break out of their traditional "boxed-in" way of thinking.

The tendency to base current plans on past practices alone was exposed in a textile machinery company when each business unit manager was asked by top management to outline alternative strategies for developing his or her assigned business and to summarize the commitments (e.g., financial, personnel, facilities) required and the payoff expected (sales, profit, return on investment). The request drew a complete blank. Despite all the new technology in textile manufacturing, massive textile plant closings, and declining domestic markets for textile machinery, these managers were so locked into their accustomed ways of thinking about their business that they could not conceive of a different approach that made any commercial sense at all. How can a company improve or even survive in such a different environment when its managers fail to recognize how the business has changed and what must be done differently?

This problem stems from a deficiency that has plagued business seemingly forever. Far too many managers have let their businesses "die on the vine" or have completely missed major opportunities because they thought only about making and selling their existing products and technologies instead of serving target markets with whatever it takes. Admittedly, it is difficult to think about moving away from traditional products, technologies, and business beliefs to preserve or secure a stronger position in selected markets. However, the tendency to limit one's thinking to existing products and technologies without regard for the realities of the market segment is a critical weakness. The CEO of a major chemical company stressed the importance of this point when responding to a question about the loss of vitality in American industry:

> To my mind, one central reason is this—our strategies have become too rigid. In trying to make our companies more manageable, we've constructed formula after formula which tell us how to run our businesses, and too often we get so tied up in the formula, we forget the changing real world that can break any business. We're too much like a football team that sticks to its game plan in the fourth quarter—even though it's losing 21-0.

Insufficient or less-than-candid analysis is a prime cause of unimaginative planning. Many managers either misjudge or fail to understand the underlying economics of the business and the changes occurring in the marketplace (e.g., competitive moves, shifts in usage or technologies) that call for new strategies. Others appear reluctant to face up to unpleasant truths about their competitive position (such as high cost and price, inferior product performance, or poor service) that place the company in an unattractive market position. Without a thorough and objective appraisal of the marketplace and of how the product or service really stacks up against competitive offerings, the need for fresh ways of running the business goes unrecognized. Instead of being able to choose among alternatives, top management all too frequently has to settle for a single recommendation that usually calls for the continuation of a stale strategy that offers little chance for improvement.

PROVEN PRACTICES

The most successful companies concentrate on developing market-driven plans that are part and parcel of the management process of each market/ product business. Planning is largely a bottom-up process and not a stifling bureaucratic one. These companies are not hung up on forms or formal planning procedures. Instead, they place major emphasis on outside-in planning from the market in, utilizing information about market segments, key customers, and cost-profit facts. We now look at each of these vital factors closely to see how they can lead to better ways of doing things.

Planning Based on Hard Facts

Companies that excel never let emotions or wishful thinking influence their plans and decisions. Their managements are well aware of several truisms that greatly influence the outlook for most industrial and high-tech companies, and they ensure that market/product strategies are consistent with them.

Strategic thinking must always start with the defined market segments. This is particularly true now when market growth is no longer given. In the 1970s and 1980s, it was not unrealistic to think in terms of 4 percent to 5 percent real growth for most businesses since gross domestic product was growing close to that rate in real terms in the United States and Europe. Now global, regional, and country differences in segment growth rates must be recognized in any planning and resource allocation process. Global competition has increased, and an increasing number of industrial market segments are likely to be flat or shrinking in some regions and countries of the world and rapidly growing in others. This does not mean that growth is impossible or should be forgotten as an objective. But it does mean that market/product strategies must be realistically geared to several facts of life:

1. *Rapid growth for an industrial or high-tech product is always limited.* New products and many new competitors will generally find their way into attractive growth markets. No market in any country is forever a high-growth one. The high market growth in certain Asian countries will eventually slow. However, any boom market can mislead management in its strategic thinking and planning. The importance of market share is often overlooked when sales are growing rapidly with the market. The need for fully competitive costs and products is often obscured because a growth market will absorb marginal producers and products. But the euphoria of a growth market will never continue forever, and marginal producers and products will fail as the market moves into a mature stage with limited growth characteristics.

2. *Rapid growth usually does not return to a mature industry.* Although it is possible for a mature or declining market to experience short growth spurts, strategy should be guided by the market's long-term prospects. There are exceptions to this generalization in developing countries, and when rapid growth does return to a mature industry, it is usually due to some structural change in the underlying technology or economy. For example, from 1950 on, the industrial scale market was essentially saturated, showing very limited unit growth. In the mid 1980s, however, the technology shifted from mechanical to electronic. The significant advantages of electronic scales, which offered a computing capability, motivated many customers to replace mechanical scales that were still perfectly usable. The combination of a large number of replacement sales plus higher unit volume triggered a growth rate in the market that was significant for the next 10 years, and then maturity again occurred. Similarly, the market for automatic boring machines has been flat to declining for the past 10 years. However, these automatic machines are the most efficient means known to produce small-arms munitions. If a major war should break out, the market demand for these machines would grow dramatically.

3. *Competition is typically more intense in low-growth markets.* A company in a high-growth environment can increase its sales without taking market share from its competitors. When a market is flat or declining, however, growth occurs only at the expense of others. Capturing market share in such an environment is not easy because competitors retaliate viciously to preserve their market position, utilize their capacity, and absorb their costs. A business unit facing a stagnant market is generally a

much greater managerial challenge than one in a high-growth market. A great deal of company weakness and management incompetence are masked in a rapid-growth market. In fact, we would argue that it is impossible to tell how good managers really are until they have proved themselves in a flat or declining market.

4. *Innovation continues even in mature industries.* Technology improvements, both in product and process, and continuously lower costs provide customers with greater value. For instance, the technology for producing steel and automobiles has improved dramatically during the past decade, despite greatly increased global competition and unfavorable market trends. Stagnant demand, therefore, does not mean stagnant technology; it does not mean management can forget or downplay the need for continuous product and process innovation. Companies that underinvest in innovation may never catch up. Furthermore, the development of new technology is now occurring all over the globe.

5. *Product performance, service, and price are the basics of any industrial or high-tech business purchase.* A competitive disadvantage in any one of these areas simply cannot be offset by hard work, a company's past image, or having bright people. In situations where competitive disadvantages exist, the market/product strategy must focus on ways to correct or overcome these deficiencies or you will face a "no-win" result.

Given these facts of life, a successful market/product strategy must be developed around a demonstrable competitive advantage, such as offering products with distinctive performance or cost benefits, improving the customer's manufacturing process, offering superior postsale service, or achieving a cost advantage by some other means.

Whatever the approach, the objective is always to establish a clear and favorable advantage over competitors. Without such an advantage, it is unlikely that any market/product strategy will allow the business to compete effectively and generate satisfactory profit growth over the long term.

Companies that compete most successfully in the industrial world develop their strategies around three approaches, all designed to achieve and sustain a competitive advantage:

1. *They concentrate on growth market segments within the industries they serve.* Even the most stagnant markets generally offer a segment—a particular customer group, specific countries, or specific geographic areas that offer better-than-average rates of growth. Electronic test and measurement equipment sales, for example, have sustained attractive growth rates during periods when total industry sales were flat by focusing on hospital and medical laboratory segments that were growing.

2. *They emphasize consistent quality and product/service that provide demonstrable value to market segments.* They avoid any business that is sold only on unit price. Innovations, especially proprietary expertise, are difficult and expensive for competitors to imitate. More importantly, they keep a product from becoming a commodity with services and thus allow a company to compete on a basis other than just price. Toledo Scale took the lead in moving the very mature and slow-growing mechanical weighing industry into electronics and enjoyed a proprietary product advantage for several years. The company picked up significant market share and profits by introducing sophisticated computing scales for parts counting and other industrial applications that no one else could match.

3. *Even though they steer away from straight "price business," they continuously strive for operating efficiencies.* Such companies automate to reduce unit costs, consolidate facilities, prune product lines, redesign products, and seek broader and more efficient sales approaches. In short, they recognize the need to drive every area in the organization toward the lowest possible unit cost and to be a cost-effective competitor over the long term.

Many managers talk a good game about making a factual assessment of the performance, competitive standing, and outlook for their business, but few really do it in a realistic manner. Instead, too much emphasis is placed on excuses of why sales have not materialized, why profit returns are low, or why competitors seem to have an edge. The objective should be to strip away all the rhetoric and rationalizations that generally accompany any evaluation of business performance and to simply look at the cold, hard facts. Probably the best way to examine the facts is to plot historical growth and profit patterns for each product line, customer, or market segment on a grid of sales growth and profit targets. Plotting average performance over some period of time, or even last year's results, will show how well each product/customer/market segment has performed against corporate profit targets and how much improvement is required to bring the business up to par.

The two axes of the grid in Exhibit 8–2 reflect the company's return-on-assets (ROA), compounded growth rate targets (16 percent return on average net assets and 14 percent on sales growth). The grid is divided into four quadrants: high profit/low growth, high profit/high growth, low profit/low growth, and low profit/high growth. The ultimate aim, of course, should be to move all of the product/market businesses into the upper left quadrant—the high profit/high growth category in a north-by-northwest direction. Businesses in the lower right quadrant—low profit/low growth—should obviously be under pressure for significant improvement as strategic plans are developed. Arrows can be used, as

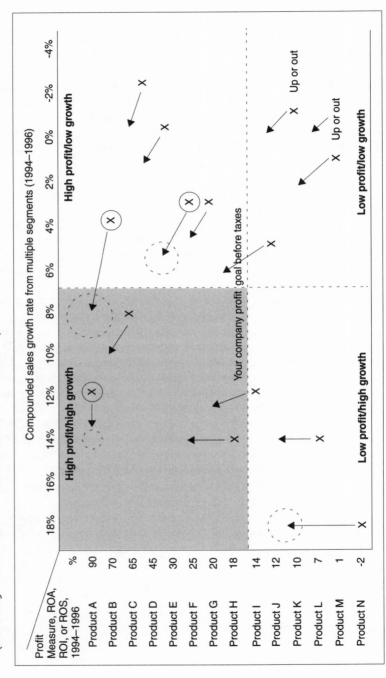

EXHIBIT 8-2

Product-Line Profit and Sales Growth
(North-by-Northwest—Current and Future Positions)

shown, to indicate the direction management intends to go with any particular product, and circles can be drawn to show the current and potential profit.

This analysis is always a good starting point for planning because it does avoid the rhetoric of why things are better than they look; it simply shows the facts as they are. Moreover, it provides a useful framework for demonstrating how a business team and plan will move the business toward the company's performance standards, and the analysis can help top management decide on resource allocations and the fate of poor or marginal performing units. Parker Hannifin uses this grid across their 90 divisions and business units. When Parker's CEO, Duane Collins visits a company facility, he often asks to see their "north-by-northwest" roadmap. This same grid can be used to plot and develop strategies for key customers.

Direction from Upper Management

General management personnel in leading industrial companies clearly recognize the strong role they must play in the planning process if they are to be effective. This doesn't mean they do all the planning, but certainly they are the ultimate architects of the plans for their business. Product, market, business unit, or general managers must lead the development of strategies and implementation programs across the departments. One general manager within the test and measurement group of Hewlett-Packard demonstrated the importance of this point with the following comment:

> It took me three years to realize that our people couldn't come up with the kind of plans I wanted for our products and markets unless I worked closely with them. They have always been able to develop a picture of where our markets are heading, identify the opportunities that exist, and interpret what we have to do to build the business. The many considerations and options require a general management approach to marketing that no one department can come up with. Unless I set the basic direction and targets for our business, specify who is to plan what, see to it that technical, manufacturing, and sales really work together to provide what is needed, and then challenge and contribute any ideas on how our business can be developed, the whole planning effort is nothing more than a paperwork exercise.

This statement underscores several ways in which general management must participate in the planning process to make it successful.

The Cabot Corporation, a global specialty chemical company based in Boston, has evolved from developing large annual business plans to having a group of more-focused business plans for specific market segments. Ken Gilson, the Cabot officer who drove this evolutionary change in their business planning states:

> Multiple mini-business plans become essential when there are many different product/markets or applications, each with its own customers and competitive offerings. The division and corporate management add little value to planning for these business applications: the goals and results are most effectively set and achieved by the team/people directly involved. This in turn means that greater planning capability needs to be developed in depth and that the application teams expect to draw in needed additional resources (trials, studies, R&D, capital). Next, this means middle and senior management often need to get out of the way—by supporting the teams, not controlling them.

Top Management Guidelines

"If only top management would tell me what they want!" is a common complaint among division and middle managers with major planning responsibilities. Perhaps some of them expect too much. But they are right in asking for guidelines from top management that spell out the rules of the game. Everyone must know the profit goals set by top management and what are acceptable and unacceptable profit returns. For example, the Andrew Corporation, a high-tech global manufacturer of wireless phone and data networks has developed the following minimum long-term goals:

15% increase in annual sales	**15%** increase in annual earnings	**7%** annual return on sales	**16%** annual return on stockholder's equity

The top management of the Andrew Corporation communicates these minimum goals to each of the 4,000 employees. These goals also appear in bold print on the inside cover of every annual report to show the company's commitment to achieving them.

It is also extremely important for everyone in the organization to know what products, markets, and customers should be emphasized; what kinds of businesses and customers should be avoided; and what capital availability or constraints exist. Planning guidelines are essential to provide parameters for people actually doing the planning in the various business units. The key here is to make sure that the criteria are rational, in line with the realities of the business, and that they make people stretch.

A good example of top management guidelines to help set the stage for effective planning is provided in the following letter from the president of an industrial automation firm to the company's division managers:

As you know, our end purpose is to earn a return for our shareholders that is more attractive than they could expect from other investments with similar risks. To do this means we must consistently compound our earnings at a rate that is 3 percent to 5 percent higher than inflation and achieve a return on stockholder equity in excess of 22 percent. For the corporation to achieve this kind of performance means that each operating unit must compound its earnings growth at the same rate and achieve an after-tax return on assets of at least 15 percent. In most cases each business unit will need to improve our after-tax return on sales to 5 percent or better to achieve the target return on net assets. These goals are mathematically compatible given our capital structure, debt limitations, and dividend requirements. Even more important, they are achievable. In fact, the leader companies in our industry have done better over the past several years.

It should be obvious that we need to refocus several parts of our business to achieve these profit goals. As you commence your planning assignments, be sure to keep the following eight corporate goals in mind:

1. We want to reduce our dependence on the automotive industry specifically and OEM markets in general (to no more than 40 percent of sales) so that we can achieve a more stable earnings pattern from after-markets and less cyclical industries.

2. We want to shift our focus from building and selling products to nearly everyone to serving selected markets (e.g., coatings, oil field, copiers, medical equipment) that we believe have more attractive growth prospects than the overall economy.

3. We want to grow our business in these target markets at the expense of our position in our traditional businesses, and we want to recover capital that is marginally employed in any of our current operations.

4. We want to set up most of our technical service and repair operations as discrete profit centers and grow these businesses faster than our total business; we will enter new service and repair areas to do so.

5. We want to have at least 55 percent of our sales from outside the United States within the next three years, and we are especially interested in rapidly growing our positions in southeast Asia, China, and central Europe.

6. We want to achieve a goal of 40 percent of sales from products introduced in the last five years (in our electronic imaging businesses that could be 60 percent and in our fluropolymers businesses about 30 percent).

7. We don't want to put new capital into any market/product business that does not offer the possibility of achieving our profit goals within the next three to four years.

8. We will accept a negative cash flow to support growth as long as earnings projections grow faster than 20 percent each year and there are no shortfalls from plan.

This letter does an excellent job of providing focus and direction without putting anyone in a straightjacket. Continuing emphasis on these kinds of targets and guidelines forces the strategic thinking and planning in each business unit into areas of business with the potential to accomplish corporate objectives and out of areas of business where this possibility does not exist.

Define Planning Units
As we have said, it is usually unrealistic to develop plans for an industrial or high-tech business as a whole. It makes more sense to segment the business according to some combination of product, market, customer, or application. These segments should be the building blocks for planning rather than the large operating units typically shown on corporate organization charts. "Small is beautiful" is an appropriate reminder to any business planning team. It is much more meaningful to develop strategies for many discrete market/product segments than for a big organization unit that houses multiple market/product businesses with quite different customers, competitors, product requirements, and growth prospects.

Companies that are successful at strategic planning often break five or six major organization units down into 50 or more discrete chunks for strategic planning purposes. Reliance Electric is a case in point. Although the company is managed around five major organization units (Electrical Products, Mechanical Products, Toledo Scale, Telecommunications, and Federal Pacific), the business is planned and controlled around more than 100 separate product centers, each with its own plan and net profit responsibility. The "small is beautiful" motto applies to the need for smaller planning units. The goal is to create the spirit, soul, and speed of a focused, small company but with the resources of a large company.

Define the Expected Format
In companies with many divisions or business units, a wide variety of interpretations is possible if top management does not provide direction as to the end products expected. The trick is providing adequate direction without confining anyone. The following memorandum sent to all operating managers by the president of a multidivision company serving the petrochemical industry illustrates how direction can be provided without an elaborate set of forms and procedures:

> As we move toward our plan review dates, it is important to agree on what your end products should look like. I think you can summarize everything I want to see on a few slides.

1. Define in a paragraph or two what it is your division is seeking to do in a way that provides the rationale for the growth and profit goals you have set. In other words, state the overall mission you have defined for your business unit and how you intend to accelerate sales and profit growth.

2. Show a five-year history of sales, market share, earnings before taxes, return on sales, return on net assets, and cash flow and compare with our corporate targets. Do this for your division overall and for each market/product segment for which you have prepared a strategic plan.

3. Show three-year projections of sales, market share, earnings before taxes, return on sales, return on net assets, and cash flow for your division overall and for each market/product segment.

4. List the key strategic decisions, commitments, and programs required for your division and for each market/product business. If major capital or expense commitments are required, be sure to highlight these and indicate the probable timing. Also, be sure to comment on your priorities in the event that corporate cannot fund everything you want to do.

5. Describe what strategic alternatives you could pursue to accelerate your profit growth, assuming no constraints on capital or short-term profit requirements.

Be sure to have the backup detail to respond to questions that are sure to be raised during your presentation. You will undoubtedly want to have your whole management team with you so that questions can be directed to those most directly responsible.

The actual format may vary somewhat from industry to industry. However, the objective should always be to avoid unnecessary details, forms, and schedules and to concentrate instead on end products that bring the strategic issues and options into sharper focus.

Cross-Functional Linkages

If we could stress only one point in this chapter, it would be this: Any planning in industrial or high-tech companies that does not actively involve a cross-functional team is an exercise in futility. There are many departmental barriers and blinders to effectively involving an entire cross-functional team in developing sound business plans. As a result, many departmental or functional managers do not know how to translate their responsibilities into the needs of customers. Far too many departmental managers view other departments as necessary evils or adversaries. However, collectively these managers shape, make, sell, and service the products that provide competitive value to customers.

The rewards in many companies reinforce the organizational barriers to cross-functional linkage. The rewards are often at odds with customer needs and competitive performance. Engineering is rewarded for developing the best product, which may or may not be what the customer needs. Manufacturing is rewarded for high output, asset utilization, and unit costs, regardless of what the customer needs or what global competitive costs are. Sales is rewarded for volume goals, regardless of profitability and customer satisfaction. And finally, controllers are rewarded for balancing the books by generally accepted accounting principles (GAAP) rules, no matter what the true product/customer costs are.

In order to plan and execute as a cross-functional team, all the people involved with a product line or customer need to communicate continuously about *customer* needs, *competitive* solutions, product-line *costs*, and the business unit's *capabilities*. These same people must all be involved in identifying and prioritizing the key issues in each target market segment. Next, the same group of people must be involved in developing the strategy, goals, and cross-functional plans. The development and implementation of the strategy is also done by the same team of people. Finally, this cross-functional group of people must communicate the focus and priorities of the business unit to many others in the organization so that they understand their role in implementation programs.

Cross-functional teams are essential to creating a market-driven business unit and developing sound business plans. Sales, manufacturing, engineering, marketing, quality assurance, customer service, and controllers must work together as a team to develop market-focused plans rather than write memos defining functional programs that are then assembled into some kind of a bureaucratic plan. Cross-functional business teams must be actively involved in mapping out implementation programs to ensure coordination, buy-in, commitment, and successful execution.

If a technically based company does not recognize the need for closer links among its functions, any talk about market-driven management will be just that—talk. Just as all key functions in a company must unite to improve product quality, market-driven management also requires all key functions to unite to develop and share common plans. When a cross-functional team of people in a business unit have input in a product/market plan, the process will inevitably require more front-end time. But this is time well spent because the team-developed plans will be more speedily executed across the organization.

Cross-Functional Team Leaders

After participating in one of our workshops that emphasized the power of cross-functional teams, a product manager from Hewlett-Packard said:

I first realized that my sales forecasts must be more accurate, detailed, and responsive to market changes or else I'll lose total credibility with all other functions. No longer do manufacturing and materials management develop their own forecasts. We now hold our monthly operating meetings at the plants so more people can be involved in discussing and solving the key issues. The cross-functional process has caused many engineering and manufacturing people to spend more time in the field with customers and distributors. Our new-product designs now have more of a customer focus, and the final designs are more closely integrated with manufacturing capabilities and cost targets. Overall, our cross-functional approach to being more market driven has resulted in a sensitivity to customer needs and competition advantages, costs, and capabilities that just weren't here before. Problems are even informally raised in the hallways and right then discussed and brainstormed until a good solution emerges. But before we adopted a cross-functional team approach, I was, as a product manager, nothing more than a glorified scheduler or a special accounts salesman.

The use of a cross-functional team should not be limited to once-a-year meetings to develop business plans. The more successful companies involve a mix of people from different disciplines to structure and carry out market research, competitive analysis, new-product development, and cost-reduction projects. In every cross-functional team, all members should have an equal say in what should be done and how. It is the power of ideas, not organization authority or position, that is key. For this reason, the more autocratic manager is often opposed to the leadership style needed to put market-driven management to work with cross-functional planning teams. The "one-man-show" manager who sees his primary responsibility as "giving orders to the troops" will have great difficulty changing to the more participative and team-consensus method of developing market/product strategies. Rather than be a take-charge gladiator, the cross-functional team manager must be skillful at group problem solving, reaching consensus, and managing differences of opinions.

Some managers may think that the use of cross-functional teams to develop and implement market-driven plans involves giving up one's authority. The opposite is true—cross-functional teams more clearly identify the responsibilities of each person, thereby increasing the manager's influence on each team member. When a team of people is involved in selecting target markets, setting sales and profit goals, and developing action programs, more people will be committed to and feel responsible for the results. A great leader manages the team process and measures the results.

Contribute Ideas and Alternatives

If top management truly wants to find ways to improve profits and growth, it must actively participate in the development of market/

product strategies by challenging underlying assumptions and by contributing alternative ideas. Most strategic decisions, particularly those that involve a change in direction, require the experience, perspective, and "feel" of top management—not just its blessing. To be sure, many top executives try to do this, but the *way* they do it often stifles rather than encourages new ideas. They must avoid any atmosphere of an inquisition and, instead, encourage an open exchange of ideas and opinions. In such an environment, one idea leads to another, and the management team soon finds itself exploring new and imaginative ways of developing the business.

A cross-functional give-and-take discussion led a high-speed elevator manufacturer to adopt a new marketing strategy that gave its parts operation a chance for survival:

> In this company, as in many others, parts sales had traditionally been a major source of profits. Now management was concerned because "parts pirates" (local parts producers) were cutting sharply into their business. Asked to develop a marketing strategy that would reverse the trend, the parts manager first came up with a plan that called for adding three salespeople and cutting prices on a large number of parts to be more competitive. As he acknowledged, his plan was essentially no more than a holding action.
>
> During the planning review session, in which all functions took part, the company president encouraged everyone to take an entrepreneurial look at the parts business and to try to think of various ways to grow it. Predictably, fresh ideas were hard to come by in a business that had been run the same way for years. But eventually three embryonic ideas emerged that were considered worthwhile: (*a*) build a service organization and sell contracts for maintenance service instead of just parts, (*b*) decentralize the parts business and set up local parts and repair shops to compete head to head with local competitors, and (*c*) start to buy and sell parts for other manufacturers' equipment in order to spread overhead costs and service other manufacturers' products.
>
> The long-time parts manager was naturally somewhat reluctant to do any of these things, since they would revolutionize his end of the business. But with top management backing and encouragement, he did the required analytical work and came back with two possible strategies, based on the first two ideas, that offered a much more attractive outlook.

This process does not always lead to a viable market/product strategy since it is not always possible to overcome the scarcity of fresh ideas characteristic of a business run the same way for years. Moreover, alternative strategies are not always visible on a first pass. But management in the more successful companies insists on seeking alternative strategies and avoids getting locked into a self-defeating business-as-usual pattern of thinking.

Give and take among the entire cross-functional business team is really the heart of the market-driven planning process: It is during these discussions that marketing presents the requirements of the marketplace and the other functions discuss feasible responses. With all the opportunities and constraints out in the open, top management has a good basis for deciding how to allocate resources. Once the best combination of ideas is agreed on, the various functions are then in a position to make commitments on the timing and costs of the alternative actions that underlie the business plan. Leading company executives insist this is the best vehicle for triggering new ideas and ensuring cross-functional buy-in and implementation.

Regional and Global Business Teams

Dr. Harald Wulff, president and CEO of Henkel Corporation, the $10 billion chemical company based in Dusseldorf, Germany, has done a good job of creating decentralized business units. Each business unit develops business plans for discreet target markets and key accounts in the emphasized market segments. Each business team leader has full control of all the major cost factors related to managing the business, and each team is accountable for the profitability of each unit. Cross-functional business teams helped Henkel change from a strong hierarchical emphasis with "silos" in manufacturing, sales, and technical to a horizontal organization as shown in Exhibit 8–3. In the new cross-functional business team organization, target market plans and customer selection were more focused, and faster decision making took place. Customers were served faster, and customer satisfaction became a shared responsibility of each business team. The formation of global business teams followed. The regional and global business planning teams helped accomplish the following:

1. Develop common bottom-up country and regional plans that, in turn, helped the company move from being a multinational to a truly global enterprise.

2. Reduce the duplication of R&D efforts, and develop more global products.

3. Share market segment and application knowledge among countries and regions of the world.

4. Create centers of excellence in one country for businesses with global opportunities.

5. Follow and service large global customers anywhere in the world.

E X H I B I T   8–3

Aligning the Organization to Serve Target Market Segments
and Key Accounts

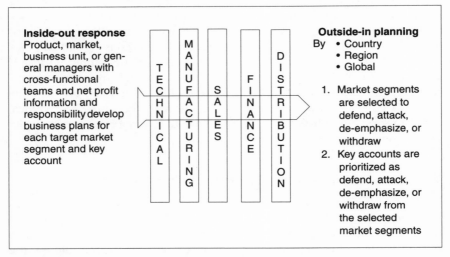

Inside-out response
Product, market,
business unit, or gen-
eral managers with
cross-functional
teams and net profit
information and
responsibility develop
business plans for
each target market
segment and key
account

TECHNICAL

MANUFACTURING

SALES

FINANCE

DISTRIBUTION

Outside-in planning
By • Country
    • Region
    • Global

1. Market segments
    are selected to
    defend, attack,
    de-emphasize, or
    withdraw

2. Key accounts are
    prioritized as
    defend, attack,
    de-emphasize, or
    withdraw from
    the selected
    market segments

Source: Adapted from a presentation by Dr. Harald Wulff, president and CEO, Henkel, North America, 1996.

SUMMARY

Business planning is undoubtedly one of the most important, if not *the* most important, activities in the whole process of management. Who would consider for a minute supporting anyone interested in any type of a business venture without some kind of a business plan? Some companies' bureaucratic plans are nearly useless. We have, however, observed and worked with many companies that talk a good game of planning and go through all the motions required to develop plans for their business. Yet, when the facts are known, many of these plans have little impact on the way the business is conducted. We strongly suggest the need for many discreet business plans for specific target markets rather than a thick plan that quickly dies on a shelf. The prescriptions outlined in this chapter can help any company avoid this problem and achieve improved results through better strategies and plans on a country, regional, and global basis.

Winning Plans

While management in most industrial and high-tech firms recognizes the importance of planning and prepares both long-term strategic plans and annual operating plans, there are wide variations in the quality of the end products. Some are very useful instruments that provide the basis for communicating a direction, pulling the organization together, controlling the business, and dramatically improving results. Unfortunately, many others lack the substance to be a useful management tool.

Of course, no one can guarantee the success of any plan, and there is no ready-made checklist that will show absolutely whether a plan is a winner or a loser. There is, however, a logical thought process that will greatly assist management in deciding whether a plan is a solid vehicle for moving the business ahead or just a lot of words and numbers without real substance. Our intent in this chapter is to describe how to use this thought process to determine whether proposed plans are soundly conceived and worth the commitment of resources or whether they should go back to the drawing board for more work. There is nothing sophisticated about the procedure. It simply requires getting answers to three general questions:

1. Is the plan properly structured and focused?
2. Is there anything about the plan that detracts from its credibility?
3. Is the business team's attitude and approach to planning sound?

Although these broad questions may be obvious, the answers are often obscure, and it frequently takes much digging and detailed questioning to bring the answers to these questions into focus.

STRUCTURE AND FOCUS

To start with, the plan should be a complete and self-explanatory document, which means that even without prior knowledge of the business, anyone should be able to read the plan and decide whether it makes sense. That is, they should be able to understand the direction the business team has in mind for the business, why this direction was selected, and how it will be pursued. We are not suggesting that simply because a plan is understandable and reads well, it is necessarily sound. However, unless it has these attributes, it isn't worth further review. Far too much time will be wasted trying to figure out what the plan really means, what the cross-functional team intends to do, and whether the proposed actions are worthwhile.

Strategy Statement

The plan should be prefaced by a brief summary or strategy statement explaining what type of business the team is trying to build, what market(s) has(have) been selected as targets and why, and the basis for believing the plan can be accomplished. All that is needed here is a summary of the team's intent and the underlying rationale. Why waste time wading through a total plan if the basic intent and rationale do not make sense? Here is a well-worded strategy statement from a plan to build a business in the telecommunications equipment market:

> Our continuing objective is to build a $300 million business in the telecommunications equipment market within the next three years. We intend to concentrate our efforts on the equipment area involved in the "subscriber loop," where we have a significant technical base. We do not intend to get into switching or toll transmission, nor do we intend to get into the interconnect business.
>
> We will achieve this objective by introducing several new products with significant cost and/or performance advantages that will help telephone operating companies hold down or cut back their labor costs and prolong the useful life of their existing plant and equipment. These new products will account for 50 percent of our volume growth each year through 1999. We will also have to acquire several new products and pools of technology that we do not now have to serve this market.
>
> Accomplishing this plan will enable us to sustain a real growth rate of better than 10 percent a year, bring our after-tax ROS to 10 percent and our after-tax ROA to 25 percent.

A clear directional statement such as this one, which explains in broad terms what the cross-functional team is seeking to do and how it intends to do it, is the hallmark of any good business plan. It states a precise objective and a time frame for reaching it. It defines the market segment the team has targeted and explains the competitive basis for believing the business can be enlarged. It defines the focus of attention—both what will be done and what won't be done. It states the type of action the business team intends to take, and it states the expected financial results. Finally, it provides an initial perspective on whether those responsible for the plan have a concept for running the business that makes sense.

One point about defining a concept for the business is worth emphasizing. It is equally important to define what you don't want to do as it is to define what you do want to do. Defining what you don't want to do is like getting a no answer in the old game of 20 Questions. Even though a no answer is negative information, it often provides useful insight into the ultimate solution. Similarly, a statement defining what you *don't* want to do in a business helps bring into focus the strategic direction you *do* want to take. Note how the telecommunication strategy statement achieved precision by naming the business (interconnect) in which the company would not participate.

Now let's look at a not-so-good example. Here is a statement that management in a programmable-controller business prepared on a form that allowed about one inch for a strategy statement:

> We intend to grow our business in programmable controllers at the fastest possible rate and maximize profits. We intend to broaden both our distribution and customer base and gain market share. We will continue to reduce costs and build value into our products with world-class manufacturing. We will need an especially strong selling effort and will achieve this through superior sales training.

As you can see, this statement doesn't really describe any kind of a business concept. It doesn't establish any parameters on the size or scope of the overriding business objective, does not define any target market segments, makes no attempt to define a strategy for accomplishing this objective, and says nothing about financial implications.

The lack of thought in this statement is highlighted by testing it against the obverse. This test holds that if a statement doesn't make much sense when the obverse is stated, it probably isn't worth saying. Now, think of the mission statement for programmable controllers. Does it make sense to think in terms of growing the business at the "slowest possible rate," to make "minimum profits," or to "increase costs" supported with a "very weak selling effort" or "inferior sales training"? Hardly. And yet, the phrases "fastest rate," "maximum profits," "reduce costs," and "superior sales training" don't mean much more. And finally, the buzzword "world class" is so vague it says nothing.

Initiatives

Following the strategy statement, the plan should outline a series of initiatives linked to the business concept or objective. Given the summary statement for telecommunications, you would expect to see recommended actions and programs designed to develop new or improved products for the subscriber loop market and thus improve profit margins to the 10 percent level. If planned actions and programs do not fit this pattern, the logic is faulty, and there is something fundamentally wrong with the plan.

To be meaningful, all the recommended actions and programs should be defined in sufficient detail to provide the basis for effective execution and management control. For example, do the key programs proposed to improve performance show the major steps to be taken, the costs involved, the timetable for accomplishment, and the personnel responsible for each step? This level of detail is important. How else can you be sure that there is reason for successful execution? Moreover, it is the only way to ensure that appropriate corrective actions can be taken if something goes wrong before an accounting "scorecard" comes out at the end of a period.

Another question to consider is whether there are any parts of the plan in which actual performance cannot be measured. Many companies are saddled with information systems that do not provide the means of tracking costs and profits for individual products, customers, or markets or that have other critical gaps. If this is the case, plans to improve sales and profits for these individual product or market segments—or for anything else in which actual results cannot be determined—cannot be measured or controlled. Since it doesn't make sense to plan something you can't measure and control, any part of a plan that falls into this category should be discounted until some basis for control is defined.

Finally, the plan should be summarized in a series of cost and profit projections that are also consistent with the strategy statement. In the case of the telecommunications plan, these projections should reflect a growth pattern that heads toward a $300 million business in three years. Profit results should show a 10 percent after-tax return on sales (ROS) and a 25 percent after-tax return on assets (ROA). If the projections show a different picture, there is obviously something wrong that needs to be corrected before the plan is subjected to detailed review.

Summing up, Step 1 in distinguishing winning plans from losers is to quickly examine the plan document for completeness and logic. Is it understandable and does it make sense? Is there a brief summary statement that clearly explains what management is trying to do with the business? Does this statement sound reasonable, and is it supported by recommended actions and programs that are logical and cost effective? Are recommended actions and programs sufficiently detailed to ensure effective execution and control? Do sales, cost, and profit projections make sense in light of what management wants to do and the actions and programs that are proposed?

Clearly, this first step in the review process does not entail any kind of in-depth analysis. It shouldn't take more than half an hour or so to do. If it takes longer, the plan is too complicated and verbose. There is no use spending time getting into details if the basics are not right. And any plan that cannot pass this initial examination of its structure and content should be reworked before more management time is wasted reviewing a product that is inherently unsound.

CREDIBILITY ISSUES

Assuming the plan is structurally sound, Step 2 should be to look for weaknesses or inconsistencies that detract from the plan's credibility. Six questions will help ensure that there are no fatal flaws in the plan: (*a*) Is the plan's fact base sound? (*b*) Do the sales, cost, and profit projections make sense? (*c*) Are key physical ratios reasonable? (*d*) Does the risk/ reward ratio make sense? (*e*) Has adequate allowance been made for contingencies? (*f*) Have subplans been developed for each key function and project?

Fact Base

A solid fact base is crucial to good business planning. It is the whole foundation for management's evaluation of the product, market, and competition and, ultimately, cost and profit projections. Few will disagree with the importance of solid facts to good planning, but very few managers are sufficiently tough minded when searching for the real facts. Over the past several years, we have seen many presentations presumably based on facts. However, when many of these purported facts were challenged and the truth really emerged, we found that purported facts were not facts at all. Instead they were statements that fell into some of the following categories:

1. *Folklore facts* have grown up with the business and have never really been challenged. One such example is, "We have the best product or offer customers the best value." It is hard to think of any division manager that doesn't make such a claim. But, in most cases, such a claim doesn't stand up when the necessary digging and comparative analytical work are performed to get the real facts.

2. *Assumed facts* are necessary assumptions about the future, but not facts. For example, statements that GDP will grow or inflation will run at a certain rate, costs will increase by a certain amount, or competitors will react in a certain way should be clearly labeled as assumptions and not presented in any way as facts.

3. *Reported facts* tend to be given unwarranted validity simply because they have been published by some association or industry expert. Who published the data? What is the source? How valid or complete is the source? Until these questions are answered satisfactorily, the data should not be regarded as factual.

4. *Hoped-for facts* represent situations management would like to believe but that do not accurately reflect the situation. "We are the most profitable company" or "We have the best salesforce" are typical examples.

5. *Half-true facts* have a certain amount of validity to them but are misleading. For instance, "The market has grown at an average rate of 10 percent a year over the past five years" may be a true statement, but it is misleading if five years ago this market dipped to an unusually low level and much of the 10 percent growth was simply catching up to where the market should have been. What is the base point? Where is it in the secular trend? What is the growth rate if we shift the base point back or forward?

In many situations, these distinctions between facts that are real and facts that are not so real may not be important. But in business planning, the distinctions are critical. The whole plan is worthless if it is based on anything other than real facts. There is no way to make certain that proposed actions and programs are based on incontrovertible facts without hard-nosed questioning that challenges some of the facts and places the burden of proof on those presenting the plan. What are the data to support this statement? What is the source for these data? What is the proof that we are competitive or have a demonstrable advantage? These are all fair questions that must be answered to prove that facts are truly facts.

Sales, Cost, and Profit Projections

How do you determine whether a plan's sales, cost, or profit projections are sound? What do you look for when making this kind of an evaluation? You don't have to be a financial wizard, but you do have to have a solid understanding of cost and margin relationships and how they change or should change as volume moves up or down. Exhibit 9–1 shows several red-flag indicators of weakness in the sales, cost, and profit projections that management should look for any time a plan is being evaluated.

A few caveats are worth emphasizing. First, watch out for sales projections that call for a faster rate of market growth than historical patterns show or that require a significant gain in market share. Market growth rates or share positions may increase, but not as easily or as quickly as those presenting the plan expect. New or improved products with clearly demonstrable cost and profit advantages seldom affect the market the way their sponsors think they will. Moreover, every perceived opportunity for market gain is usually accompanied by some risk or threat that could cause a decline. In most cases, risks or threats are overlooked and only opportunities are emphasized. When the success of a plan depends on accelerated sales growth, especially with market share improvement, it is crucial to explore the reasons the change is projected, ensuring that they are valid. It is generally much safer to bet on a business plan geared to a conservative sales forecast—and then scramble to exceed the plan if the market opportunity develops—than on a plan with a higher sales forecast that will require a cutback in costs and operations if the anticipated market opportunity does not occur. Losing sales dollars because a market opportunity is missed always hurts. But it is

E X H I B I T   9–1

Red-Flag Indicators

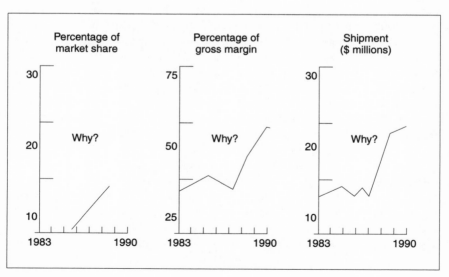

not as painful as the losses that occur and the explanations that go with those losses when the whole plan is based on a sales forecast that is far too optimistic.

Also, if cost and profit projections show sharp improvement from past patterns, look for the reasons for this change. Remember, cost and profit patterns do not improve unless someone does something to make it happen. Who is going to do what? When will it be done? What is the evidence that it can be done and will yield the desired result? Watch out for long-term projections (three to five years) that are much more favorable than projections for next year. Long-term projections are easy to make; it is difficult to hold anyone accountable for them. Long-term improvements usually represent wishful thinking rather than a concrete plan.

Be wary of an abrupt change in operating rate that causes profits to improve sharply over an immediate prior period. Operating managers frequently overlook the practical problems involved in stepping up production and jumping from one operating level to another without allowing sufficient time to gear operations to a higher level of business. This oversight appears most frequently when a much higher operating level for the year is planned and then spread evenly, by a computer or an accountant, over the 12-month period. As a result, first-quarter profit projections tend to be overstated because planned operating rates cannot be achieved.

Be sure that gross margins are adequate to cover all related expenses and generate a satisfactory profit margin. Of course, gross margins vary widely across businesses, but it pays to be very suspicious of the profit potential of any industrial or high-tech business with a gross margin (sales dollars less all manufacturing costs [including variances] to convert the product from raw material to finished product) that is much less than 30 percent. In some cases, particularly in a process industry or where the business is based on the sale of a relatively few high-ticket products or systems, sales, marketing, and administrative expenses may be sufficiently low to permit a satisfactory profit level with a lower gross margin. Nevertheless, a gross margin under 30 percent should be viewed as a red flag and should be examined to determine whether the entire cost-profit structure makes sense with the lower ratio.

Check to see that anticipated cost changes for labor, materials, and outside services are adequately reflected in profit-and-loss projections. In today's volatile economic climate, it is all too easy to underestimate cost changes up or down, leading to erroneous profit projections. The only way to avoid this possibility is to ask very specific questions about the allowances for cost changes that have been factored into profit projections. For example, ask purchasing what price changes are expected on raw materials and other purchased items and when. Ask human relations management what kind of wage or benefit increases are anticipated for both hourly and salaried workers and when. Ask insurance management how much allowance has been made for increasing costs of medical, disability, and liability insurance and why. Obviously, all of the responses must be checked for consistency with current market and economic conditions. The controller should then ensure that all of these allowances have been correctly factored into the plan.

Examine expense levels for key areas to ensure that they correctly consider prior spending patterns and the job that needs to be done. In some cases, planned expenses may be too low. There is a tendency on the part of some managers to cut back on expenditures that should be made in critical areas so that their current profit looks good, even though this may jeopardize the long-term health of the business. In other cases, planned expense levels may be too high, especially with an overly optimistic sales forecast. Sloppy planning practices enable many managers to automatically increase their budgets for advertising, promotion, sales, and other areas that can move up or down very easily without regard for what is really required to support the plan.

Industry comparisons that will help determine whether a particular expense level is too low or too high are generally available through competitor reports, trade association data, or industry publications. If sales, advertising, or product development expenses are out of line with published industry data, it is important to ask why. An answer frequently given to this question is that the comparisons are not valid; apples to oranges is a common claim. Don't settle for this response. There may very well be differences in what different companies include in various expense categories, but if the ratios are significantly different, there is a good chance that something is fundamentally wrong.

Finally, be sure that profit on incremental volume is satisfactory. In any business with a sound economic structure, higher volume should generate higher profit margins, hence, significantly higher earnings, since it should be possible to achieve leverage on the fixed-cost component. Unfortunately, most costs tend to be far too variable as volume increases and far too fixed when volume declines. As a result, the profit gain from added volume does not vary as directly with volume as it should. It is reasonable in most manufacturing companies to look for a 30 percent increment of profit on incremental volume and to insist on a clear explanation whenever this is not projected. Conversely, if volume should decline, it is reasonable to expect the same profit margins to be maintained, and profit dollars should not be any lower than they were when the business grew through this volume to a higher level.

Risk/Reward Ratio

A long time ago, some wise person stated, "Risk and opportunity usually go hand in hand." This is terribly important to keep in mind when reviewing any business plan. It should be obvious that every plan involves some degree of risk—no one can predict future events with absolute certainty. However, the degree of risk varies widely from plan to plan, and it is essential to ensure that the opportunity for reward is commensurate with the degree of risk involved. Let's examine two plans to determine how the degree of risk varies and what the factors are that cause these differences.

1. Example A—A business team for a manufacturer of electronic communications equipment submitted a plan to double sales volume for one of its new, high-growth product lines. Doing so required a plant addition involving a $2 million investment and an equal investment for added working capital. The company's sales of this product had doubled during the previous four years, and the total market was projected to more than double during the next five years. This total market projection was not out of line with past growth trends and was supported by a growing customer base that perceived real economic advantages in the company's product. Product cost estimates had proven to be valid, and projected profit returns on sales and investment were well in excess of the company's accepted hurdle rates. Payback on the new plant addition was planned in 2.4 years.

2. Example B—A business team in a machine tool company presented a plan to take the company into robotics. The plan emphasized the growing interest in robotics in both foreign and domestic markets and projected a dramatic increase in robotic sales during the next decade. The company's product development group had developed a modular concept for a line of robotics that appeared to offer opportunities for major cost savings in the manufacturing process. Product development also claimed that their line of robotics would have better speed, range, and load-carrying capability than any other competitive offering. Pictures of a design or break-board prototype were presented to prove the feasibility of product development claims. Continuation of the program required additional funding of $2.7 million for further product development activities and a joint venture with another independent research firm to ensure the necessary control capability. The product development group was committed to having a prototype for the machine tool show in the fall of the following year, and marketing expected to capitalize on the introduction of the new robot with an integrated sales and promotion campaign to major potential users. The company had manufacturing capacity available to meet projected sales requirements, and no immediate investment was required for new plant or equipment. Total costs of pursuing the plan were about $5 million, with product development and market development expenses accounting for the great bulk of this sum. A payback period of 4.5 years was projected, and profits beyond that point were expected to grow at a much faster rate than anything the company had ever experienced.

It doesn't take much insight to see that the potential risk/reward ratio in Example A is much more attractive than that in Example B. Both situations are based on exciting market characteristics, and both appear to offer attractive growth opportunities. However, the plan in Example A is based on a proven product with an attractive sales and profit history, while the plan in Example B is based solely on claims by the product development group of what they can do against a formidable array of competitors. Moreover, the payback period in Example A is of much shorter duration, and the company's exposure to potential loss is much less.

All of these points are relatively easy to see when the examples are succinctly described on paper. They are not nearly as easy to see in a real-life situation, especially when the plan is presented by an enthusiastic and articulate management team, who, quite rightly, has the utmost confidence in their abilities. Therefore, it is always worthwhile to ask two specific questions: (a) What is the risk/reward ratio; that is, how many dollars of gain can we expect for every dollar at risk? (b) What happens if customers or competitors react differently than anticipated?

Clearly, the degree of acceptable risk, regardless of potential rewards, varies from company to company, depending on its size and financial condition. In a high-risk situation, the potential reward should be 6 to 10 times the dollars placed at risk in a relatively short time frame. Isn't this what you would want if you were investing your personal money in a high-risk situation? When the risk is less, you can settle for reduced reward opportunities because of the greater certainty of achieving planned results. In any event, a plan should never be approved unless those proposing the plan can respond to questions about the risk/reward ratio in a manner that demonstrates they have given it serious consideration.

Allowances for Contingencies

Many business plans compare their explanations to a road map, and, for the most part, this analogy is correct. Like a road map, the plan shows where you want to go and how you should get there. However, you can be much more certain that you will get where you want to go when following a road map than when following a business plan, no matter how brilliantly the plan may have been conceived and prepared. Unexpected road construction or detours might keep the driver from following the route exactly as planned. But these difficulties are minor compared with the roadblocks that any business plan is likely to encounter. Unforeseen changes in economic climate, competitor actions, customer or user requirements, and internal performance or capability breakdowns all represent uncertainties that are much more severe than those facing a driver trying to follow a map.

Unless adequate allowances are made for these contingencies when the plan is developed, it is almost certain to be too optimistic. It is not prudent to accept any business plan when successful execution requires all the pieces to fall into place exactly as planned. There must be some margin for error. How much depends on the penalties involved if the plan is not successful. When the penalties are very severe, the plan should not be accepted unless there is a high probability of success. Murphy's Law (everything that can possibly go wrong will) will prevail more times than not, and results will not be achieved as expected.

The best way to make this determination is to ask a series of what-if questions. For example, what happens to planned results if:

1. Sales volume is 5, 10, or 20 percent below forecast?
2. Critical costs are above estimates by a significant amount?
3. Deadlines for product development are missed?
4. Material shortages or unusually slow deliveries occur?
5. Competitors cut their prices by a significant amount?

Naturally, the questions will vary with each situation, but the technique remains the same. Simply look for the key variables and ask what happens if any of them go wrong. Inadequate answers probably indicate that insufficient thought was given to the possibility of things going wrong as the plan was developed.

Cross-Functional Plans

Most plans include expectations of major improvements in many areas. It is common to find statements such as "Manufacturing costs (or cycles) will improve by X;" "Inventories will be reduced by Y;" "Product redesign will take Z out of total costs;", or "Time to market will be cut by 50 percent." While these are certainly admirable objectives, they are nothing if not backed by detailed plans showing who is going to do what and when and the specific result that will be achieved. And, it is very easy to be misled into believing improvements will be made because objectives such as these are included in a plan presentation when, in fact, nothing has really been planned to make the improvements.

In short, cross-functional plans should exist for every key function and project:

- Research and development and engineering.
- Manufacturing.
- Inventory.
- Procurement.
- Cost reduction.
- Productivity improvement.
- Quality improvement.
- Sales and distribution.
- Manpower.
- Capital expenditures.
- Cash flow.

All of these plans should be developed and ready for review and discussion.

MANAGEMENT APPROACH AND ATTITUDE

Two final points must be considered to complete the evaluation. First, it is important to determine whether the plan is integrated and truly reflects the thinking and requirements of the entire business team or whether it is simply a brainchild of one person or group that none of the other departments know anything about. It is also important to determine whether the entire cross-functional team believes in and is committed to achieving the planned results.

Integrated across Functions

One of the most common and serious deficiencies of industrial and high-tech plans is that they are not integrated; they do not have input from all key functions of the business. This is the primary reason so many plans have so little meaning and make so little contribution to management and the decision-making process. When plans are developed in a vacuum, sales forecasts are discounted or second guessed by manufacturing, and inventory levels inevitably get out of line. Product development activities are too technically directed and thus out of phase with market needs and what the other departments should do. The salesforce operates with an unhealthy emphasis on volume and too little focus on selected customer groups or market segments that could make the business stronger and more profitable.

It is not difficult to determine whether a plan is an integrated instrument to help manage the business. The first clue is the name of the plan. If it is called a marketing plan, it probably is just that, and it probably has all the shortcomings identified earlier. The second clue is how it is presented. If it is written and presented completely by traditional marketing people, it is a fair bet that other functional departments have not been adequately involved.

Another way to check if a plan is integrated is to ensure that all functional departments are represented when the plan is presented and to ask relevant questions. For instance, ask manufacturing if they agree with the sales forecast and if their inventory and production plans are actually geared to it. Ask if the planned mix of sales is comparable with existing production capabilities or if this factor was even considered when the sales plan was developed. Ask the controller if the department has determined the relative profitability of alternative sales strategies and if this information was considered as sales plans were drawn together. Ask engineering to identify their planned project priorities and show how engineering labor-hours will be allocated to these projects. Then ask marketing to explain how these priorities and allocations tie into their assessment of marketing needs and opportunities. The answers to such questions will clearly and quickly indicate if the plan is based on a true cross-functional business team effort. If not, it isn't worth much and should be rejected.

Business Team Commitment

Commitment to a plan is a difficult concept to define and probably the most difficult area to probe. At the same time, it is, in many respects, the most crucial area. A deep-rooted sense of commitment is why certain business teams are able to overcome all obstacles and still achieve planned results. It is the same ingredient that enables a team to win against tough competition even though their best players are injured or all the breaks in the game go against them.

Without attempting to be a psychologist, there are several things to look for to determine whether this sense of commitment exists. What has been the track record of those submitting the plan? It is a positive sign if they have a history of fulfilling commitments. Conversely, if the group has not met its commitments in the past, it is essential to find out what has changed to make their commitment to the current plan any more meaningful. Is there evidence that individuals understand how a failure to meet their personal or functional commitments would jeopardize the ability of the whole group to accomplish its plan? Is there any indication that anyone in the cross-functional team feels that their function has over-committed or that they have been pressured into making commitments that are unrealistic?

It is unlikely that anyone will admit they are not committed to a plan they developed and recommend. But questions directed to each functional area about the certainty or difficulty of achieving its part of the plan help everyone see what must be done to successfully implement the plan. Such questioning helps to establish the importance of each individual's personal commitments, not only to the plan but to the rest of the organization. In a sense, it helps to develop a form of peer pressure, which is just as important in the execution of the business plan as it is in other walks of life. No one enjoys being in the position of having let team-mates down.

EMERSON ELECTRIC COMPANY—A SHINING EXAMPLE

Emerson Electric Company is a $9 billion manufacturer of electrical, electro-mechanical, and electronic equipment that employs over 75,000 people. In 1996, Emerson marked its 36th consecutive year of improved earnings per share—performance matched by only a handful of manufacturing companies in the world. According to a study by A.T. Kearney, Emerson is one of only eleven U.S. corporations that out-earned its cost of capital during each of the past 25 years. Their business units are very decentralized and autonomous, with names such as Alco Controls, Skil, Rigid, Rosemount, Appleton Electric, and Micro Motion. Emerson's 50 divisions make a wide range of industrial products that are not household names—even though Emerson is one of the better-run companies in the world. Emerson consistently makes profits in a manufacturing business that many observers consider mature and not glamorous.

Emerson's corporate headquarters is small. In order to avoid bureaucracy, the company has no published organization chart. The company does not have groups or sectors or other combinations commonly found in large, diversified companies. Emerson's CEO, Chuck Knight describes their planning process:

At Emerson, developing business plans is a line job, not a staff function. The people who develop the plans must be the people who

(continued)

(continued)

implement the plan. We also believe in keeping our plans simple, our communication simple, our implementation simple, and our organization simple. It takes a lot of discipline to keep planning and implementation simple. Emerson's planning process emphasizes setting firm financial targets, planning carefully, and following up closely. This process is fueled by dynamic annual planning and control cycles.

Set Financial Targets

The first step in our planning is to set financial targets. Consistent high performance requires ambitious and dynamic targets. Once we fix our financial goals, we do not consider it acceptable to miss them. The financial targets drive our strategy and determine what we have to do, the kinds of businesses we are in, how we organize and manage them, and how we pay the management team.

We have not modified our other financial goals, despite pressure to do so. During the 1980s, for example, we were criticized because we refused to increase our debt position. Given the then-prevailing attitudes toward leverage, our financial position appeared unduly conservative. But we regard our finances strategically: maintaining a conservative balance sheet is a powerful competitive weapon. When we see an opportunity that we can finance only by borrowing, we have the capacity. By the same token, we're not encumbered by interest payments, which are especially burdensome during economic down-turns.

Identify Investment Opportunities

The second step in our planning process is to identify specific market/product opportunities that will meet or exceed our criteria for growth and returns. In other words, we identify business investment opportunities. It is the role of our division presidents and their business teams to bring forth the better business investment opportunities. Since we are a big decentralized company, this bottom-up process of identifying opportunities that meet our top-down financial goals is the only way we know to run a large, close-to-the-customer company. We push the divisions to think through different scenarios and to plan actions that will reach our financial goals. We require only a few standard planning formats. While there are only a few planning formats, they require substantial planning and backup data to develop the small number of exhibits. To prepare properly requires the division general managers and their business teams to really understand the customers, technology, competition, and economics of the business.

(continued)

(continued)

Competitive Analysis

Our third step is to stress the importance of analyzing and under-standing the competition in each attractive market segment. Simply comparing ourselves with ourselves teaches us nothing of value. We use the products and the cost structure of our competitors as the mea-sures against which we assess our performance. We do this in detail, legally and ethically, taking apart competitors' products, analyzing the cost of components, knowing regional labor rates and freight costs, and more. If we want to make intelligent decisions about invest-ing millions of dollars in a new plant to make circular saws we must assemble as clear a picture as possible of the cost structures and over-all plans of both our domestic and global competitors.

When most companies consider adding capacity, they typically compare the anticipated returns for the new facility with the existing plant's return. But at Emerson, the management demands that the proposed capital expenditure for a new plant be compared to the return at the lowest cost competitor's plant anywhere in the world. In one situation, if the business team requesting the capital could not beat the lower cost of a Taiwan competitor, they could not get the funds. Before Emerson added the capacity, through judicious intelli-gence gathering, they knew what Makita's, Bosch's and Black and Decker's costs were. At Emerson, we figure out what the competitor's costs are before building any new plants.

Focused Strategy

Once we understand the needs of our customers and the plans of our competitors, we develop a focused strategy to develop better prod-ucts, produce more competitively, and provide better service. Among other things, this strategy means staying close to customers and ven-dors and helping them achieve their goals as well as our own. The financial targets are the parameters for the strategies. We don't have any grand corporate strategy—that's determined by each division and business units within each division. However, we have recently adopted strategies to exploit common sales and distribution channels and share technologies. Our division strategies are often based upon both product design and process improvements.

Successful Implementation

Once we identify the most attractive investment opportunities in each division, the next step is to successfully implement. This is where many companies fail. Often implementation goes astray because the people who plan are separated from the people who have the responsibility to

(continued)

(continued)

make the plans work. The plans too often go to the bottom of an operations manager's drawer, and that's the end of them. At Emerson, the
people who plan are the people who execute. They have ownership
and involvement; it's their plan, not a corporate plan. That ownership
makes all the difference.

Sometimes people fail to execute because the same people who
developed the plan are not permitted to complete the implementation. Many companies put high-potential people on a fast track by
giving them more responsibility and promoting them. For the benefit
of implementation, we avoid moving people who are in the middle of
implementing business plans. We focus on the person's projects
rather than status; we compensate people based on the importance of
their job, not on the number of people reporting to them or the arbitrary need for a promotion.

For implementation, we use a technique called ABC budgeting: an
A budget applies to the most likely scenario, a B budget to a possible
lower level of activity, and so on. As a result, our managers know well
ahead that, if their business environment changes, they have a well-
thought-through set of actions they can take to protect profitability.
This contingency planning is particularly helpful in an economic
downturn; we are not paralyzed by bad news because we've already
planned for it.

Tracking Performance

Our next step is to closely track performance and address deviations
immediately. Each division submits monthly operating reports indi-
cating how well they are doing, the criteria being sales growth, profitability, and return on capital. Each division has a board that meets
monthly to review and monitor performance. In addition, the president and chief financial officer of each division meet quarterly with
corporate operating and financial management to discuss short-term
operating results. Each division president along with their appropriate staffs, meet once a year with seven corporate officers for corporate
financial reviews. These reviews occur late in the fiscal year and are a
review of performance against the financial plan.

Management Development Planning

The last step in our annual business planning reflects the importance
we place on human resources. This part of the planning process usually requires an additional half-day meeting centering on the human
resource issues in each division. In preparation, a division will evaluate all managers who are department heads or higher. We talk about
each manager's length of service in a particular assignment and his or

(continued)

(concluded)

her potential to move to a more difficult job. We try to identify those people who look like future "high potentials," and we develop career plans to offer them a series of assignments and training programs to enhance and augment their skills. We maintain an organization room at headquarters, where we keep personnel charts on every management team in the entire company. Every year we update this information, which covers more than a thousand people, on the basis of organization reviews. The charts include each manager's picture and are color-coded for areas such as function, experience, and career path. They provide a powerful visual aid to human resource planning. When a position opens, we know quickly which candidates are most qualified and which people might succeed the candidates we move up. For the purpose of follow-through and implementation, this approach also lets us know which people should not be moved.

Since about 95 percent of all our promotions come from within Emerson, we believe that this approach to management development, as part of our business planning process, helps to create continuity, maintain our culture, and foster high morale. All of our general managers come from within the company or from an acquisition we made. We only hire from the outside when we need specialized experience.

SUMMARY

None of the approaches raised in this discussion should be difficult to achieve if the company's plan has been properly put together and is integrated across all key functions of the business. The cross-functional business team should be able to answer these questions clearly and directly. Long, vague, or indirect answers are a good indication that the plan is not solid and should not be approved until the right answers are in place.

Finally, a straightforward and relatively simple planning cycle should exist in every organization. The guidelines described in the previous chapter (Putting It All Together) and the many examples should help any company develop a better planning process.

CHAPTER 10

Working Smarter

In this final chapter, we come full circle back to the market-driven rating scale introduced in Chapter 2. The previous chapters described what it means to be market driven in all aspects of the business, pinpointed common problems that interfere with the concept in most companies, and described some of the practices that leading companies have followed to make the concept pay off. After reading these chapters, you should be in a much better position to employ the rating scale as a diagnostic tool to assess market-driven performance in your own company.

We have discussed the problems of being a market-driven business with hundreds of managers from a broad range of industries at my training workshops. We have drawn two conclusions from working with a cross section of managers. First, since most managers rate their performance for most factors on the low side, there appears to be a huge need for improvement in most companies. Second, even those managers that were generally positive about their performance were still very critical about certain factors and felt major improvements were needed.

Let's examine the underlying reasons for the weaker ratings on each of the 14 factors and some of the comments made by workshop participants to describe the situation in their company.

Factor 1: Market Facts

Liabilities	-5	0	+5	Advantages
1. Market facts are nonexistent, unverified, or underutilized in planning and decision making.	I I I I I II I I I I			1. The value of market facts is widely recognized as the foundation for all planning and decision making.

Many managers are unaware of the importance of market information about customers, market segments, and competition as a basis for all plans and decisions. Too few companies invest the time or effort required to obtain critical market intelligence. These same uninformed managers do not see the value of market facts as key to selecting a focus in the business unit. With global markets and more rapidly changing customer requirements, the need for facts about customers and competition is greater than ever. Some typical comments from our workshops are given here:

> Our general managers and product managers don't believe that fact-based market information is key to market/product selection and don't budget any significant time or money to get it, and they often waste big money without these vital facts.

> The value of marketing research is simply not appreciated by middle or top management, and legitimate studies or findings are often dismissed in favor of gut feelings, hunches, or folklore.

> We need to know more about market trends, and our salesforce needs to do a better job of gathering and sharing competitive intelligence.

Factor 2: Market Segment Priorities

Liabilities	-5	0	+5	Advantages
2. Market segment definitions are too broad or based on an industry, products, technology, manufacturing, or customer sizes in each country and region.	I I I I I II I I I I			2. Market segments and key accounts are defined by common needs and grouped as attack, defend, de-emphasize, and withdrawn in each country and region of the world.

Market segmentation as a business practice has long been recognized and accepted in the consumer goods sector, but among industrial and high-tech manufacturers there has been no corresponding level of interest and rigor. However, the identification and selection of market segments is the most important strategic decision facing every industrial firm. Everything else follows this strategic decision. The following comments demonstrate this common weakness:

> No one here realizes that the choice of market segments determines the competitive and technology race we are in and the capabilities we must have in place.
>
> We think too broad about market segments and, as a result, miss the attractive opportunities our smaller competitors capture.
>
> The value of our products and services vary greatly between applications or different market segments.

Factor 3: Side-by-Side Competitive Comparisons

Liabilities	-5	0	+5	Advantages
3. Side-by-side competitive comparisons are nonexistent, unverified, too broad, and underutilized in decision making.		I I I I I II I I I I I		3. Side-by-side competitor analysis is done by segment, country, and region of the world and is used to develop market/product strategies.

Most managers are routinely required to make some kind of competitive statements in their planning process. However, it is usually a superficial listing of presumed strengths and weaknesses made with very little factual information, a reluctance to pinpoint fundamental advantages of competitors, and an exaggerated opinion of their company. Very few suppliers routinely do side-by-side comparisons of themselves and competitors on key dimensions. Here, again, are typical comments:

> We do broad-brush competitive analysis when it needs to be done by each application or market segment and in each region of the world.
>
> We need to compare ourself to segment competitors on product performance, service, price, and profitability.
>
> We need to learn about the fastest-growing competitors in each market segment, not just the biggest or oldest players.

Factor 4: Accounting Systems

Liabilities	-5	0	+5	Advantages
4. Accounting systems driven by generally accepted accounting principles and upward reporting rather than for management decision making.		I I I I I II I I I I I		4. Net profitability is reported, shared, and reviewed regularly for each product line, customer, market segment, and distributor.

Many companies have incredibly inaccurate accounting information for decision making. Too many managers are still willing to settle for a profit report at the gross margin level or for profit-and-loss statements that relate to big families of products. They fail to realize that gross margins, at best, tell only half the story and that individual products within families often have significantly different cost-profit structures. When there are large pieces of shared costs that are not allocated, it is a sure clue that the supplier does not know its costs. Few companies know what it really costs to serve their key accounts. Typical comments include the following:

> Our controller says that he cannot and will not even try to allocate the costs necessary to give me a true product-line profit-and-loss statement. We need to sit down with all the business managers and match the costs to the real activities.

> We really don't work too closely with our controllers. We simply take the reports they give us as gospel. We have little confidence in the data.

> My overhead charge is calculated on a formula basis. I know it is way too high and the main reason my reported profit is so low.

Factor 5: Lower-Cost Claims

Liabilities	-5	0	+5	Advantages
5. Lower cost claims are limited to manufacturing, are unsupported, and competitor actions and results imply otherwise.		I I I I I II I I I I I		5. Documented side-by-side comparisons show total unit costs are in line with or better than the regional and global segment competitors.

Most managers too often make self-serving statements about being a lower-cost producer without having a factual basis for making this claim.

It may sound good to top management and stock analysts, but it is a highly suspect claim when margins are slim and competitors are selling the same product at a lower price. Many managers still don't know their own costs and even fewer know their competitors' costs. Here are representative comments:

> We have always claimed to be the lower-cost producer, but some of our competitors have fewer management levels, less overhead, state-of-the-art manufacturing, and higher prices.
>
> We need to realize that being a lower-cost supplier without sufficient gross margins will not result in profitable top-line growth.
>
> Since we know so little about our competitors' cost structures, especially the foreign ones, how can we really know where we stand?

Factor 6: Quality

Liabilities	-5	0	+5	Advantages
6. Quality goals, product performance, and customer satisfaction measurements are nonexistent or talked about without programs for continual improvement.		I I I I I II I I I I I		6. Superior quality is relentlessly demonstrated through global side-by-side comparisons of yield rates, product performance, services, and customer satisfaction.

Every company we know talks a lot about quality and being a "world-class supplier." The fact is only a very few companies can clearly show that they do have superior quality or that they are "world class" in anything. Few companies identify sources of customer dissatisfaction and turn them into sources of satisfaction. Typical comments include the following:

> All the emphasis we have placed on quality has not shown up in results. We still have too much scrap and rework, too many customer complaints, high warranty costs, and too many competitors with equal or superior performing products.
>
> We have talked a lot about quality, but our priorities have been on cost reductions, and our design engineers and manufacturing people rarely consider global quality standards.
>
> We forget that quality standards are a moving global target. Sure we have improved, but some of our competitors, especially foreign ones, have improved faster, and we have higher warranty claims.

Factor 7: Manufacturing Efficiency and Capacity

Liabilities	-5	0	+5	Advantages
7. Machine efficiency and capacity utilization considerations dominate product line and customer mix decisions.		I I I I I II I I I I I		7. Manufacturing is committed to continuous productivity gains that lower costs and seek a richer product and customer mix.

Despite continuing improvements in manufacturing efficiency, most managers believe that too many manufacturing decisions are made independently and often at odds with market segment priorities, key accounts, and profit objectives. They are usually very reluctant to consider alternative approaches that would better serve customer needs and too quick to say something can't be done even though competitors are doing it. Here is what managers said:

> Our manufacturing investments and programs are not linked to the business plan, pricing strategy, superior quality, or market priorities.

> Our manufacturing resists sourcing from Central Europe and Southeast Asia like the plague. They claim it doesn't make sense when we have open capacity. Yet our competitors are doing this and have a much lower cost as a result.

> Our manufacturing people just want to keep the plants filled and add more capacity when we could probably make more money with fewer products, fewer customers, and less production capacity.

Factor 8: Response and Cycle Times

Liabilities	-5	0	+5	Advantages
8. Response and cycle times in many departments are lagging, and measurement and improvement programs are not in place to reduce response times.		I I I I I II I I I I I		8. Response and cycle times in most departments are equal or superior to the best competitors, and the organization relentlessly searches for more improvements and increased speed.

Improvements have been made in manufacturing and delivery cycles, but not enough to catch up with many foreign and some smaller domestic competitors. Also, far too little time and attention has been directed toward improving response time in the service side of the business. It still takes too long to respond to customer questions or requests for special quotes, solve customer problems, and so on. Typical comments are listed here:

> Our setup and cycle times are still too long and unpredictable. We repeatedly miss promised dates because we can't ship to schedule.

> Our response to customers' requests on specials takes three to five days. Our toughest competitor does this the same day.

> Our sales guys have claimed we lose a lot of profitable business because we don't respond to or solve problems quickly, but nothing has been done to document their claims.

Factor 9: Existing Products and Technology

Liabilities	-5	0	+5	Advantages
9. Existing products and technology suppress thinking about new market needs and new opportunities.	I I I I I II I I I I I			9. People are willing to think beyond existing products and technologies to serve present and new market segments and customer needs.

A deep-rooted commitment to existing technology, heavy investments in special-purpose plant and equipment, and a general discomfort with the idea of moving into any completely new product or process combine to make most managers uneasy about even considering a departure from the status quo. And blindly sticking with existing products and technologies while these market changes occur is a sure prescription for failure. The following comments from our workshop participants indicate the types of problems that exist in this area:

> When an attractive market segment begins to move to a different product form, material, or technology, we usually continue investing in yesterday's technology.

> Most of our senior management have backgrounds in yesterday's products and technologies. They give lip service to new technologies but won't seriously consider anything new.

Our technical service and salespeople are well schooled in our existing technology. Shifting to anything new would require a big change.

Factor 10: New Products

Liabilities	-5	0	+5	Advantages
10. New products are too late, too costly, or not demonstrably better for target customer groups and are not a major source of sales and profits.		I I I I I II I I I I I		10. New products are guided by cross-functional teams and are a major source of sales and profits.

New-product activities continue to be a contentious area largely because technical development groups are perceived as too independent in setting priorities and establishing their own pace. This perception is held by both marketing and manufacturing managers, who claim that the research and development group doesn't listen to them. R&D managers also have their complaints. They say manufacturing never meets cost targets, marketing never achieves their projections, and many salespeople lack the aptitude to sell the new products:

Our technical people are isolated from customers and marketing. They operate in a cocoon with no sense of urgency.

Our R&D people don't get close enough to customers—it is why they develop differentiated products that are not better in the customer's eyes.

We can't take forever to develop new products. Life cycles are shrinking, and we have to get demonstratably better new products out much faster and launch them as if they were perishable fruit.

Factor 11: Salesforce

Liabilities	-5	0	+5	Advantages
11. Sales training is uneven and mostly product- and feature-driven, and at odds with target market priorities, company goals, and customer needs.		I I I I I II I I I I I		11. All sales training activities are highly focused to communicate tangible and intangible customer benefits to target markets and key accounts.

The problem in this area is that most sales training and promotion programs are product and feature driven. Markets have not been segmented, so there is no basis for designing sales programs that relate to the specific customer benefits or applications. These same companies rarely know the benefits of their products and services to their customers' customers. Thus, most sales training and promotion materials are tied to general product features and undocumented claims. Typical comments include these:

> We do product feature training with our factory and distribution salespeople. We do little, if any, training on how to identify customer problems and how to document the tangible and intangible benefits of our products and services.

> Many of our sales representatives are in the comfort zone with their old accounts, and some are having difficulty with the increased complexity of our products and the customers' applications. We don't provide salespeople with any direction, selling tools, profit information, or incentives to improve the sales and profit of their accounts and territories.

> Our best competitors do problem solving and reference selling with a laptop computer. They also trust their salespeople with profit information and make them the account team leader.

Factor 12: Organization

Liabilities	-5	0	+5	Advantages
12. The organization is too structured around functions, wide families of products, large accounts, and too many management levels and meetings.		I I I I I II I I I I I		12. The organization is relatively flat, informal, and focused on small families of products or markets, and net profit responsibility is assigned for each major product, market, and key account.

Many companies have done a reasonably good job of stripping away or cutting back staff groups and management layers that were obviously redundant, unneeded, or bottlenecks. However, it is apparent that a lot more work needs to be done. Far too many managers still complain about bureaucracy, interfunctional friction, and high overhead costs. Some representative comments are given here:

We are still missing major opportunities because our decision-making and response time is too slow. Just look at all the long-winded meetings and lengthy memos that are a waste of time.

All our cost-reduction savings last year were more than offset by increased overhead charges that provided no customer or shareholder value.

Our managers are more loyal to their department than they are to the company or business unit. We just manage department silos and don't work well across functions.

Factor 13: Planning

Liabilities	-5	0	+5	Advantages
13. Planning is done sequentially by individuals and functions, and without necessary market focus, cross-functional integration, or team commitments.		I I I I I II I I I I I		13. Cross-functional teams develop and implement business plans for each product, market, and key account with horizontal commitments to achieve the planned sales and profit goals.

Most companies go through some type of formalized planning process. Planning schedules are published, planning meetings are held, planning forms and schedules are completed, and planning presentations are made. All this involves a great deal of work from many people, and there is an audible sigh of relief when the ritual is completed for another year. Unfortunately, in most companies all these efforts are long on form and frighteningly short on substance. Typical comments include the following:

Our planning is a form-filling exercise for budgeting purposes with little cross-functional input and team buy-in.

Our planning is done almost exclusively by department heads with baton-like hand-offs. We are then given marching orders, and we wonder why implementation is weak or nonexistent.

Our planning is still too top-down and around division activities as a whole. We need to do more bottom-up market/product planning for smaller pieces of business and then measure the cross-functional teams by their planned results.

Factor 14: Incentive Systems

Liabilities	-5	0	+5	Advantages
14. Recognition and reward programs are not aligned to market priorities, to short- and long-term goals, and to individuals, business teams, and business unit results.		I I I I I II I I I I		14. Recognition and reward programs reward both shorter- and longer-term results and are aligned with market priorities that recognize individuals, business teams, and the business unit performance.

Most managers are very critical of their incentive systems, claiming they are much too short-term oriented, usually paying off for quarterly or backward-looking annual performance. Others complain that the pay system resembles a nonprofit bureaucracy. Cross-functional teams are not accountable for results. There is no alignment with individuals, teams, or business unit performance. Frequent comments include the following:

> To make this concept work, we need both individual and business team incentives. Otherwise, team efforts will be subordinate to the functional or department interests.

> Our performance and pay systems recognize mediocrity and seniority. We need more variable pay based on goals, plans, and results.

> Accountability is inversely related to your organizational position in the hierarchy—there is no reward for hustling or taking risks at the lower levels.

Getting consensus agreement on the ratings for each of the 14 factors is only the starting point within each division or business unit and region of the world. Next comes the far more difficult task of determining how deficiencies can be corrected.

OVERCOMING DEFICIENCIES

Consensus agreement means that the division or business unit team has made a collective judgment that their business unit's performance on various factors is good or bad or needs improvement in certain areas. The profile they develop defines the problem areas and indicates the magnitude of improvement needed. If the ratings made by managers in our workshop are an indication of the norm, major improvements will be necessary in multiple areas.

General managers must lead their team in deciding which problems are most serious, what priorities should be established, and who should be assigned responsibility for corrective programs. Assuming strong general management leadership in this cross-functional team process, our experience suggests several guidelines that should be helpful to any management team seeking to improve their position:

1. There are no quick fixes to low ratings on any of the factors. Deficiencies will probably take many months to correct and will require fundamental departures from past management practices.

2. It doesn't make sense to tackle all the low ratings at once. Because of the time commitment and degree of change involved, most organizations can only digest corrective efforts in two or, at most, three areas at once. This means priorities must be set.

3. It is better to assign major problem areas to small cross-functional teams rather than individuals. Doing so encourages a broader evaluation of the problems and helps avoid functionally biased solutions.

4. Team assignments must not be taken lightly. Each team should come up with concrete improvement programs that are acceptable to the entire management team and be held accountable for progress throughout implementation.

5. Don't look at the rating scale as a one-time tool. It should be institutionalized as part of the planning process and used repeatedly to measure performance and progress and to determine whether and where further improvements are needed.

ROLE OF TRAINING AND MANAGEMENT DEVELOPMENT[1]

In most cases, becoming a more market-driven company requires a fundamental cultural change throughout the organization. As we all know, cultures don't change easily, and it is unlikely that many companies will be able to make the transition entirely on their own. The deficiencies that typically surface on the rating scale are deeply entrenched in the organization, and the attitudes of many people must be changed before meaningful improvements can be made.

Since our business environment has become increasingly turbulent, managers in any business must continually learn and make good decisions

---

1. The remainder of this chapter was developed by Dr. Jim Hlavacek who has over 25 years of experience in designing and presenting market-driven workshops for cross-functional business teams. As he sees it, many companies fail to implement the concepts described in the preceding chapters if they don't embark on training their people. The remainer of this chapter was intentionally written as a strong wake-up call for companies that are committed to significantly changing their people and implementing these concepts.

much faster if their organization is to survive and prosper. Market-driven management is a proven concept to help managers succeed with increased turbulence. We defined market-driven management around 14 factors that help a cross-functional business team identify their weaknesses and areas for improvement. However, the task of overcoming the identified weaknesses usually requires major cultural changes throughout the organization.

CULTURAL CHANGES

Basically, most people don't like change. Because the necessary changes are always difficult to bring about, I have written this section as a "how to" on changing your culture with high impact training.

Several comments from managers who understand the importance of becoming more market driven, but are frustrated by their inability to make the changes that are necessary on their own, reflect the magnitude of the problem. The following statements from top management describe the common dissatisfaction at many organizations before a market-driven transformation occurred:

> Many of our upper-level executives still operate as though nothing has changed. They haven't accepted the realities of our markets, and a sense of urgency is nonexistent. Unfortunately some come from the old school of intimidation, command, and control.

> Middle management inhibits the new ideas, changing priorities, and new directions that market-driven management implies. Some of our managers are fossils when it comes to developing and implementing strategies with cross-functional business teams.

> Some of our business unit managers and their people act more like functional bureaucrats than decision makers and profit-minded businesspeople.

> Executive speeches or slogans are not substitutes for reprogramming outdated and often autocratic managers at any level. Many of our managers are unable to break out of their technical or sales-driven mind-sets.

These statements describe the Herculean challenge to make a company more market driven. Furthermore, there are some fundamental hurdles to overcome and avoid before the actual transformation can begin.

SHORT-TERM AMERICA

It typically takes at least two to three years of training to change a company culture from being product, manufacturing, or sales driven to one that is market driven. In large and old organizations, the transformation process may require three to four years of extensive training, and, in some cases, personnel changes eventually have to be made. Unfortunately, too few publicly held American companies strike a healthy balance between the short and long term. Said another way, too many U.S. companies are obsessed with quarterly earnings and the daily stock price.

Most of the practices described in the previous chapters will not get implemented in an organization unless it embarks on an intensive and long-term training program of many people. Since training, like R&D, is a long-term investment that doesn't immediately improve bottom-line profit, it is often neglected. Training is the software that makes companies work smarter. As long as training is perceived by top management as a short-term expense and not a long-term investment, the company's software will always be outdated and the potential of their people will never be realized.

The short-term emphasis in America causes executives to look for quick fixes or "silver bullets," which they mistakenly believe will instantly change people's attitudes, knowledge, and behavior. Business schools, headhunters, and consultants are three common quick fixes that U.S. managers seek out, but that usually fail to help make their companies more market driven.

The Business School Fix

Organizations in every industry have a tendency to turn to what they consider centers of academic excellence and then graft the needed knowledge onto their organization. A physician turns to medical schools and teaching hospitals for practical state-of-the-art help in a specialty. If someone is deficient in an area of engineering, they turn to the specialists in engineering schools that can help. When industrial marketing help is needed, some companies logically turn to business schools for courses and to faculty members for seminars. Many hire business school graduates to bring practical and state-of-the-art industrial marketing expertise to their company.

Unfortunately, when companies turn to business schools, they find that most of the faculty and students have little or no industrial marketing background. If the faculty know anything about real-world marketing, it consists of a lot of household goods examples and retailing principles that have little or no application to industrial companies. Bob Jasse, the founder and builder of Chomerics, the high-tech Electro Magnetic Interference shielding manufacturer on Boston's high-tech Route 128, sums up the barren desert at even the most prestigious business schools when it comes to practical and current industrial marketing expertise.

Chomerics pioneered a technology that required developing new industry standards; getting specified by users all over the world; hiring, training, and motivating the right people; and focusing business units and sales and application teams on clearly defined industrial market segments. Our rapid growth was dependent upon having the right people in the right places and at the right time. I felt more confident when hiring chemists and engineers, but had no idea what to look for when promoting or hiring industrial marketing people. My MBA degree in marketing from a well-known business school in Pennsylvania was useless to build this $50 million industrial business to a market value of over $105 million. All of their marketing courses were geared to staff jobs for consumer marketing of pantyhose, diapers, and Coke.

The majority of marketing professors have never worked full time in a for-profit organization, and even fewer have ever worked at an industrial firm. The few that have worked in industrial firms often had limited staff jobs or bad experiences and retreated to academia. Many who failed in business went to academia, which only reinforces the adage, "Those that can, do, and those that can't, teach."

Tenure and a lack of hands-on experience are at the heart of why business schools largely ignore the needs of industrial marketers. Life-long tenure, which exists at all public and private business schools, typically begins at the age of 35 and lasts until declared retirement or death. During the 35 years most faculty have tenure, there is minimal accountability. Tenure, like a closed-shop trade union, discourages learning about a new field such as industrial marketing, which also requires hands-on experience. Therefore, the cycle of emphasizing retail marketing over industrial marketing will never be broken as long as faculty have tenure, which often eliminates any need to learn about state-of-the-art industrial marketing and retool.

It is no wonder that the people coming out of most business schools and entering industrial businesses are unprepared to solve the complex industrial marketing problems companies face today. Sending people to evening or weekend executive MBA programs, or a week-long university program, won't do much for the industrial company since many students in these courses have much more experience than the consumer goods–oriented and limited-background instructor at the front of the class. When I conduct workshops for Japanese and German industrial companies all over the world, their leaders proudly remind me they have no business schools in Japan or Germany. Do the Japanese and German business leaders, who are often global powerhouses, know something that executives in many other countries don't? Phil Hofmann, who was the former CEO of Johnson & Johnson during ten years of J&J's greatest global growth, described why Japan and Germany have no business schools:

Many Japanese companies realize that the best business schools are the great corporations that consistently perform well. Two of the many concepts that the Japanese brought to management practice, benchmarking and continuous improvement or *kaizen,* are based upon learning from the great for profit corporations, not the business schools. The German emphasis on technical knowledge and the hands-on apprenticeship orientation flies in the face of the business school belief that you can be a good general manager of anything in a few weeks. Frankly, for Johnson & Johnson's more technical businesses, we have not been terribly impressed with the impatience, arrogance and shallowness of many business school MBAs when we needed sound industrial marketing know-how. In these businesses, a passionate understanding of customers, competition and the technologies is mandatory before you can make any sound decision.

The Headhunter Fix

Some companies spend millions of dollars on placement recruiters, or headhunters, each year in a futile attempt to improve their industrial marketing capabilities. These same companies usually spend far more on headhunters every year than they do on training their own people and are rarely the high-performing companies that practice promotion from within. While headhunters can sometimes be helpful in finding the right person for a specific job, the basic assumption that they can be used in lieu of providing industrial marketing training is far off base. We are concerned about the imports' knowledge of the industry and their industrial marketing skills.

Many headhunters claim that the hands-on and intimate knowledge of a given industry is not important. They claim a bright person can be a "quick study" and can rapidly learn any business. This may be true in a consumer goods business that is heavily dependent upon common advertising decisions. Industrial firms don't hire marketing and profit-center managers from advertising agencies, as often happens in consumer goods companies for their "brand" managers. I don't know of any industrial companies that have brand managers. We contend that it takes years, not months, to learn about any industrial business. No one can simply parachute into an industrial company and instantly know its business, products, technology, customers' needs, and how to develop winning strategies. The need for in-depth knowledge of the industry and industrial marketing skills applies to any competent business unit, product, or market manager.

When companies go outside and hire people for their marketing expertise from unrelated industries through headhunters, they have usually failed to invest in developing their own people. There are some exceptions: for example, a supplier may carefully hire someone from his customer base to get closer to certain market segments. In a few situations, the company may be growing so fast that they may have to go outside to supplement their promotion-within policy. In contrast, consider rapidly growing great companies such as Hewlett-Packard and Johnson & Johnson. For decades they have had an informal rule that before any profit-center manager is promoted, there must be an identified and qualified successor. This policy has made managers at all levels think first and foremost of their people's skills, deficiencies, and training needs. Hewlett-Packard and Johnson & Johnson don't apply succession planning only to finding the next CEO; they apply it to every line or operating position in the company. Furthermore, they don't always replace the profit-center manager with a clone of the previous manager. They identify and groom people with the right skills for each situation. Leading companies grow nearly all their people from within. Great companies rarely go outside the organization for profit-center management jobs. To go outside is seen as a major failure of upper management.

In great companies, top executives view themselves as personnel managers and realize that their primary job is to place the right people in the right jobs at the right time and with the right skills. These few companies spend many days every month discussing their people, assessing their ability to be promoted, and determining what kinds of training they need. Bob Hennessy, vice president of human resources at well-run National Starch and Chemical, says it well:

> All of our senior executives see themselves as talent scouts. They are constantly assessing people's needs and areas for improving their deficiencies. As a result of this nonstop work, we try very hard to have future managers ready for broader responsibilities. Every manager at National Starch knows that in order to continue our excellent record, we must have competent and highly skilled professionals in place and cadres of people in various stages of development. Our senior executives and general managers spend at least 20 percent to 25 percent of their time on questions of management readiness and development.

The Consultant Fix

The third questionable substitute for sound industrial marketing training is the consulting fix, which is often doomed to fail for one simple reason: Most consultants perform studies; they don't train people in industrial marketing. After thousands and sometimes millions of dollars, the consultant study might point you in the right direction or conclude that "your marketing is weak." In addition to having the same industrial marketing limitations of business school graduates because most management consultants were indoctrinated there, they exhibit additional shortcomings.

Many industrial companies find that industrial marketing consultants spout canned and simplistic "raise prices, cut costs, or sell the business" strategies. The canned solutions also tend to be "one size fits all." Unfortunately, the consultants aren't the ones who have to live with the decisions they recommend, even if the decisions are wrong or lead to a even worse state of affairs. Few consultants have the industrial marketing knowledge base and executive teaching skills to spend days leading a workshop with a room full of experienced managers asking specific "how to" questions.

Once a consulting firm's senior partner snags a job, they usually send in young and inexperienced MBAs, straight out of business school, who have little depth in industrial marketing. Rarely do senior partners dive in and get their hands dirty. The senior partners reappear to sell the follow-on studies. The CEO of ABB, the Swiss-based $40 billion industrial manufacturer and former major consulting firm partner, says this about industrial marketing consultants:

> If you want a good business decision, you don't want a superficial consultant to tell you how to run it. They will mess it up for you. We don't use consultants. If someone in our company says they want a consultant, I ask them five questions:
>
> Do you have a clear idea of precisely what you want done?
> Why that consultant?
> What has he done lately that will help us?
> Will he bring in inexperienced MBAs right behind him?
> Can you use him to train our people or train our trainers?
>
> If they can't clearly answer these questions, I say no. I might let them pick a consultant to do a very specific and tightly defined task. But few can ever meet the test of these questions, so we usually stay away from consultants.[2]

A major difference between management consultants and management trainers goes back to the hackneyed, but true, idea about the difference between just giving someone a fish versus giving someone a fishing pole and training him or her how to use it. Hiring the industrial marketing consultant or broad-brush strategy consultant who does not train a company's people to analyze, develop, and implement sound product, market, and key account strategies is like dropping a big sack of money (often millions) down a large rat hole.

After failing to transform the industrial organization with consultant studies, consumer goods MBAs, and outside hires from headhunters, the top management often embark on one or a number of mediocre training

---

2. *Swiss Air In Flight Magazine,* August 1995.

programs for their employees. Let's examine some of these training approaches that usually continue to waste shareholder money.

WASTED TRAINING APPROACHES

When top management finally decides that marketing training is needed, they call on their people in either human resources, sales training, or sales management to "make our marketing stronger!" The elitist, perk, SOS, and train-the-salespeople approaches are common knee-jerk reactions to filling the huge industrial marketing voids spotted by top management.

Elitist

A small number of fast-track, rising star employees are sent to big-name college campus training programs for weeks or even months. They never attend programs as a cross-functional business team with an existing problem they all face. They return to their companies from college campuses with many approaches that don't address their companies' current needs. In the event that some of the approaches can be applied, they encounter resistance from upper management or coworkers when they try to implement the changes. These bright, impatient, and elite employees quickly see glass ceilings and glass walls all around them. The more ambitious ones leave the organization for greener pastures—and often go to competitive companies, where they are the most marketable. These elite and fast-track employees help create a "we and they" attitude throughout the company.

No follow-up evaluations are conducted to see if there was any positive or negative effect on job performance once the employee returned to the office. The era of sending managers off one by one to a bucolic college campus to read and answer generalized case studies should be reevaluated because it usually only adds a line to the elite employee's resume. This training approach often does more harm than good to the organization.

Perk

In good economic times, employees are allowed to attend public programs; even if any in-house training is offered, it is quickly turned off like a faucet in soft economic times. Many employees perceive these programs as a free company benefit or time to rest and dream. Upper management sees these programs as a benefit for employees, like the company picnic and a free Christmas turkey. People attend the programs on a random basis without cross-functional representation from their business unit. They don't bring real problems with them to discuss at the workshop. Very few of the new approaches later get discussed back on the job, and even fewer get implemented in the business units.

Most evening and weekend college courses in marketing for which the employer reimburses the employee, with no questions asked, also fit into this category. The company has no control over the content and practical value of such programs. If these programs are conducted by universities, they usually have all the limitations of the "business school fix" previously discussed. These same companies usually see training as a means of perpetuating their old ways. The companies then brag about the number of people that have attended over the years, but no one ever asks, "What has been the impact?" Follow-up evaluations are never conducted. Any training that resembles this smorgasbord approach should be ended in both good and slow times.

SOS

Many companies that consistently underperform see training programs as a quick fix or silver bullet for their major deficiencies. These naive and often desperate companies usually take a "theme of the month" or "flavor of the week" approach to training programs. They quickly jump from one faddish program to another. One employee at a large compressor and construction equipment company told me:

> We are again reading simultaneously out of three different management bibles, and the way we jump from one program to another, it's not surprising that we are known for mediocre results. We don't stay with any program long enough to really make it stick.

Such companies are forever catching up, and usually never go anywhere, because they do not understand the longer-term development role of training programs. The impact of training programs at these companies is usually too little and too late. When these companies uncover some budget money for training or when the CEO mandates training, they think they're doing "just in time" training when it is usually decades too late.

For example, the new CEO of a well-known conglomerate in the aerospace, automotive, and chemical business requested a series of one-day sessions to help his people rapidly grow the company. When he was advised that his company required several four- to five-day sessions to change the attitudes and behavior of dozens of cross-functional teams, he reverted to more short-term downsizing and sold off more of the underperforming businesses. The CEO eventually found some people to conduct his mandatory one-day events on various marketing topics, which jokingly became known as "birdbath feeding sessions for the survivors on the Titanic."

Train the Salespeople

In companies using this approach, top management doesn't realize that industrial marketing is first the general manager's or profit manager's role and then every department's responsibility for implementation; it is never the job of just the sales or marketing department. A closer look at these companies reveals that most CEOs and upper management incorrectly see industrial marketing as a subset of sales, and the even less informed CEOs perceive industrial marketing as largely sales promotion.

Many people with marketing titles are professional salespeople with the word "marketing" added to their title, and then they are vice president of sales and marketing. When they learn a little about industrial marketing, they reverse the words "sales" and "marketing" in their title. These salespeople are instructed by the CEO to get stronger in marketing, as was the case at a major chemicals and air products company. When the CEO compared the profitability in their chemicals group to their old-line gas businesses, he became disenchanted and ordered the gases group to improve their marketing with training. The gases group saw marketing as advertising, deal making, and aggressive selling for the salespeople. The top and general managers in the gas group had no idea that marketing was a general management and cross-functional responsibility. The general managers, engineering, manufacturing, and finance people were not seen as part of the needed industrial marketing transformation. Their sales training department, which was totally inexperienced in management development, sent all the sales and "marketing" people to an off-site academic program that emphasized an esoteric computer model of an unrelated industry. They returned to the workplace with a lot of keyboard typing experience from the course and joked that the warm chocolate chip cookies were the big highlight of each day. The company wasted more than $250,000 on a program that was doomed from the beginning. The ineffective training program contributed to the declining credibility of management in this underperforming area of the company.

These wasted approaches to industrial marketing training should be replaced with hard-hitting, high-impact in-house programs. Let's now see why the trend toward sound in-house programs is accelerating and how committed companies support and implement a market-driven change process with well-conceived training workshops.

TRENDS IN MANAGEMENT TRAINING

An extensive study in the United Kingdom revealed that there is a major trend across the globe to move toward using experts for management learning rather than the academically driven business schools.[3] A landmark study of management education interviewed more than 200 U.S. corporations that were recognized as very active in supporting management development activities. CEOs, senior executives, general managers, and vice presidents of human resources were interviewed. Porter's respected study is excerpted here:

> The fastest growing source of management development education is comprised of independent individuals who spend most of their time developing and presenting customized in-house workshops. They are full-time trainers, not B-school academics moonlighting between classes and university vacations. Most of these people have had full-time industry experience in their specialty. They have perfected excellent presentation skills with a constant and wide array of managerial audiences. A major advantage of these independent providers is that they are working with a wide number of companies at any one time. This advantage results in two major benefits. First, it keeps their programs very practical or "how to" oriented. Secondly, their exposure to many different companies, cultures, and practices allows them to develop training materials and examples from the very best approaches.
>
> Because these independent suppliers are so specialized in their full-time training, they usually have greater knowledge beyond that typically found on a university campus where they are not constantly engaged and challenged by practicing managers in their field. These third-party or external providers are able to continually see, experience, and try different executive education formats and facilitator approaches. Their workshop materials and workbooks are usually very concise, instructional, and professionally packaged. In other words, they are usually expert at developing, conducting, and "putting on" well-organized, current, and practical management development workshops.
>
> Most CEOs, upper management, and VPs of human resources stated to us that they will significantly increase their use of these independent niche providers in the future. These corporate buyers stated that the independent suppliers offered a level of expertise unobtainable elsewhere. Our interviewers and data all indicate that the independent or external providers of management development programs will gain an increasing share of the continuing executive education market. They have made great in-roads into executive education, and we see nothing on the horizon to reverse or even slow up this strong trend.[4]

3. "Business Schools Need to Learn," *EuroBusiness*, February 1996, pp. 46–50.
4. Lyman Porter, *Management Education and Development: Drift or Thrust into the 21st Century* (New York: McGraw-Hill, 1990).

The Porter study on management training trends can be summarized in four key points:

1. Companies are participating less in university business school training programs that are mostly a rehash of MBA programs.

2. Companies are demanding that management training workshops be conducted by highly experienced, practical, respected, and cutting-edge full-time trainers.

3. Companies are engaging market niche trainers who will do a needs analysis and tailor a workshop to their industry, cross-functional team needs, and company situations.

4. Company top management is taking a proactive role in demanding practical training and is highly supportive of and engaged in making the long-term training process a success.

I firmly support Porter's conclusion that well-developed and implemented in-house programs are the best way to go. They are cost effective for large, medium, and even smaller sized firms. Using Porter's study as a building block, let's now see what progressive companies do to train their people and make their organizations more market-driven.

Role of Top Management

Peter Drucker said, "The first and most important job of management is training."[5] We reaffirm Drucker's point and stress that management development and training sponsored and firmly supported by top management is the catalyst for implementing market-driven management practices in any organization. Unfortunately, most industrial manufacturers spend too little time and not enough funds on management training. The few that do spend money on marketing and management training waste most of it on esoteric, quick fix, or elitist programs. However, there is a small and growing number of high-performance industrial companies that have embarked on training to make the marketing department encompass the whole company and thus are becoming market driven. Their top management is always involved in the process.

Far too few CEOs and upper management see the nonstop learning of managers as their responsibility. Even fewer senior executives realize that management training is the only way to really change and improve the culture up, down, and across a large organization. At the end of the day, every company's competitive strength rests within its people. How

---

5. Peter Drucker, *The Wall Street Journal*, July 28, 1987, p. 23.

competitive and financially successful a business is ultimately depends on the climate that top managers create for their people to learn, experiment, and try new ways of doing things.

The majority of top management personnel in U.S. industrial companies turn management training on and off (mostly off) like an occasional advertising campaign. Ask most CEOs and upper management what they spend yearly on management training and they will look down and murmur, "Very little," "Not enough," or "Spotty." The annual amount spent on training is so small they often can't even begin to calculate it. When business slows, training programs are quickly terminated when, in fact, training, like plant maintenance, should be increased in slow times because the opportunity cost is less. The upper management in these companies does not realize that management training is constant and is the basis for our fifth market-driven C—continual improvements. Therefore it's not surprising that we hear the following comments in some lagging companies:

> We don't spend money on training because many people only leave and join a competitor. We stopped training the enemy 10 years ago.

> Since we can't measure the immediate results of training on the bottom line, why bother with it?

> We believe in informal self-learning rather than formalized instruction.

> We never budget for this because we see it as a luxury and something we can only do in good times—which we haven't had for some time.

> We used to send people off to all sorts of training programs, and they'd come back all charged up with new ideas of how things should be and try to change things, which they couldn't.

Great Companies

Unlike the companies just discussed, which don't understand the need and role of training, progressive companies invest in industrial marketing workshops tailored to their industry- and company-specific needs. People usually attend the workshops in natural cross-functional work teams. Each company's cross-functional teams bring real situations and information to the workshop. A major by-product of these workshops is the team-building experience from working in cross-functional teams, on a real company situation. There is extensive prereading and prework involving the participants' company before they arrive at the workshop. The few smart companies that engage in this type of training and development see it as the foundation for continual improvements and a means of sustaining their existing success. These hallmark companies encourage people to break out of their mind-sets, to question everything, and to have an open mind toward proven industrial marketing approaches used throughout the world. They see themselves as a good company, but never the best, and believe they must continually improve by learning better approaches. They are never satisfied with their results. Arrogance and complacency are not tolerated in these companies. They see two kinds of companies—the smart ones and the dead ones. Sealed Air, National Starch, Unilever, 3M, Parker Hannifin, and Hewlett-Packard are clearly in a special category in which they see practical training as a nonstop process that helps their organizations work smarter.

Top Management Commitment

For any successful market-driven training program, top management must be totally committed to the program. Like the quality movement, top management has to be behind the training to make it happen. Memos, mandates, pep talks, and even threats will never substitute for training people to work smarter around the industrial marketing concept. Upper and top managers must realize that training is one of the few ways they have to really change the people or the culture. As a good example, at the kickoff of each industrial marketing training workshop for Unilever's industrial companies, their chairman, Dr. Ian Anderson, often states:

> You have no idea how little influence I have here. Training is the only way we can continually move ourselves to the forefront of practice and results. With just one better decision, we will get the investment back from this workshop. If you think of this workshop as an expense—just try ignorance as an alternative.

Dr. Anderson not only understands what a learning corporation is, he realizes it must occur at all levels, and especially with the people that are the closest to the products, customers, laboratories, and plants. Decentralized and very global Unilever Industrial provides information, tools, authority, and accountability to their greatest asset—their people—who then manage close to the customer.

The power of a high-impact training program on a global organization can be enormous. After conducting market-driven management training sessions for more than 400 people at the Cabot Corporation in the Americas, Europe, and Asia, their CEO, Dr. Sam Bodman, said:

> This market-driven management is seen as such a practical and powerful process throughout our organization that I doubt I could stop it if I wanted to. The training has created a common language, some common values, and more sharing between our business units across the globe.

To be a continuously outstanding business unit, a company must be open to changing anything, even some of the company's basic beliefs if they are out of alignment with the realities of today's customers and global competition. Top or general management that have tried to change a strong culture know that it is easy to talk about what should be done but far harder to get people to shed their inward-looking focus and historical approaches that no longer work. In companies that we work with in an effort to improve their market-driven capabilities, there are often decades of old culture to change. Because industrial marketing is not one department but the whole company, cross-functional teams must be involved in real issues at the workshop, and then they must immediately apply the better practices learned at the workshop to support the old training point, "You must use it or you will lose it."

There are six top management "musts" to make in-house market-driven management training successful. They are as follows:

1. Top management must see training as a way to maintain high performance over the long term and as a way to change the culture.

2. Top management must see industrial marketing as a general management or profit-center responsibility and a cross-functional team process, not just as one department or limited to the sales and marketing people.

3. Top management must participate in the needs analysis and open the company up to an outside review of their marketing and management practices.

4. Top management must participate in an executive overview or, ideally, experience the entire workshop.

5. Top management must be part of the opening and especially the ending of each workshop session, where each cross-functional team's presentation about the company's product line, market segment, or key account strategy is reviewed.

6. Top and general management must become partners with the workshop leader before and after the pilot session and during the entire training transformation process.

The workshop leader must team up with top and general managers to create change. Top management and people lower in the organization are usually very eager to consider and embrace the new ways. The source of greatest resistance is often middle and department managers and some of the salespeople masquerading behind marketing titles. Their lukewarm support, resistance, or even sabotage is embedded in the possibility of losing respect, power, status, and (ultimately) their jobs. There will always be people who mourn the good old days and old ways, but when you want people trained to be more competitive today and tomorrow, they cannot drive an organization into the future with both eyes on their rearview mirrors. Top management must change these people with training and new business processes, or else they must eventually make personnel changes. Ken Burns, the president and chief operating officer of Cabot Corporation, a $2+ billion specialty chemical company, said it well at the beginning of each market-driven management workshop we conducted for his company at each of its global locations:

> The purpose of this training investment is to increase the intellectual knowhow and change our people. You will find this workshop interesting, challenging, practical, and fun. However, if this training doesn't change all the people, we will then change some of the people.

False Starts

Most industrial companies have good intentions when they start customized in-house training. Unfortunately, a large percentage, probably more than half of the $15 billion U.S. firms spend annually on executive education, is wasted and that includes many in-house programs. Far too often companies sponsor in-house programs with little linkage to the individual's or company's needs. Furthermore, rarely is an attempt made to follow up and determine if the program was of value back on the job.

Parker Hannifin, a $4 billion manufacturer of motion control systems and components, embarked on an ambitious executive training program with a large university in Michigan. After three groups of managers completed the program, Parker Hannifin canceled it when employees found it off base, slow moving, and mainly just a lot of canned and warmed-over MBA material. Parker has since elected to work closely and long term with full-time management trainers who know their company and who develop Parker case studies around their products, markets, and company needs. Pat Parker, the chairman, summed up the situation:

> We are a very decentralized company with about 90 little PT boats led by general managers and their business teams. If the general managers and their business teams don't see the practical value of any training program, we at corporate headquarters will not continue to sponsor it.

In contrast to Parker Hannifin's sound approach to industrial marketing training, a paper manufacturer has for years been bringing in 20-year-old business school cases and semiretired college teachers to their corporate training center for a two-week session. One of the general managers who attended said:

> This is just another "event of the month" training program—if we wait long enough, this event, like all the others, will go away. You can hide in the case study groups that just B.S. about the old and unrelated case studies. I do a lot of crossword puzzles at our corporate-sponsored training events and play a lot of cards or pool in the evenings. The human resources people always complain about our bar bills.

Many entry-level and important basic training needs such as selling skills, effective presentations, and negotiation and listening skills can usually be done cost effectively and in-house by a company's own people. For example, John O'Rourke, director of training at National Starch and Chemical, who personally conducts (not just administers) face-to-face selling skills, value selling, and negotiating skills workshops around the world, stated:

> Training and development at National Starch is a permanent process that occurs during lean as well as prosperous times. We conduct over 30 different in-house training programs that address our practical needs. We do not cover the short-lived management fads and fashions we often see advertised.

On the other hand, National Starch also realizes that middle and upper management education is usually best done with outside help because of the specialized expertise and cutting-edge content needed from other companies' best practices. For decades IBM's own people did most of their in-house executive education. Unfortunately, IBM was reinforcing their own culture when they needed to be changing their culture by changing their people with challenging training. They wasted millions of dollars on management development programs every year. The main deficiency of using your own instructors for a change program is that they inevitably overemphasize the current way of doing things within your organization. Sound management training helps reinforce what is good about your culture while it forces people to ask how the company should improve and continually evolve. Every management training program must cause people to think outside of how things are currently done. The training should break down the resistance to changing the old ways that no longer work well, and it must show people how to work smarter.

Practical industrial marketing training creates a thirst for continual learning and sharing better business practices within your company and from other industrial companies. High-impact in-house training is the catalyst and glue for becoming and staying market driven by learning how to adapt to a faster-moving environment.

High-Impact Training

Leading companies are increasingly searching for practical and customized industrial marketing training programs that address the needs of their cross-functional business teams. Many Japanese companies have worked at this for years. Their nonstop investment in in-house training programs makes many U.S. and European firms look pale. Training allowed the Japanese to learn about quality while the rest of the world was napping. In Japanese, *kaizen* means unending improvement, doing things better, and setting and achieving even higher standards—and it can't be done without an open mind and a willingness to continually learn.

When top and upper management take a proactive role in the development, support, and funding of practical industrial marketing training for cross-functional business teams (never for just the sales and marketing people), it is off to a good start. Assuming that top management know their supportive role and real commitment to make the organization more market driven with training, there are eight key implementation steps to follow:

1. *The workshop leader.* Before embarking on any training effort, it is wise to spend considerable time identifying the person who will design, develop, and present the workshops in your company. Don't allow any hand-offs, which is the approach most consulting firms take with their clients—after the senior guy sells the job, the junior associates do the rest. This one person will provide continuity and must be very knowledgeable about your organization. Don't just blindly engage a name brand organization or institution and accept whoever appears on your corporate doorstep. Engage the most qualified person (regardless of the person's affiliation), who will do the work, become very knowledgeable about your company, and be willing and able to become a long-term partner with the top and general management in your company.

You should also choose the person with the greatest practical and current industrial marketing expertise. Look for some previous full-time industrial marketing line experience in the workshop leader's background. Ask for and thoroughly check out the workshop leader's current and former industrial training clients and references from general managers with whom he or she worked closely. If the prospective workshop leader has written any industrial marketing articles or books, ask for copies and review them for their practical or how-to value. The chosen person must also have excellent executive workshop skills. If the candidate does not meet the litmus tests of being practical, current, and dynamic, do not engage the person.

2. *The needs analysis.* Once you have identified the best possible person to be your workshop leader, have him or her sign a confidentiality statement. Then open up the organization for the needs analysis. By asking many questions—including how you plan, identify trends, develop and launch new products, set prices, organize and pay sales people, evaluate competitors, and use cost-profit information—an experienced industrial marketing workshop leader can quickly identify common market-driven deficiencies in any organization. Before conducting any face-to-face or telephone interviews, the workshop leader should review your business plans, sales literature, and any former studies and internal documents. Invite the workshop leader to sit in on business planning and review meetings. In the needs analysis, people should be interviewed from all functions, not just sales and marketing. People at different levels must also be interviewed. As a result of reading company documents, asking the right interview questions, and listening aggressively, a competent workshop leader will develop a fairly clear picture of your organization's common needs. If the workshop leader is unwilling or unable to conduct such a needs analysis, rethink your choice of workshop leader.

3. *Program development.* The next step in the process is to select the program topics and develop the workbook for the in-house program. Typically, 60 percent to 70 percent of any industrial marketing training firm's topics and workbooks are already developed. Furthermore, a leading-edge workshop leader is constantly learning and updating 20 percent to 30 percent of the material every year. The leading industrial marketing trainers have separate topics and workbooks for chemical and material firms, for component parts manufacturers, and for equipment manufacturers because the marketing approaches are significantly different in these businesses. The workshop leader then configures the workshop and workbook to your industry's and company's needs. The program development should result in a workbook for each participant of all the workshop leader's materials used and shown at the workshop. The workbook should serve as a future reference manual for each participant. A program should be developed for three to five days of intensive training around your current needs and real-life problems. If a training program is less than three days, significant attitude change isn't likely to occur.

4. *Company case studies.* Some companies develop small and very focused case studies around common problems in their company. Company-specific case studies help address the needs analysis, they significantly increase participant involvement and retention, and they help the workshop leader learn about your technologies, markets, and company culture. Seasoned managers like their own company case studies because it allows them to analyze, discuss, and solve real issues in their business.

Company cases help people see the common weaknesses in their organization. Sensitive market, customer, and cost-profit information must be shown within each case study. These confidential cases are the intellectual property of the company and should be treated as such by the participants.

The Cabot Chemical Corporation is a 115-year-old Boston landmark. When the company wanted to improve its marketing prowess in 1991, they went down the street to a well-known Boston business school. When the professors made canned pitches for Cabot's industrial marketing training business, the general managers were unimpressed. The general manager of one of Cabot's high-performance chemical businesses said:

> The somewhat arrogant faculty only wanted to use their dated MBA cases about marketing chain saws, motorcycles, and Odor Eater shoe inserts. We are an industrial materials supplier that makes and sells 200 different grades of carbon black into the tire, ink, paint, plastics, and copier toner markets. They didn't understand our industrial business, and no one wanted to or had the time to learn about our marketing needs. One very experienced industrial marketing trainer, with extensive experience in the chemical industry, first did an analysis of our marketing needs throughout the Cabot Corporation. He then developed Cabot case studies and presented workshops to many cross-functional business teams in North America, Europe, and Asia. The case studies, frameworks, and approaches used at the workshops have had a tremendous impact on our marketing attitudes, skills, and business planning approaches across the globe.

5. *Workshop preparation.* For every one day of workshop time, there should be about one-half day of individual prereadings and questions about their company practices before participants arrive at the industrial marketing workshop. Therefore, for a four-day training workshop, each participant should have at least two full days of preparation before they arrive. Advance preparation by each participant achieves many objectives. The advance reading and study questions enable each cross-functional team member to have a fairly clear understanding of what the workshop is all about. Next, it lets each participant think about the business unit's current practices and deficiencies. Furthermore, in situations where English is the second or third language of the participants, advance preparation is a major need. Finally, the advance preparation allows the participants to arrive with a closer "band of common understanding," regardless of their functional background and previous length of experience.

6. *Target audiences.* The basic audience for any market-driven training workshop includes the natural cross-functional business teams responsible for developing a focused business plan, developing a new product or market, or having responsibility for a major customer. A core of two to three people should be close to the company situation, which the five- to seven-member cross-functional team will then attack, defend, de-emphasize, or withdraw from. The key functions (technical, manufacturing, sales, and finance) should be represented on each team. No workshop or team should ever consist of or be dominated by only sales and marketing people. If only the sales and marketing people attend, the necessary cross-functional input, give and take, and integrated implementation programs will be lacking. Training with people from different disciplines is a key way to improve our sixth C, working in cross-functional business teams.

The top management of the company should be exposed to either an executive overview of the workshop, or they should participate in the full fledged three- to five-day workshop. Future workshop sessions should move down and across the entire organization. To maintain the dialog and the give-and-take of a workshop (not just a lecture that does nothing to encourage adults to share experiences), each session should have no more than 24 people, and the size of each cross-functional team should be five to seven people.

7. *Live company problems.* Each cross-functional business team must come with information about a real product, customer, market segment, or situation for which the team is currently facing a decision to defend, attack, de-emphasize, or withdraw. Templates used during the workshop will help each team understand and frame the specific information needed. At the end of the workshop, each cross-functional team should develop and present a preliminary strategy and business plan for the situation it brought to the workshop. This training process builds upon the premise that you must put it to work or lose it when it comes to remembering materials from a workshop. And since all the cross-functional teams make presentations about their real situation at the end of the workshop, there is healthy peer-group pressure and peer-group learning when this process is repeated as each team uses the same framework in their presentations. When the teams know upper management will be present at the presentations, there is even more peer-group pressure to learn throughout the workshop and excel in the final presentations.

8. *Workshop outcomes.* Every workshop should immediately be evaluated at the end and then again six months to one year later. If only the immediate outcome or "applause meter" evaluation is done, a company may never know the more important longer-term impact. The follow-up results are measured by determining if many of the frameworks, concepts, and approaches are being widely used by the participants when they return to their work environment. As senior executives visit various

operating units, they should inquire about the practical value of the workshop from past attendees. Follow-up measurements should be taken to see if a common market-driven language is evolving throughout the organization and to determine if some of the frameworks are being used. Longer term, some of the frameworks used in the workshop should be incorporated into the company's annual business planning process to develop market/product plans. Some companies have all participants write a half- to one-page critique of workshops five or six months after attending to determine the practical value of the workshops and to see if there are problems implementing the approaches in their work environment. There is always the risk that when people return to their jobs, the daily pressures in an operating unit will drive out the time needed to put the better practices to work. In short, urgent pressures often drive out doing the important things. Tom Strouble, an officer at The Timken Company, ended each in-house market-driven management workshop with the following statement:

> How will you *find time* to do many of the very practical approaches you learned at this workshop? If they are practical and useful approaches, you and your associates will *make time* to use them when you return to your work environment.

PARTNERSHIPS WITH YOUR EMPLOYEES

There may never again be life-long job security in most companies. However, as long as a person is cost effectively adding value to the organization, job security will probably exist. Training is key to remaining a value-added employee. Today, anyone who wants to keep a job must be continually updated in that job and be prepared before being given wider responsibilities. Even if the person goes to another company, training is necessary in order to be employable elsewhere.

As industrial marketing knowledge and skills become antiquated at a faster rate, smart companies realize they have no choice but to invest more in training their cross-functional business teams. There are no quick fixes for continually developing and updating your people. Hiring bright or smart people is never enough. High graduate entrance exam scores and degrees from prestigious universities are never substitutes for working smarter and more efficiently and for continually learning practical new industrial marketing approaches. There is no one more stupid than a bright person with little or no common sense—and the best industrial marketing practices make a lot of common sense; unfortunately they are not always commonly known or practiced.

Unless more companies begin to treat employees as vital assets to be developed rather than just costs or head counts, they will probably not remain competitive in the long term. The industrial world is not a steady state. User needs are changing more frequently. Global competitors are constantly on the prowl for your customers. Markets fluctuate and technologies continue to change in even the most mature industrial markets. The longer any industrial manufacturer rests on its laurels, self- and public praise, and outdated management practices, the more likely it will be to fall behind and never catch up. The industrial firm must constantly learn how to work smarter.

SUMMARY

Clearly, reading about what it takes to create profitable top-line growth by being market-driven and actually doing the things necessary to become market driven are two different things. We have shown how many great companies achieve outstanding top-line results, even in depressed industries, by being more market driven. There have been and always will be many opportunities for these very same great companies to fail during the life of this book. Ever-changing markets and product technologies are capable of breaking any business organization if it is unprepared for change and has not developed the necessary mechanisms for anticipating and responding to change. Organizations that are truly market driven don't just react to the future; they create it by working smarter.

Many industrial companies in Europe and Asia invest significantly more in training per employee than many U.S. companies. Managers in these countries don't just pay lip service to the value of employees. Festo, the German-based world leader in the design and manufacturer of pneumatic and electronic motion control systems, has one of the better in-house training programs for a company of its size. The importance of all types of training for all people at Festo was summarized by the director of the Festo Learning Center:

> We have never been impressed by the content of U.S. and U.K. business schools. We prefer focused short programs of three to five days in length that are run by world experts and that address the practical needs of our experienced managers. The focal point of Festo's training is that it must be practical and tailored to our needs. We have been a world leader in training for over 30 years. Our training center is organized around four areas: technology, computing, software, and management. Most of our management training is done with interdisciplinary or cross-functional teams. The Festo

Learning Center is a modern, two-floor complex with seminar rooms, instructors' offices, a library, and a computer center. With this investment in training, we expect that all of our employees will keep up with the latest ways of doing things and acquire and share the needed information to keep us innovative in technology and management know-how. Only by having constant training can we secure our future. We have now begun to offer many of the Festo training programs to our suppliers and subcontractors. This knowledge and continual learning with employees and suppliers has been and will be a key factor in our success.

Festo's management and employees in their plants, laboratories, and the field echo the sentiments of their training director. Festo's nonstop training has built a real spirit and atmosphere of trust, open-mindedness, and sharing among employees. Self-initiative, creativity, and cross-functional teamwork is very high. Festo is widely recognized around the world as a leader in motion control. Festo, like any company, doesn't do everything well, but it is one of those few industrial companies that realizes that management learning is like rowing against the current in whitewater rapids. As soon as you stop, you will start going backward, and you may never catch up.

INDEX

ABB, 214
Abbott Laboratories, 54, 119
ABC budgeting, 194
Account analysis, 147
Accountability, 7
Accounting practices, 52
Accounting schedules, 160
Accounting schools, 57
Accounting systems, 60, 200
Acquisitions, 88, 93, 112
Activity-based costing approaches, 63
Administrative costs, 5, 58, 60
Administrative expenses, 184
After-market categories, 84
Agreed-upon market priorities, 110
Airborne, 70
Alco Controls, 191
Allaire, Paul, 54
Alternatives. *See* Business situations
    contribution, 173-175
    strategies, 153, 174
Amerace Corporation, 21
AMP, 127
Anderson, Dr. Ian, 221
Andrew Corporation, 168
Apple Computer, 52, 53
Appleton Electric, 191
Application knowledge, 134-135, 175
Assets, 13, 14
Assumed facts, 182
AT&T, 100
Attack, 90, 156, 228
Attitudes, shifting, 94-95
Average costing, 55

Balance sheet, 5, 52, 68
Baldor Electric, 110
Bandag, 89
Bankruptcy, 51
BASF, 76
Bayer, 76
Bedrock fixed costs, 62, 63

Betz Laboratories, 45, 131, 135
Bigness mentality, 81
Black & Decker, 193
BMW, 118
Bodman, Dr. Sam, 221
Boeing, 127
Borch, Fred, 41
Bosch, 193
Bottlenecks, 53, 205
Bottom-line growth, 68
Bottom-line profit, 53
Bottom-up approach, 158
Bottom-up market/product planning, 206
Bottom-up process, 162, 192
Bottom-up sales forecasts, 159
Branch managers, 146
Brand managers, 36, 212
Breakeven point, 12, 56
Broad-based strategy, 83
Broad-brush strategy, 214
Bureaucracy, 26, 205. *See also* Nonprofit
    bureaucracy
Bureaucratic management approaches, 5-7
Bureaucratic organizations, 31
Bureaucratic plan, 172
Burke, Jim, 104
Burns, Ken, 223
Business base, 4
Business conditions, 2
Business cycle, swings, 88
Business economics, 45
Business focus, 46-47
Business objectives, 39
Business plan, 114, 171, 176, 178, 187, 188,
    202
Business planning, 11, 168, 181
    example, 191-194
    importance, 151-152
    pitfalls, 152-162
    process, tailoring, 153-155
    role, 148-149
Business planning consolidation, 151-176

summary, 176
Business results, 1
Business schools, 210-212, 214, 216, 223
Business situations, alternative, 160-162
Business strategy, 17, 37, 59
   foundation, 83-84
Business teams, 179. *See also* Cross-
   functional business teams
   commitment, 190-191
Business unit, 63, 64, 93, 94, 96, 102, 112,
   143, 157, 172, 193, 198, 222. *See also*
   Market-driven business unit
   capabilities, 172
   manager, 15, 44, 77, 91
Buyer-seller process, 121

Cs (6 Cs). *See* Market-driven company
Cabot Corporation, 135, 167, 168, 221, 223,
   227
Call report, 147
Canon, 81
Can't-win strategy, 17
Capabilities, 19, 23
Capacity utilization, 56, 58
Capital expenditure proposals, 67
Capital expenditures, 189
Capital investments, 72
   decisions, 68
Capital spending, 57
Capital structure, 58
Capital use, 70-71
Career ladder. *See* Sales career ladder
Carrying costs, 68
Carver, Marty, 89, 90
Cash, management, 67-68
Cash flow, 52, 71, 169, 189
Cash management, 68
Cash returns, 67
Cash-carrying costs, 67
Cash-flow outlook, 157
Caterpillar, 2, 3, 127
Chevrolet, 118
Chomerics, 107, 108, 210
Chrysler, 119
Claims. *See* Lower-cost claims
Close follower strategy, 59
Codman & Shurtleff, 135
Collins, Duane, 38, 167
Commissions, 142
Commitments, 171, 191

Common ranges, 57-60
Communication options, 145
Companies. *See* Great companies
Company case studies, 226-227
Company culture, 209
Company databases, 136
Company goals, link. *See* Sales
   compensation
Company weakness, 164
Compaq computer, 52, 53, 114, 115, 137-139
Compensation. *See* Sales compensation;
   Seniority-based compensation
   system, 144
Competent people, 43-46
Competitive activity, 88
Competitive advantage, 11, 82, 91, 97, 100
Competitive analysis, 193
Competitive comparisons. *See* Side-by-side
   competitive comparisons
Competitive decay, 60
Competitive edge, 24
Competitive environment, 42
Competitive information, 46
   understanding, 128-130
Competitive intelligence, 198
Competitive offerings, 19
Competitive output, 76
Competitive product. *See* Side-by-side
   competitive product
Competitive statements, 199
Competitiveness, 31
Competitors, 1, 4, 7, 10, 15, 16, 18, 20, 22, 49,
   52, 54, 56, 69, 79, 101, 107, 112, 120, 125,
   142, 165, 199, 201, 203. *See also* Foreign
   competitors
   actions, 158
Complaints, 9, 101
Complex customers, 122-123
Complex products, 122-123
Concept, implementation, 43-47
Consensus agreement, 207
Consultants, 213-214
Consultative salesforce, 121-150
   concerns, 123-124
   special situations, 132-133
   summary, 150
Consultative selling, 122, 147
Consumer goods, 211
   company, 32, 36, 212
   sector, 199

segmentation, 85
Consumer retailing approaches, misuse, 84-85
Contingencies, allowance, 187-188
Contingency planning, 151, 194
Continuous improvement, 19
Controller. *See* Marketing controller
Convergent Technologies, 92
Copier strategy, 59
Cordiner, Ralph, 41
Core managers, 29
Corning Glass, 101
Corporate earnings target, 158
Corporate goals, 157
Corporate planning, market/product planning comparison, 155-156
Corporate profit targets, 165
Corporate strategy, 157-158
Correnti, John, 74
Cost advantages, 183
Cost averaging, 55
Cost categories, 60-63
Cost competitiveness, 55
Cost control, 60
Cost effectiveness, 41
Cost improvement, 37
Cost information. *See* Reordering cost information
Cost projection, 182-185
Cost reduction, 189
    programs, 106
Cost reductions, 55, 201
Cost requirements, 128
Cost structure, 53, 56, 57, 75, 156, 193, 201
Cost targets, 21, 204
Cost-effective solutions, 22, 122
    determination, 126-128
Cost-plus reimbursement industry, 54
Cost-profit components, 57
Cost-profit economics, 43
Cost-profit facts, 57, 162
Cost-profit information, 37
    sharing, 72-74, 141
Cost-profit pictures, 56-68
    improvement, 64-65
Cost-profit structures, 57, 59, 60, 72, 200
Credibility issues. *See* Plans
Crosfields, 135
Cross-functional approach, 39

Cross-functional business planning process, 35
Cross-functional business teams, 23, 46, 47, 113-115, 175, 190, 195, 209, 215, 227-229
Cross-functional business units, 93
Cross-functional buy-in, 175
Cross-functional cooperation, 39-40
Cross-functional discussions, 149, 174
Cross-functional group discussions, 29
Cross-functional input, 206
Cross-functional linkages, 105, 171-172
Cross-functional new-product teams, 114
Cross-functional plans, 172, 188-189
Cross-functional representation, 215
Cross-functional responsibility, 217
Cross-functional team approach, 114
Cross-functional team leaders, 172-173
Cross-functional team process, 208
Cross-functional teams, 15, 19, 63, 107, 111, 113, 148, 172, 173, 178, 189, 191, 206, 207, 222, 228, 231
Cross-functional work teams, 220
Cultural changes, 72, 208, 209
Current profits, matching. *See* Future products
Customer complaints, 201
Customer delivery, 56
Customer demands. *See* Performance; Prices; Response times; Services
Customer dissatisfaction, 201
Customer groups, 9, 23, 35-37
Customer information, understanding, 128-130
Customer needs, 19, 36, 40
Customer price sensitivities, 55
Customer problems, 21, 114
    focus, 126
    identification, 107-108
Customer profit information, 141
Customer profitability, 66-67
Customer requirements, 36, 45, 86
Customer returns, 106
Customer satisfaction, 143
    ratings, 141
Customer segments, 54
Customer value, 19, 22, 23
Customers. *See* Complex customers
Cycle costs, 104
Cycle of decay. *See* Decay cycle
Cycle times, 13, 104, 202-203

Debt leverage, 58
Decay cycle, 60-62
Decision-making authority, 72
Decision-making process, 6, 7
Decision-making responsibility, 7
De-emphasis, 90, 91, 156, 228
Deere, 2
Defense, 90, 156, 228
Deficiencies, 9, 26, 38, 42-43, 109-110, 164, 216, 227. *See also* Performance deficiencies
  overcoming, 207-208
Delivery cycles, 21, 203
Demand curves, 20
Demands, conflict, 146
Demosthenes, 79
Department expenses, 75
Design engineers, 201
Design requirements, 128
Design trade-offs, 118
Development cycle. *See* Product development
  problems, 102-106
Developments, help, 115-117
DHL, 70
Digital, 52, 138
Direct variable costs, 62, 63
Distributor analysis, 147
Distributor management, 141
Divide-and-conquer strategy, 79
Division controller, 154
Division general manager, 42, 43, 87
Division plans, 158
Downcycle, 57
Downsizing, 56, 216
Drucker, Peter, 113, 219
Dumphy, Dermot, 104
DuPont, 71, 88

Earnings opportunity, 144
Economic information, 46
Economic facts, 40
EG&G Idaho, Inc., 93, 94
Electronic data interchanges, 136
Electronic networks, 74-75. *See also* Global electronic networks
Electronic technologies, 136-140
Elitist approach, 215
Emerson Electric Company, 99, 191-194
  implementation, 193-194

management development planning, 194
  performance, tracking, 194
  strategy, 193
Emery, 70
Employees, training partnerships, 229-230
End-use customers, 38
End-use markets, 140
Engineering costs, 5, 60
Engineering hours, 75
Equipment methods, 5
Errors, 85-88
Existing products, 46, 203-204
  satisfaction, 7-8
Existing technology, 203-204
Expense reductions, 56

Fact base. *See* Planning; Plans
Fact facing, reluctance, 3-4
Failure rate, 128
Federal Express, 70
Feedback, 38, 128
  loop, 148
Festo, 230, 231
Financial goals, 192
Financial managers, 63
Financial targets, setting, 192
Finished stock, 11
First-line sales manager, 146
Fixed costs, 57. *See also* Bedrock fixed costs; Managed fixed costs
Fixed-to-variable cost relationship, 11
Fluke Corporation, 104
Folklore facts, 181-182
Follow-up evaluations, 215, 216
Ford, 118
Foreign competitors, 1
Foreign sources, 4
Foreign suppliers, 124
For-profit organization, 211
Front-line salespeople, 141
Fry, Art, 108
Fujitsu, 22
Full-cost allocations, 64
Future products, current profit matching, 112-113

GAAP. *See* Generally accepted accounting principles
General costs, 58

General Electric (GE), 41, 100, 101, 110, 113, 137
General management, 35, 75, 91, 111, 153, 159
  direction, 167-175
General manager, 44, 46, 77, 83, 91, 149, 167, 198, 208, 218. *See also* Division general manager
General-level manager, 82
Generally accepted accounting principles (GAAP), 172
Geography, 130
Gilson, Ken, 135, 168
Global competition, 2, 20, 162
Global competitors, 193, 230
Global customers, 175
Global electronic networks, 74, 164
Global environment, 52
Global opportunities, 175
Global teams, 175-176
GMC, 118
Goals. *See* Sales compensation
  setting, 140-141
Golden Step Award, 114
Government assistance, 3
Government-funded contracts, 116
Great companies, 220-221
Grimm, Richard, 113
Group-level marketing, 5
Grow-and-divide philosophy, 93
Growth markets, 92, 163
Growth opportunities, 187
Growth rates, 182
Growth trends, 186
GTE, 123

Half-true facts, 182
Hannifin, Parker, 38, 93, 94, 130, 131, 167, 221, 223
  Corporation, 33
Hardware, obsolescence, 1
Harris, 116
Hayes, Dennis, 49, 51
Hayes Microcomputer Products, 49, 51, 67
Headhunters, 212-213
Henkel Corporation, 23, 175
Hennessy, Bob, 213
Hewlett-Packard (HP), 52, 73, 74, 81, 92, 102, 104, 106, 119, 123, 126, 127, 138, 141, 167, 172, 212, 213, 221

High-cost countries, 75-76, 111
High-impact training, 225-230
High-tech business purchase, 164
High-tech companies, 1, 33, 34, 36, 41, 60, 121, 153, 161
High-tech global manufacturer, 168
High-tech growth businesses, 94
High-tech industries, 112
High-tech manufacturers, 127
High-tech products, 50, 163
Hitachi, 2
Hoechst, 76
Hofmann, Phil, 44, 104, 113
Hoped-for facts, 182
Houghton, Jamie, 101
HP. *See* Hewlett-Packard

IBM, 49, 52, 73, 81, 82, 100, 123, 138, 141, 224
Ideas, contribution, 173-175
Illinois Tool Works (ITW), 93
Implementation. *See* Concept
  plans, 167
  programs, 172
Incentives, 142. *See also* Sales team
  incentives; Team-based incentives
  programs, 147, 159
  systems, 207
Incremental cost, 56
Incremental profit, 56
  rate, 12
Industrial business, 32
Industrial buying situations, 143
Industrial companies, 1, 33, 41, 45, 60, 82, 109, 121, 148, 150, 153, 161, 212, 231. *See also* Outside-in industrial companies
Industrial manager, 85
Industrial manufacturing company, 33
Industrial market position, 41
Industrial market segments, 83, 88
Industrial marketing, 31, 32, 47
  concept, understanding, 35-38
  consultant, 214
  difficulty, 32-34
  expertise, 211
  failure, 34-43
  implementation, 38-39
  practices, 10
  segmentation, 86
  suppliers, 36

training, 224
Industrial markets, 85, 89
Industrial products, 50, 122
Industrial scale market, 163
Industrial selling, 121
Industrial suppliers, 123
Industry averages, 69
Industry comparisons, 185
Industry knowledge, 134-135
Inflation, 13, 54, 55
    rates, 9
Inflation-adjusted costs, 52, 54
Information networks, 136
In-house industrial marketing, 229
In-house marketing research, 85
In-house programs, 217
In-house training, 215
    false starts, 223-229
Innovation, 13, 164
Inside-out, 20
Installation costs, 39
Intel, 106
Internal growth, 31
Intuit, 81
Inventories, 75
Inventory, 189
    write-offs, 106
Investment opportunities, identification,
    192
Issues, defining, 12-14
ITW. *See* Illinois Tool Works
Iverson, Ken, 80, 104

Jasse, Bob, 107
JCB, 2
Johnson & Johnson, 45, 92, 93, 102, 104, 113,
    131, 135, 212, 213
Jones, Reginald, 41
Justice, Dick, 127

Kaizen, 225
Keiretsu, 117
Kennedy, Jim, 59
Kimberly Clark, 117
Knight, Chuck, 99, 191
Knowledge worker, 75
Kodak, 88
Komatsu, 2

Labor costs, 5

Labor and sales efficiency, 75
Layering, 6
Lexmark, 81, 92
Liebherr, 2
Life cycles, 9, 56, 100, 204. *See also* Product
    life cycle
        problems, 102-106
Life-cycle cost, 128, 131
Liquidity, 13
    management, 67-68
Loctite, 23
Long-term strategic decision, 84
Long-term strategic plans, 177
Lotus, 81
Lotus Development product, 119
Low-cost offshore employees, influence, 1
Low-cost supplier, 4
Low-growth markets, 163-164
Lower-cost claims, 200-201
Lower-cost countries, 75-76
Lower-cost producer, 55
Lower-cost supplier, 4-5, 51-55
LSI Logic Corporation, 79, 80, 107
Lubrizol, 95

Macro-analysis, 83
Maddock, Sir Levan, 17
Makita, 193
Managed fixed costs, 62, 63
Management. *See* Cash; Liquidity; Market-
    driven management; Top management
        approaches, 189-191. *See also*
            Bureaucratic management approaches
        attitude, 189-191
        demands, 193
        development, role, 208-209
        education, 218
        guidelines, 168
        mind-set, 13
        personnel, 167
        practices, 208
        principles, 51-52, 67
        responses, 10-17
        tool, 177
Management teams, 5, 12, 60, 187, 194, 208
Management terms, 18
Management training
        programs, 38
        role, 208-214
        trends, 218-229

Managerial finance, 73
Manhattan projects, 118
Manufacturing capacity, 2, 186, 202
Manufacturing cells, 53
Manufacturing companies, 125, 159
Manufacturing costs, 60, 158, 188
Manufacturing cycles, 203
Manufacturing economics, 40
Manufacturing efficiency, 202
Manufacturing manager, 204
Manufacturing methods, 5, 87
Manufacturing process, 109, 164, 186
Manufacturing requirements, 87
Manufacturing technology, 51
Manufacturing-oriented company, 47
Marginal customers, 42
Marginal products, 36, 42
Marginal returns, 68
Market analysis, 89, 147
Market development, 60
Market facts, 85, 198
Market focus, 105
Market information, 46, 198
Market intelligence, 124, 198
Market managers, 34, 44, 77, 154
Market needs, 10, 15, 39
    response, 92-94
Market opportunities, 92
Market position, 54, 90
Market priorities, 202
Market segment, 23, 36, 38, 57, 66, 82-86, 88,
    109, 114, 130-132, 134, 135, 156, 158, 162,
    165, 175, 180, 193, 198, 199, 203. *See also*
    Industrial market segments; Product/
    market segment
        priorities, 198-199
        prioritizing, 90
        strategy, 95
Market segmentation, 10, 83, 84, 96, 199
Market share, 42, 100, 171
Market trends, 198
Market-driven approach, 20
Market-driven business, 26, 197
    unit, 18, 37
Market-driven capabilities, assessment, 26-
    30
Market-driven change process, 217
Market-driven company, 86, 125, 208
    6 Cs, 23-26
Market-driven entity, 29

Market-driven factors, 29
Market-driven focus, 21
Market-driven language, 229
Market-driven management, 19, 21, 26, 29,
    30, 173, 208, 209
    definition, 21-23
    team, 150
    training workshop, 33
    workshops, 223
Market-driven managers, 30
Market-driven performance, 29, 197
Market-driven planning process, 175
Market-driven plans, 173
Market-driven rating scale, 197-231
    summary, 230-231
Market-driven training
    program, 221
    workshop, 227
Market-driven transformations, 135
Market-focused approach, 133
Market-focused plans, 172
Marketing. *See* Group-level marketing;
    Industrial marketing; Proactive
    marketing
Marketing concept, 38, 46
Marketing company, 33
Marketing controller, 49-77
    summary, 76-77
Marketing decisions, 41
Marketing departments, 39
Marketing director, 44
Marketing effectiveness, 32
Marketing manager, 44, 204. *See also*
    Product-line marketing manager
Marketing objectives, 144
Marketing opportunity, 183
Marketing plan, 190
Marketing programs, 22
Marketing skills, 34
Marketing strategy, 126, 174
Marketing success, principles, 124-125
Marketing training, 219
Market-oriented commitment, 40
Marketplace, 13, 22, 81, 88, 96, 101, 140, 148,
    150, 162
Market/product business, 11, 153, 170, 171
Market/product planning. *See* Corporate
    planning
Market/product plans, 229
Market/product requirements, 153

Market/product segments, 153, 170, 171
Market/product selection, 198
Market/product strategies, 60, 156-157,
162-164, 174
Markets. *See* Turbulent markets
segmentation, 10-11
product confusion, 85-86
Market-share losses, 110
Market-specific selling approach, 132
Material costs, 39, 75
Maturity stage, 26
MBAs, 34, 45, 154, 214, 223
programs, 211, 219
Mercedes Benz, 127
Merck, 111
Micro Motion, 191
Microsoft, 81
Miller, Henry, 82
Miller Group, 93
Mistakes, 84-88
Motorola, 51, 116
Mousetraps, 99-120
summary, 120
Multidisciplinary team approach, 114
Multi-product-line businesses, 57

Nalco, 119
National Starch and Chemical (NSC), 23,
38, 39, 60, 104, 117, 119, 213, 221, 224
NEC, 114
Needs analysis, 226
Need-to-know management, 73
Need-to-know mentality, 46, 72
Networks. *See* Electronic networks
New products, 100-102, 204
activities, 113
odds, improving, 106-120
New-process technology, 105
New-product development, 99, 111, 149
New-product introductions, 134, 144
New-product launch/meeting, 115
New-product orders, 101
New-product sales, 141
New-product success, 112, 117-118
New-product teams. *See* Cross-functional
new-product teams
New-product technology, 105, 117
New-production plant, 155
NIH factor. *See* Not invented here factor
Nonprofit bureaucracy, 207

Not invented here (NIH) factor, 116
NSC. *See* National Starch and Chemical
Nucor Corporation, 37, 74, 80, 102, 104
Nypro, 80

Objectives, tailoring, 143-144
Odell Associates, 81
OEM. *See* Original equipment
manufacturer
Off-the-shelf components, 52
Ongoing training, organization, 133-136
Open-book culture, 46, 74, 75
Operating efficiencies, 165
Operating managers, 60
Operating programs, 152
Operating plan, 156
Operating rates, 184
Operating results, 194
Opportunities, 79-97
summary, 96-97
Opportunity cost, 220
Oracle, 81
Order-entry workers, 15
Organization, 205-206
realignment, 14-16
schemes, 14
Original equipment manufacturer (OEM),
84, 128
markets, 169
Out-of-pocket costs, 11
Outside-in industrial companies, 21
Outside-in management, 19-30
summary, 30
Overhead, 54, 201
charge, 200
costs, 55, 58, 66, 205
Overstructuring, 6
Owens-Corning Fiberglas, 149

Paine, Thomas, 10
Pall Corporation, 23, 107, 131
Paperwork, 147-148
Parallel method, 114
Partnerships. *See* Employees
Patent life, 112
Payback cycles, 56
Payback period, 187
Peer-group learning/pressure, 228
Performance. *See* Emerson Electric
Company

claims, 125
customer demands, 1, 2
deficiencies, 107
indicator, 70
measures, 68-72
ratios, 69
Perk, approach, 215-216
Personnel decisions, 68
Pfeiffer, Eckard, 115, 138
Physical ratios, 181
Pioneer Hi-Bred, 137, 139-140
Plan document, 180
Planning, 206. *See also* Business planning;
Emerson Electric Company; Production
planning; Strategic planning
  activities, 155
  comparison. *See* Corporate planning
  consolidation. *See* Business planning
    consolidation
  fact base, 162-167
  guidelines, 13
  presentations, 206
  process, 206, 208. *See also* Cross-
    functional planning process
  proven practices, 162-176
  role. *See* Business planning
  schedules, 206
  strategies, 125
  systems, 68
    overemphasis, 160
  types, confusion, 155-159
Planning units
  defining, 170
  format, defining, 170-171
Plans, 177-195. *See also* Cross-functional
plans; Sales compensation
  credibility issues, 181-189
    fact base, 181-182
  focus, 178-181
  initiatives, 180-181
  integration, 189-190
  projections, 182-185
  structure, 178-181
  summary, 195
Plant capacity, 156
Plant methods, 5
Platt, Lew, 119
Pooled salesforce, 131
Porter, Lyman, 218, 219
Post-It-Notes, 108

Postsale service, 56
Postsale support, 11
Preparation, 146-147
Price business, 165
Price increases, 20, 54
Price pressures, 53
Price schedule, 43
Prices, customer demands, 1
Pricing decisions, 68
Pricing strategy, 202
Priorities, defining, 12-14
Proactive marketing, 31-47
  summary, 47
Process technology, 30, 58
Procurement, 189
Producers. *See* Results producers
Product cannibalization, 118
Product confusion. *See* Markets
Product costs, 39
Product definition team, 114
Product design, 37
Product development, 1, 8, 9, 110, 188, 189
  cycles, 14, 92, 101, 102
  groups, 105, 186
  priorities, 95
  problems, 102-105
Product enhancement, 106
Product features, 114
Product knowledge, 133
Product life cycle, 1, 20, 58, 105-106
Product lines, 12, 13, 43, 63, 124, 131, 165
  rationalization/shelving/
    cannibalization, 117-119
Product managers, 34, 44, 77, 149, 198
Product performance, 49, 164, 199
Product range, 130-131
Product technology, 30, 58
Product training, 96, 124
Product types, 21
Product/account/market businesses, 62
Product-driven company, 135
Product-driven industrial firms, 86
Production activities, 94
Production assembly lines, 53
Production capacity, 202
Production costs, 54
Production planning, 95
Productivity, 12, 19, 23, 52, 70, 125, 128, 137,
149
Productivity gains, 13, 52, 55

Productivity improvements, 5, 31, 37, 68, 124, 189
Productivity information, 143
Productivity measurements, 69-70
Productivity results, 74
Product-line costs, 66
    differences, 55
Product-line information, 141
Product-line marketing manager, 45
Product-line profit, 66
Product-line profitability, 66
Product-line profit-and-loss statement, 200
Product/market focus, 107, 120
    defining, 108-109
Product/market segment, 10, 66, 95
Product/market strategies, 107, 111
Product-oriented company, 47
Products. *See* Complex products; Existing products; Future products; New products
Product/service offerings, 124
Product/service package, 15, 20, 22, 23, 35, 38, 85, 125
    design, 37
Profit. *See* Cost-profit pictures
Profit advantages, 183
Profit center managers, 45
Profit centers, 7, 15, 92
Profit economics, 10
    understanding, 11-12
Profit goals, 37, 168, 173
Profit growth, 11, 32, 90, 112
Profit history, 187
Profit improvement, 37
Profit margins, 2, 4, 22, 52, 53, 59, 185
Profit matching. *See* Future products
Profit performance, 70
Profit potential, 66, 91, 156
Profit projection, 181-185
Profit responsibility, 15, 66
Profit sharing, 82
Profit structure, 156
Profitability, 76, 84, 194, 217. *See also* Customer profitability; Product-line profitability
Profit-and-loss projections, 184
Profit-and-loss responsibility, 59, 66, 74
Profit-and-loss statement, 12, 200. *See also* Product-line profit-and-loss statement
Profit-center management jobs, 213
Profitless prosperity, 52

Program development, 226
Project management, 114
Project manager, 115
Promotion, 204-205
Promotion-within policy, 212
Proprietary information, 119-120
Proprinter, 92
Purchase order, 121

Quality, 165, 201
    assurance, 172
    improvement, 189
    standards, 21, 201
Quest, 132, 135
Quick fixes, 210, 216
Quick study, 212
Quicken, 81

Ranges. *See* Common ranges
Rapid-growth market, 164
Raychem, 89
Raytheon, 116
Real costs, 67
Reference selling, 205
Regional teams, 175-176
Reliance, 110, 126, 170
Reordering cost information, 62-64
Reorganization schemes, 14
Reported facts, 182
Reporting systems, 68
Research and development (R&D), 3, 11, 47, 97, 189
    activities, 8, 58, 94
    costs, 52, 58
    efforts, 175
    expenditures, 9, 108, 111
    expense, 59
    focus/speed, 8-9
    function, 8
    managers, 204
    programs, 8, 95, 111, 118, 155
    projects, 21, 117, 118
    reports, 105
    staff, 5
    strategy, 8
Resegmentation, 88-95
Response times, 13, 202-203
    customer demands, 2
Results producers, 71-72
Retail segmentation approaches, 84-85

Return on assets (ROA), 58, 180
Return on sales (ROS), 180
Rigid, 191
Risk/reward ratio, 181, 186-187
Risk-taking culture, 104
ROA. *See* Return on assets
ROS. *See* Return on sales
Rosemount, 191
Rubbermaid, 106

6 Cs. *See* Market-driven company
Sales activities, 94
Sales agents, 125
Sales arm, urgency, 9-10
Sales assignments, 129
Sales career ladder, providing, 144-148
Sales compensation, 147
    company goal links, 140-144
    plans, 9
Sales competency quizzes, 136
Sales costs, 60, 149
Sales department, 44
Sales development, 60
Sales expense, 58
Sales force, tie in, 158-159
Sales forecasts, 105, 158, 183
Sales, general, and administrative (SG&A), 66, 139
    costs, 51
    overheads, 64
    requirements, 59
Sales goals, 140
Sales growth, 32, 90, 156, 165
Sales history, 187
Sales management, 130, 148, 159
Sales manager, 44, 45, 145, 146, 150
Sales measures, 69
Sales organizations, 10, 130, 144
Sales performance, 148, 159
Sales personnel, 15, 147
Sales plan, 190
Sales potential, 87, 130
Sales programs, 9, 22
Sales projection, 182-185
Sales quotas, 159
Sales representatives, 137, 138, 145, 148, 159, 205
Sales revenues, 126
Sales salaries, 142
Sales segmentation, 84

Sales task, 9
Sales team incentives, 143
Sales training, 204-205
Sales volume, 37
Sales-driven industrial firms, 86
Sales-driven mind-set, 209
Salesforce, 95, 96, 122, 190, 198. *See also*
    Consultative salesforce; Pooled salesforce
    options, 130-133
    productivity, 138
Sales-oriented company, 47
Sealed Air, 96, 104, 106, 107, 136, 221
Segment priorities, setting, 89-91
Segmentation, 88-97. *See also* Consumer
    goods; Industrial marketing; Markets;
    Resegmentation; Sales segmentation
    failure, 81-83
    responsibility, 91-92
Segments, 87-88. *See also* Target segments
Self-managed work teams, 143
Self-satisfaction, 8
Selling activities, 146
Selling organization, 145
Selling skills, 224
Senior management, 203
Seniority-based compensation, 142
Service performance, 23
Services, customer demands, 2
Setting sales, 173
SG&A. *See* Sales, general, and
    administrative
Shared costs, 62-64, 66
Short-term, obsession, 40-42
Short-term America, 209-210
Short-term profits, 31, 42
    contribution, 35
SIC. *See* Standard industrial classification
Side-by-side comparisons, 22, 52, 109
Side-by-side competitive comparisons, 9,
    39, 199, 134, 136
Side-by-side competitive product, 23
Siemens, 100
Skil, 191
Small-business entrepreneur, 68
SOS approach, 216
Southwest Airlines, 70
Standard industrial classification (SIC), 10
Strategic assignment, 148
Strategic decision, 10, 97, 155, 156, 171, 174,
    199. *See* Long-term strategic decision

Strategic market segmentation, 94
Strategic marketing, 95
Strategic planning, 30, 155, 157
    gaps, 158
Strategic plans, 155, 165
Strategic thinking, 170
Strategies, reassessment, 16-17
Strategy statement, 178-179
Strengths-and-weaknesses analysis, 83
Strouble, Tom, 229
Subscriber loop market, 180
Substitute technologies, 124
Sullivan, Denny, 119
Supplier. See Lower-cost supplier
    capacity, 54
    product, 126
    profit, 36
    reductions, 31
Support costs, 72
Support services, 71, 128
Supporters, 71-72
Swagelok Company, 95

3M, 104, 106, 108, 114, 119, 132, 221
Take-order situation, 90
Target audiences, 227-228
Target customer market segments, 134
Target market segments, 52
Target markets, 10, 15, 17, 22, 95, 117, 134,
    161, 169, 173, 176
    alignment, 110-111
    plans, 148
Target segments, alignment, 95-96
TAT. See Turnaround time
Team leaders. See Cross-functional team
    leaders
Team members, 143, 173
Team-based incentives, 143
Team-based performance, 143
Technical companies, 41
Technical mind-set, 209
Technicare, 113
Technological advances, 117
Technological changes, 88
Technological developments, 99, 115-117
Territory analysis, 147
Texas Instruments, 22
Thinking, 86-87
Third-party payers, 54
Time frame, 41

Timken Company, 127, 229
    sales engineer, 128
    Select-A-Nalysis, 127
Toledo Scale, 170
    sales team, 126
Top management, 35, 45, 75, 102, 115, 161
    commitment, 221-223
    personnel, 220
    role, 219-220
Top-down approach, 7, 72
Top-level managers, 82
Top-line growth, 68, 82
Top-line results, 230
Total system cost, 128
Train the Salespeople approach, 217
Training. See In-house training;
    Management training; Ongoing training
    approaches, 215-217
    partnerships. See Employees
    programs, 133, 136, 216
    role, 208-214
    wasted, 215-217
Transformation, roadblocks, 3-10
Travel costs, 132
Travel time, 130
Trending costs, 55-56
TRW, 69
Turbulent markets, 1-18
    summary, 17-18
Turnaround time (TAT), 92

Unilever Chemicals, 90, 132, 135, 221
Unit cost, 125
Unit price, 131
Urban, Tom, 139
U.S. Robotics, 51
User performance, 42
User requirements, 21
User-friendly literature, 135

Vagelos, Dr. Roy, 111
Value system, 129
VisiCalc, 119

Wal-Mart, 138
Warranties, 56
Warranty costs, 201
Warranty costs, 75
Watch-dog attitude, 120
Westinghouse, 110

What-if conditions, 128
What-if cost, 73
What-if options, 52
Withdrawal, 90, 228
Working capital, 67, 70
    investment, 71
    requirements, 71
    yields, 71

Workshop leader, 225, 226
Workshop preparation, 227
Wulff, Harald, 174

Xerox, 54, 81, 88

Zoom Telephonics, 51
Zubin AG, 81

B. Charles Ames is a partner in Clayton, Dubilier & Rice, a New York City-based investment firm specializing in management buyouts. He also serves as director for several major companies, including Warner-Lambert, M.A. Hanna, and Progressive Insurance. He has 35 years of experience in consulting and in managing industrial and high-tech companies. Previously, he served as chief executive officer of Acme-Cleveland Corporation and Reliance Electric and as a director of McKinsey & Company, Inc., where he was the firm's practice leader in industrial marketing. He is a frequent contributor to the *Harvard Business Review*. Two of his articles are included as chapters in *The Art of Top Management* and *A Handbook of Modern Marketing*. He is co-author, with James D. Hlavacek, of three other management books.

Dr. James D. Hlavacek is the managing director of Market Driven Management, Inc., a Charlotte, North Carolina-based marketing training firm. He has over 25 years of experience designing and developing industrial marketing training programs for cross-functional business teams. He served as head of the marketing department at Case Western Reserve University and was director of the Institute for Executive Education at Wake Forest University. He was previously the editor-in-chief of *Industrial Marketing Management* and was vice president and a director of the American Marketing Association for many years. Dr. Hlavacek now conducts training programs for industrial manufacturers around the world and is on the board of directors of Nucor Corporation, a leading manufacturer of carbon, alloy, and specialty steel.

For information about public or in-house training, call 800-322-3540, or 704-366-9024.

Market Driven Management, Inc.

Phone: 800-322-3540 / 704-366-9024 - Fax: 704-366-8933

Yes, I would like information about the following workshops:

Please ✔ the appropriate boxes and mail or fax:

❑ The Best and Worst Industrial Marketing Practices

❑ Industrial Pricing Strategy and Tactics

❑ Team Marketing with Industrial Distributors

❑ In-house sessions for the above workshops

❑ Annual Seminar on New Product Development

❑ Please add my name to the Market Driven Management, Inc., mailing list:

Name: _____		Title: _____	
Company: _____		Division: _____	
Address: _____			
City: _____	State: _____	Zip: _____	Country: _____
Telephone: ( ) _____		Fax: ( ) _____	

Your company manufactures:

❑ Chemicals or Materials   ❑ Equipment or Systems

❑ Components or Parts   ❑ Service or consulting business

Total number of people employed by your company:

❑ under 100   ❑ 100-500   ❑ 500-1,000   ❑ 1,000+

Total annual sales of your company:

❑ under $100 million   ❑ $100-$500 million   ❑ $500-$1,000 million   ❑ $1+ billion

Market Driven Management, Inc.

Phone: 800-322-3540 / 704-366-9024 - Fax: 704-366-8933

Yes, I would like information about the following workshops:

Please ✔ the appropriate boxes and mail or fax:

❑ The Best and Worst Industrial Marketing Practices

❑ Industrial Pricing Strategy and Tactics

❑ Team Marketing with Industrial Distributors

❑ In-house sessions for the above workshops

❑ Annual Seminar on New Product Development

❑ Please add my name to the Market Driven Management, Inc., mailing list:

Name: _____		Title: _____	
Company: _____		Division: _____	
Address: _____			
City: _____	State: _____	Zip: _____	Country: _____
Telephone: ( ) _____		Fax: ( ) _____	

Your company manufactures:

❑ Chemicals or Materials   ❑ Equipment or Systems

❑ Components or Parts   ❑ Service or consulting business

Total number of people employed by your company:

❑ under 100   ❑ 100-500   ❑ 500-1,000   ❑ 1,000+

Total annual sales of your company:

❑ under $100 million   ❑ $100-$500 million   ❑ $500-$1,000 million   ❑ $1+ billion

Market Driven Management, Inc.
P.O. Box 470188
Charlotte, NC 28247-0188

Market Driven Management, Inc.
P.O. Box 470188
Charlotte, NC 28247-0188